WHAT EVERY SPECIAL EDUCATOR MUST KNOW

ETHICS, STANDARDS, AND GUIDELINES FOR SPECIAL EDUCATORS

Fifth Edition
2003

Council for
Exceptional
Children

The voice and vision of special education

Library of Congress Cataloging-in-Publication Data

Council for Exceptional Children.
What every special educator must know : the international
standards for the preparation and certification of special education
teachers.
5th ed.
p. cm.
Includes bibliographical references (p.)
ISBN 0-86586-993-6 (paper)
1. Special education teachers—Training of—Standards. 2. Special
education teachers—Certification Standards. I. Title.

Stock No. R5644
Printed in the United States of America.

10 9 8 7 6 5 4 3 2

One of the original aims of CEC:

. . . to establish professional standards for teachers in the field of special education.

First CEC meeting, 1923

She insisted that "no child [is] too atypical to be neglected."

—John H. Finley, referring to Elizabeth Farrell, 1933

The quality of educational services for children and youth with exceptionalities resides in the abilities, qualifications, and competencies of the personnel who provide the services.

CEC, 1988

Table of Contents

Section 5

Appendices

Preface

It was through significant professional and personal commitment that the members of CEC crafted this product. In the process we learned not only about knowledge and skills but also about each other and developed a deep mutual respect. May those who use this [publication] experience that same mutual respect from all who serve children and their families.

Preamble to the Common Core, 2nd edition

What Every Special Educator Must Know: The Ethics, Standards, and Guidelines for Special Educators is intended to provide the kind of leadership and guidance that makes us proud to be special educators.

- For students preparing to become special educators, this publication will introduce you to the ethics and professional practice standards to which you aspire. It describes the knowledge and skills that will be the foundation of your professional practice.

- For teachers, you will not only find your professional ethics and practice standards and your professional standards, you will also find guidance in developing a plan for your continuing professional growth.

- For professors and deans developing or revising your programs, you will find the procedures for seeking national recognition of your programs either through National Council for Accreditation of Teacher Education (NCATE) and CEC or through CEC alone.

- For state directors and specialists, you will find guidance for revising state licensing standards to align with the profession's recommendations. CEC stands ready to assist you in this process.

- For parents and others from the community, you will find the ethics, professional practice standards, and the knowledge and skills that we as the special education profession use to define ourselves and judge each other's excellence.

Introduction to the 5th Edition

Like its predecessors, this edition is a collaborative product of the members of CEC and others in the wider educational community. The standards and principles represent the expertise and ideas of literally thousands of special educators. This edition, as all others have been, is based on the premises that

- Professional standards must come from the profession itself.
- Special education is an international profession, not limited to a single state, province, or location.

The standards provide to states, provinces, and nations benchmarks for developing or revising policy and procedures for program accreditation, entry-level licensure, professional practice, and continuing professional growth.

For over 75 years, CEC has worked to develop and implement standards for beginning teachers. The standards presented in this edition continue in this long tradition of leadership by providing direction to colleges and universities that prepare teachers as well as to states as they develop new licensure frameworks for special educators. The move to performance-based standards places CEC at the forefront in educational reform with other national associations seeking to improve the quality of all teachers who serve exceptional children.

The standards in the fifth edition are the result of a 3-year process to refine the 1996 CEC standards and to build on them to create standards that address changes in the field. These changes can be used by states and teacher preparation programs moving toward a performance-based accountability system. Over 100 CEC members helped directly to develop and evaluate the standards and thousands of CEC members and many other individuals affiliated with other organizations helped validate the standards. The standards, available last year on the CEC Web site for public comment, were praised for their reflection of best practice, emphasis on diversity, and for "capturing the essence of special education today."

HOW ARE THE NEW STANDARDS DIFFERENT FROM THE 1996 STANDARDS?

Changes in the Knowledge and Skill Standards

In order to provide assistance to the more than 30 states that use the 10 Interstate New Teacher and Assessment and Support Consortium (INTASC) Core Principles, the CEC Knowledge and Skills Subcommittee reorganized all of the CEC knowledge and skill standards from the eight domain areas of the current standards (Characteristics of Learners, Assessment, etc.) to the ten domain areas of the INTASC principles (e.g., Foundations, Characteristics of Learners, Diversity, Instructional Strategies, etc.). The alignment of the CEC standards and the INTASC standards is now explicit.

All of the knowledge and skills in the Common Core and the Areas of Specialization have been edited to eliminate redundancy and to increase the precision of the language. In addition, several new items have been validated and added in the areas of multicultural competence, access to the general education curriculum, technology, and collaboration.

Performance-Based Accreditation Standards

One of the primary differences between the 1996 and the new standards is the development of two levels of standards, each appropriate for a specific purpose. Over the last decade CEC has developed specific Knowledge and Skill Standards for both categorical and noncategorical licensure and preparation frameworks. These standards are particularly helpful in developing courses and curricula.

However, CEC has initiated a major change in the way teacher preparation programs are evaluated. The new standards reflect this change in the approval process. In the past, teacher preparation programs provided evidence (primarily by syllabi) that the standards were taught. Under the new system, programs must provide evidence that the standards are assessed and that their candidates perform appropriately on those assessments. To help programs develop a comprehensive effective assessment system, CEC developed Accreditation Standards to be used by teacher preparation programs seeking national recognition.

The new Accreditation Standards are divided into three parts: Special Education Content Standards, Field Experiences and Clinical Practice Standards, and Assessment System Standards (see Section 4B). A complete set of the standards is available on the CEC Web site.

The *Special Education Content Standards* were developed based on the Knowledge and Skill Standards. Instead of lists of knowledges and skills, the new Content Standards consist of ten narrative standards. These standards were written to reflect the content of the validated Knowledge and Skills Standards in each of the new ten domain areas. The Content Standards are the same for all programs.

Although program reviews will be done at the Content Standard level, it will be critical for faculty to use the Knowledge and Skill Standards in the Common Core and the appropriate Area of Specialization to inform their curriculum development and to develop assessments. This will be essential to ensure that the program's evaluation system comprehensively addresses each of the 10 standards.

In the past, CEC had 15 practicum standards. The new *Field Experiences and Clinical Practice Standards* are much briefer, focus on the kinds of experiences provided, and no longer have a requirement for a specific number of hours or weeks. They do, however, require that programs provide appropriate, comprehensive practicum experiences to ensure that candidates are prepared to enter the classroom.

The *Assessment System Standards* provide guidance to programs on the key components of their assessment systems. These nine standards require programs to build systems that are comprehensive, appropriately address the standards, include multiple measures, and collect data that are used for program improvement.

OVERVIEW

The fifth edition has been designed to provide information to a variety of audiences. It provides complete sets of the CEC Standards as well as a number of tools CEC has developed to make the standards more accessible.

Section 1. Code of Ethics and Professional Practice Standards

Central to any profession is its will to abide by a set of ethical principles and standards. As professionals serving individuals with exceptionalities, special educators possess a special trust endowed by the community. As such, special educators have a responsibility to be guided by their professional principles and practice standards.

Section 1 contains the CEC Code of Ethics and Standards for Professional Practice. The Code of Ethics is made up of eight fundamental ethical premises to which all special educators are bound. The Standards for Professional Practice describe the principles special educators use in carrying out day-to-day responsibilities. The Professional Practice Standards are how special educators are measured and in turn measure each other's professional excellence. It is incumbent on all special educators to use these standards in all aspects of their professional practice.

Section 2. Professional Standards and Practice Throughout the Career

Section 2 analyzes the role of professional standards as they impact special educators throughout their careers—from preparation to licensure to induction to professional development to advanced certification. This section provides an overview of the work CEC has done and is doing to ensure that high quality standards guide the practice of special educators at each step of their career.

Section 3. Tools and Strategies for Using the Standards

Section 3 provides tools that different audiences can use to make the standards more accessible. State personnel will find a chart to help them compare state and CEC standards. Teacher educators will find guidance on developing a performance-based assessment system, as well as a strategy they can use with teacher candidates to help them become familiar with the standards. Special education teachers will find guidance and tools for helping them use the CEC standards to develop professional development plans and advocate for the resources to implement them. Finally, students in teacher preparation programs are given a tool to help them measure their progress in developing their professional competence.

Section 4. The CEC Standards

Section 4 includes the different sets of CEC Standards. The Knowledge and Skill Standards sets are included, both for beginning teachers and for those special educators moving into advanced roles. These standards represent the knowledge and skill base that professionals entering practice or assuming advanced roles should possess to practice safely and effectively. The standards that programs are required to meet for CEC and CEC/NCATE accreditation are provided. Finally, CEC's standards for Mentorship and for Continuing Education are included.

Please note that CEC has not included information in this section to help faculty prepare for CEC and NCATE accreditation. In order to ensure that faculty receive the most accurate and up-to-date guidance, all information has been placed on the CEC Web site www.cec.sped.org.

Section 5. Standards for Paraprofessionals Serving Individuals with Exceptional Learning Needs

This section provides information about the increasingly critical role of paraeducators in special education service delivery, the CEC standards for paraeducator preparation, and tools paraeducators and paraeducator training programs can use to ensure that they are meeting the standards.

Appendices

There are several appendices that may be of interest to readers. Appendix 1 is a timeline of significant events in the history of special education and professional standards. Appendix 2 contains a brief history of the development of the CEC Standards and the procedures that CEC uses for on-going development and validation of the Knowledge and Skill Standards. CEC often gets questions regarding the knowledge and skills in several domains of interest. Appendices 3A and 3B are sets of selected CEC Common Core Knowledge and Skills that address specific topic areas. Appendix 4 provides the professional policies from the CEC Policy Manual that are policies and position statements directly related to the CEC Standards. Appendix 5 contains the National Board for Professional Teaching Standards for Exceptional Needs. Appendix 6 contains a graphic that depicts the different components of the CEC Professional Entry Level Standards.

Section 1

CEC Code of Ethics and Standards for Professional Practice for Special Educators

CEC CODE OF ETHICS FOR EDUCATORS OF PERSONS WITH EXCEPTIONALITIES

We declare the following principles to be the Code of Ethics for educators of persons with exceptionalities. Members of the special education profession are responsible for upholding and advancing these principles. Members of the Council for Exceptional Children agree to judge and be judged by them in accordance with the spirit and provisions of this Code.

A. Special education professionals are committed to developing the highest educational and quality of life potential of individuals with exceptionalities.

B. Special education professionals promote and maintain a high level of competence and integrity in practicing their profession.

C. Special education professionals engage in professional activities which benefit individuals with exceptionalities, their families, other colleagues, students, or research subjects.

D. Special education professionals exercise objective professional judgment in the practice of their profession.

E. Special education professionals strive to advance their knowledge and skills regarding the education of individuals with exceptionalities.

F. Special education professionals work within the standards and policies of their profession.

G. Special education professionals seek to uphold and improve where necessary the laws, regulations, and policies governing the delivery of special education and related services and the practice of their profession.

H. Special education professionals do not condone or participate in unethical or illegal acts, nor violate professional standards adopted by the Delegate Assembly of CEC.

CEC STANDARDS FOR PROFESSIONAL PRACTICE

Professionals in Relation to Persons With Exceptionalities and Their Families

Instructional Responsibilities

Special education personnel are committed to the application of professional expertise to ensure the provision of quality education for all individuals with exceptionalities. Professionals strive to

(1) Identify and use instructional methods and curricula that are appropriate to their area of professional practice and effective in meeting the individual needs of persons with exceptionalities.

(2) Participate in the selection and use of appropriate instructional materials, equipment, supplies, and other resources needed in the effective practice of their profession.

(3) Create safe and effective learning environments, which contribute to fulfillment of needs, stimulation of learning, and self-concept.

(4) Maintain class size and caseloads that are conducive to meeting the individual instructional needs of individuals with exceptionalities.

(5) Use assessment instruments and procedures that do not discriminate against persons with exceptionalities on the basis of race, color, creed, sex, national origin, age, political practices, family or social

background, sexual orientation, or exceptionality.

(6) Base grading, promotion, graduation, and/or movement out of the program on the individual goals and objectives for individuals with exceptionalities.

(7) Provide accurate program data to administrators, colleagues, and parents, based on efficient and objective record keeping practices, for the purpose of decision making.

(8) Maintain confidentiality of information except when information is released under specific conditions of written consent and statutory confidentiality requirements.

Management of Behavior

Special education professionals participate with other professionals and with parents in an interdisciplinary effort in the management of behavior. Professionals

(1) Apply only those disciplinary methods and behavioral procedures, which they have been instructed to use, and which do not undermine the dignity of the individual or the basic human rights of persons with exceptionalities, such as corporal punishment.

(2) Clearly specify the goals and objectives for behavior management practices in the persons' with exceptionalities individualized education program.

(3) Conform to policies, statutes, and rules established by state/provincial and local agencies relating to judicious application of disciplinary methods and behavioral procedures.

(4) Take adequate measures to discourage, prevent, and intervene when a colleague's behavior is perceived as being detrimental to exceptional students.

(5) Refrain from aversive techniques unless repeated trials of other methods have failed and only after consultation with parents and appropriate agency officials.

Support Procedures

Professionals

(1) Seek adequate instruction and supervision before they are required to perform support services for which they have not been prepared previously.

(2) May administer medication, where state/provincial policies do not preclude such action, if qualified to do so or if written instructions are on file which state the purpose of the medication, the conditions under which it may be administered, possible side effects, the physician's name and phone number, and the professional liability if a mistake is made. The professional will not be required to administer medication.

(3) Note and report to those concerned whenever changes in behavior occur in conjunction with the administration of medication or at any other time.

Parent Relationships

Professionals seek to develop relationships with parents based on mutual respect for their roles in achieving benefits for the exceptional person. Special education professionals

(1) Develop effective communication with parents, avoiding technical terminology, using the primary language of the home, and other modes of communication when appropriate.

(2) Seek and use parents' knowledge and expertise in planning, conducting, and evaluating special education and related services for persons with exceptionalities.

(3) Maintain communications between parents and professionals with appropriate respect for privacy and confidentiality.

(4) Extend opportunities for parent education utilizing accurate information and professional methods.

(5) Inform parents of the educational rights of their children and of any proposed or actual practices, which violate those rights.

(6) Recognize and respect cultural diversities which exist in some families with persons with exceptionalities.

(7) Recognize that the relationship of home and community environmental conditions affects the behavior and outlook of the exceptional person.

Advocacy

Special education professionals serve as advocates for exceptional students by speaking, writing, and acting in a variety of situations on their behalf. They

(1) Continually seek to improve government provisions for the education of persons with exceptionalities while ensuring that public statements by professionals as individuals are not construed to represent official policy statements of the agency that employs them.

(2) Work cooperatively with and encourage other professionals to improve the provision of special education and related services to persons with exceptionalities.

(3) Document and objectively report to one's supervisors or administrators inadequacies in resources and promote appropriate corrective action.

(4) Monitor for inappropriate placements in special education and intervene at appropriate levels to correct the condition when such inappropriate placements exist.

(5) Follow local, state/provincial, and federal laws and regulations which mandate a free appropriate public education to exceptional students and the protection of the rights of persons with exceptionalities to equal opportunities in our society.

Professionals in Relation to Employment

Certification and Qualification

Professionals ensure that only persons deemed qualified by having met state/provincial minimum standards are employed as teachers, administrators, and related service providers for individuals with exceptionalities.

Employment

(1) Professionals do not discriminate in hiring on the basis of race, color, creed, sex, national origin, age, political practices, family or social background, sexual orientation, or exceptionality.

(2) Professionals represent themselves in an ethical and legal manner in regard to their training and experience when seeking new employment.

(3) Professionals give notice consistent with local education agency policies when intending to leave employment.

(4) Professionals adhere to the conditions of a contract or terms of an appointment in the setting where they practice.

(5) Professionals released from employment are entitled to a written explanation of the reasons for termination and to fair and impartial due process procedures.

(6) Special education professionals share equitably the opportunities and benefits (salary, working conditions, facilities, and other resources) of other professionals in the school system.

(7) Professionals seek assistance, including the services of other professionals, in instances where personal problems threaten to interfere with their job performance.

(8) Professionals respond objectively when requested to evaluate applicants seeking employment.

(9) Professionals have the right and responsibility to resolve professional problems by utilizing established procedures, including grievance procedures, when appropriate.

Assignment and Role

(1) Professionals should receive clear written communication of all duties and responsibilities, including those which are prescribed as conditions of their employment.

(2) Professionals promote educational quality and intra- and interprofessional cooperation through active participation in the planning, policy development, management, and evaluation of the special education program and the education program at large so that programs remain responsive to the changing needs of persons with exceptionalities.

(3) Professionals practice only in areas of exceptionality, at age levels, and in program models for which they are prepared by their training and/or experience.

(4) Adequate supervision of and support for special education professionals is provided by other professionals qualified by their training and experience in the area of concern.

(5) The administration and supervision of special education professionals provides for clear lines of accountability.

(6) The unavailability of substitute teachers or support personnel, including aides, does not result in the denial of special education services to a greater degree than to that of other educational programs.

Professional Development

(1) Special education professionals systematically advance their knowledge and skills in order to maintain a high level of competence and response to the changing needs of persons with exceptionalities by pursuing a program of continuing education including but not limited to participation in such activities as inservice training, professional conferences/workshops, professional meetings, continuing education courses, and the reading of professional literature.

(2) Professionals participate in the objective and systematic evaluation of themselves, colleagues, services, and programs for the purpose of continuous improvement of professional performance.

(3) Professionals in administrative positions support and facilitate professional development.

Professionals in Relation to the Profession and to Other Professionals

The Profession

(1) Special education professionals assume responsibility for participating in professional organizations and adherence to the standards and codes of ethics of those organizations.

(2) Special education professionals have a responsibility to provide varied and exemplary supervised field experiences for persons in undergraduate and graduate preparation programs.

(3) Special education professionals refrain from using professional relationships with students and parents for personal advantage.

(4) Special education professionals take an active position in the regulation of the profession through use of appropriate procedures for bringing about changes.

(5) Special education professionals initiate, support, and/or participate in research related to the education of persons with exceptionalities with the aim of improving the quality of educational services, increasing the accountability of programs, and generally benefiting persons with exceptionalities. They

- Adopt procedures that protect the rights and welfare of subjects participating in the research.
- Interpret and publish research results with accuracy and a high quality of scholarship.
- Support a cessation of the use of any research procedure that may result in undesirable consequences for the participant.
- Exercise all possible precautions to prevent misapplication or misutilization of a research effort, by self or others.

Other Professionals

Special education professionals function as members of interdisciplinary teams, and the reputation of the profession resides with them. They

(1) Recognize and acknowledge the competencies and expertise of members representing other disciplines as well as those of members in their own disciplines.

(2) Strive to develop positive attitudes among other professionals toward persons with

exceptionalities, representing them with an objective regard for their possibilities and their limitations as persons in a democratic society.

(3) Cooperate with other agencies involved in serving persons with exceptionalities through such activities as the planning and coordination of information exchanges, service delivery, evaluation, and training, so that duplication or loss in quality of services may not occur.

(4) Provide consultation and assistance, where appropriate, to both general and special educators as well as other school personnel serving persons with exceptionalities.

(5) Provide consultation and assistance, where appropriate, to professionals in nonschool settings serving persons with exceptionalities.

(6) Maintain effective interpersonal relations with colleagues and other professionals, helping them to develop and maintain positive and accurate perceptions about the special education profession.

Section 2

Professional Standards and Practice Throughout the Career

The education of teachers must be driven by
- *A clear and careful conception of the educating we expect our schools to do,*
- *The conditions most conducive to this educating (as well as conditions that get in the way) and*
- *The kinds of expectations that teachers must be prepared to meet.*

Goodlad, 1990

It has long been common sense that children with well-prepared and qualified teachers have the best learning results. Research has recently verified that a well-prepared teacher has more influence on a child's learning than any other factor under school control (Darling-Hammond, 2000).

In most mature professions, a strong national or international professional organization sets standards that are used by institutions for preparing candidates, and by agencies for licensing individuals to practice in the profession (Connelly & Rosenberg, 2003). It is through professional standards that the public is assured individuals are qualified to practice safely and effectively in the profession.

As the largest professional organization of special educators, CEC has advocated for well-prepared and high-quality special education professionals for over 75 years. To this end, CEC develops and maintains professional standards for entry-level and advanced special education roles, as well as for guiding continuing professional growth (see Figure 2.1). CEC expects preparation programs to incorporate the CEC standards into their curricula, and jurisdictions to incorporate the standards into their licensing requirements. It is through professional standards used by preparation programs and aligned with licensing systems that the public can be assured that special educa-

tors are prepared to practice safely and effectively.

Today, the CEC professional standards for teacher quality are rigorously validated, research informed and pedagogically grounded, and performance-based for results-oriented accountability (see Appendix 6). Over the past 12 years, CEC has validated the knowledge and skills that are essential for high-quality beginning special educators and for special educators preparing for advanced roles. This process involved thousands of practicing special educators in consonance with a national committee representing the 17 national divisions of CEC. The result is the most rigorous and comprehensive set of national standards available anywhere for the preparation of high-quality special educators. (See Appendix 2 for a description of the validation process.)

The professional careers of special educators can be thought of as a continuum, including initial preparation, induction, and continuing professional growth (Figure 2.2). The standards and guidelines relevant to each part of the continuum are described in the following pages.

PREPARING TO BECOME A SPECIAL EDUCATOR

CEC expects at a minimum that entry-level special educators possess a bachelor's degree

FIGURE 2.1
CEC Professional Standards

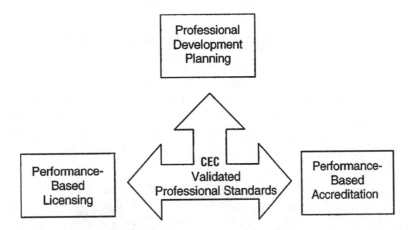

from an accredited institution, have mastered appropriate core academic subject matter content, along with the appropriate knowledge and skills for teaching.

Teaching Standards

Pedagogy or teaching skill is at the heart of special education. Special educators have always recognized that the individualized learning needs of children are at the center of instruction. The CEC preparation standards are developed around ten standards that describe the minimum knowledge, skills, and dispositions shared by all special educators. While these standards are identical across special education specialty areas, distinct sets of validated knowledge and skills inform and differentiate the respective specialty areas and provide minimum knowledge and skills that special educators must master for safe and effective practice. Each of the knowledge and skill sets is located in Section 4.

Standard #1: Foundations

Special educators understand the field as an evolving and changing discipline based on philosophies, evidence-based principles and theories, relevant laws and policies, diverse and historical points of view, and human issues that have historically influenced and continue to influence the field of special education and the education and treatment of indi-

viduals with exceptional needs both in school and society. Special educators understand how these influence professional practice, including assessment, instructional planning, implementation, and program evaluation. Special educators understand how issues of human diversity can impact families, cultures, and schools, and how these complex human issues can interact with issues in the delivery of special education services. They understand the relationships of organizations of special education to the organizations and functions of schools, school systems, and other agencies. Special educators use this knowledge as a ground upon which to construct their own personal understandings and philosophies of special education.

FIGURE 2.2
Continuum of Professional Preparation

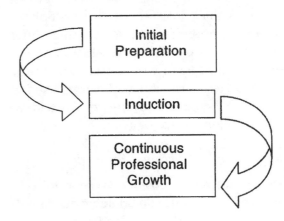

Standard #2: Development and Characteristics of Learners

Special educators know and demonstrate respect for their students first as unique human beings. Special educators understand the similarities and differences in human development and the characteristics between and among individuals with and without exceptional learning needs. Moreover, special educators understand how exceptional conditions can interact with the domains of human development and they use this knowledge to respond to the varying abilities and behaviors of individuals with exceptional learning needs. Special educators understand how the experiences of individuals with exceptional learning needs can impact families, as well as the individual's ability to learn, interact socially, and live as fulfilled contributing members of the community.

Standard #3: Individual Learning Differences

Special educators understand the effects that an exceptional condition can have on an individual's learning in school and throughout life. Special educators understand that the beliefs, traditions, and values across and within cultures can affect relationships among and between students, their families, and the school community. Moreover, special educators are active and resourceful in seeking to understand how primary language, culture, and familial backgrounds interact with the individual's exceptional condition to impact the individual's academic and social abilities, attitudes, values, interests, and career options. The understanding of these learning differences and their possible interactions provides the foundation upon which special educators individualize instruction to provide meaningful and challenging learning for individuals with exceptional learning needs.

Standard #4: Instructional Strategies

Special educators possess a repertoire of evidence-based instructional strategies to individualize instruction for individuals with exceptional learning needs. Special educators select, adapt, and use these instructional strategies to promote positive learning results in general and special curricula and to appropriately modify learning environments for individuals with exceptional learning needs. They enhance the learning of critical thinking, problem-solving, and performance skills of individuals with exceptional learning needs, and increase their self-awareness, self-management, self-control, self-reliance, and self-esteem. Moreover, special educators emphasize the development, maintenance, and generalization of knowledge and skills across environments, settings, and the lifespan.

Standard #5: Learning Environments and Social Interactions

Special educators actively create learning environments for individuals with exceptional learning needs that foster cultural understanding, safety and emotional well-being, positive social interactions, and active engagement of individuals with exceptional learning needs. In addition, special educators foster environments in which diversity is valued and individuals are taught to live harmoniously and productively in a culturally diverse world. Special educators shape environments to encourage the independence, self-motivation, self-direction, personal empowerment, and self-advocacy of individuals with exceptional learning needs. Special educators help their general education colleagues integrate individuals with exceptional learning needs in general education environments and engage them in meaningful learning activities and interactions. Special educators use direct motivational and instructional interventions with individuals with exceptional learning needs to teach them to respond effectively to current expectations. When necessary, special educators can safely intervene with individuals with exceptional learning needs in crisis. Special educators coordinate all these efforts and provide guidance and direction to paraeducators and others, such as classroom volunteers and tutors.

Standard #6: Language

Special educators understand typical and atypical language development and the ways in which exceptional conditions can interact with an individual's experience with and use of language. Special educators use individualized strategies to enhance language development and teach communication skills to individuals with exceptional learning needs. Special educators are familiar with augmentative, alternative, and assistive technologies to support and enhance communication of individuals with exceptional needs. Special educators match their communication methods to an individual's language proficiency and cultural and linguistic differences. Special educators provide effective language models and they use communication strategies and resources to facilitate understanding of subject matter for individuals with exceptional learning needs whose primary language is not English.

Standard #7: Instructional Planning

Individualized decision making and instruction is at the center of special education practice. Special educators develop long-range individualized instructional plans anchored in both general and special curricula. In addition, special educators systematically translate these individualized plans into carefully selected shorter-range goals and objectives taking into consideration an individual's abilities and needs, the learning environment, and a myriad of cultural and linguistic factors. Individualized instructional plans emphasize explicit modeling and efficient guided practice to assure acquisition and fluency through maintenance and generalization. Understanding of these factors as well as the implications of an individual's exceptional condition, guides the special educator's selection, adaptation, and creation of materials, and the use of powerful instructional variables. Instructional plans are modified based on ongoing analysis of the individual's learning progress. Moreover, special educators facilitate this instructional planning in a collaborative context including the individuals with exceptionalities, families, professional colleagues, and personnel from

other agencies as appropriate. Special educators also develop a variety of individualized transition plans, such as transitions from preschool to elementary school and from secondary settings to a variety of postsecondary work and learning contexts. Special educators are comfortable using appropriate technologies to support instructional planning and individualized instruction.

Standard #8: Assessment

Assessment is integral to the decision making and teaching of special educators, and special educators use multiple types of assessment information for a variety of educational decisions. Special educators use the results of assessments to help identify exceptional learning needs and to develop and implement individualized instructional programs, as well as to adjust instruction in response to ongoing learning progress. Special educators understand the legal policies and ethical principles of measurement and assessment related to referral, eligibility, program planning, instruction, and placement for individuals with exceptional learning needs, including those from culturally and linguistically diverse backgrounds. Special educators understand measurement theory and practices for addressing issues of validity, reliability, norms, bias, and interpretation of assessment results. In addition, special educators understand the appropriate use and limitations of various types of assessments. Special educators collaborate with families and other colleagues to assure nonbiased, meaningful assessments and decision-making. Special educators conduct formal and informal assessments of behavior, learning, achievement, and environments to design learning experiences that support the growth and development of individuals with exceptional learning needs. Special educators use assessment information to identify supports and adaptations required for individuals with exceptional learning needs to access the general curriculum and to participate in school, system, and statewide assessment programs. Special educators regularly monitor the progress of individuals with exceptional learning needs in general and special curricula. Special educators use appropriate technologies to support their assessments.

Standard #9: Professional and Ethical Practice

Special educators are guided by the profession's ethical and professional practice standards. Special educators practice in multiple roles and complex situations across wide age and developmental ranges. Their practice requires ongoing attention to legal matters along with serious professional and ethical considerations. Special educators engage in professional activities and participate in learning communities that benefit individuals with exceptional learning needs, their families, colleagues, and their own professional growth. Special educators view themselves as lifelong learners and regularly reflect on and adjust their practice. Special educators are aware of how their own and others' attitudes, behaviors, and ways of communicating can influence their practice. Special educators understand that culture and language can interact with exceptionalities, and are sensitive to the many aspects of diversity of individuals with exceptional learning needs and their families. Special educators actively plan and engage in activities that foster their professional growth and keep them current with evidence-based best practices. Special educators know their own limits of practice and practice within them.

Standard #10: Collaboration

Special educators routinely and effectively collaborate with families, other educators, related service providers, and personnel from community agencies in culturally responsive ways. This collaboration assures that the needs of individuals with exceptional learning needs are addressed throughout schooling. Moreover, special educators embrace their special role as advocate for individuals with exceptional learning needs. Special educators promote and advocate the learning and well-being of individuals with exceptional learning needs across a wide range of settings and a range of different learning experiences. Special educators are viewed as specialists by a myriad of people who actively seek their collaboration to effectively include and teach individuals with exceptional learning needs. Special educators are a resource to their colleagues in understanding the laws and policies relevant to individuals with exceptional learning needs. Special educators use collaboration to facilitate the successful transitions of individuals with exceptional learning needs across settings and services.

Core Academic Subject Matter Content

CEC expects all special educators to have a solid grounding in the liberal arts curriculum ensuring proficiency in reading, written and oral communications, calculating, problem solving, and thinking. All special educators should also possess a solid base of understanding of the general content area curricula, that is, math, reading, English/language arts, science, social studies, and the arts, sufficient to collaborate with general educators in

- Teaching or co-teaching academic subject matter content of the general curriculum to students with exceptional learning needs across a wide range of performance levels.
- Designing appropriate learning and performance accommodations and modifications for students with exceptional learning needs in academic subject matter content of the general curriculum.

Because of the significant role that content specific subject matter knowledge plays at the secondary level, special education teachers routinely teach secondary level academic subject matter content classes in consultation or collaboration with one or more general education teachers appropriately licensed in the respective content area. However, when a special education teacher assumes sole responsibility for teaching a core academic subject matter class at the secondary level, the special educator must have a solid knowledge base in the subject matter content sufficient to assure the students can meet state curriculum standards.

Assuring High-Quality Preparation Programs

There are different approaches to preparing individuals to become special educators. However, all share the responsibility to assure at a minimum that their graduating entry-level special education teachers have appropriate knowledge, skill, and field experience in content and pedagogy to practice safely and effectively.

Currently, the most common approach to the preparation of special educators in the United States (U.S. Department of Education, 2003) is through programs that prepare individuals for practice with students across a variety of exceptionalities. These approaches are usually termed preparation for multicategorical or generic practice. Regardless of the term used, it is critical that prospective special educators prepared for multicategorical practice possess the knowledge and skills to teach students with each of the relevant exceptionalities. While multicategorical preparation is most common, the challenge for preparation programs lies in preparing individuals with both the depth and spread of professional knowledge and skills.

CEC expects all preparation programs to acquire national program recognition. Recently, CEC adopted performance-based standards for the preparation of special educators. With the adoption of a performance-based approach, preparation programs now demonstrate that their graduates have mastered appropriate knowledge and skills for the roles for which they are being prepared. This includes demonstrating the positive impact of their prospective teachers on increased student learning. In national program recognition, the programs undergo a process in which the program submits evidence that the graduates of the program possess appropriate knowledge, skill, and dispositions to enter professional practice. Colleagues review the performance of the program against national professional standards to determine how well the program has prepared their prospective teachers. Only when a special education program has CEC national recognition is the public assured that the program's graduates are prepared to practice safely and effectively. For individuals looking for a preparation program, it is important for them to assure that the program is nationally recognized by CEC.

For over 15 years, CEC alone and in partnership with NCATE has provided recognition to quality special education preparation programs. Through the CEC partnership with NCATE, CEC has agreements with 47 states or territories. To date CEC has evaluated and approved approximately one-third of all special education preparation programs in the United States. Additionally, CEC has procedures in place to conduct performance-based program reviews outside the United States and in those rare instances in which a preparation program does not seek national accreditation through NCATE.

Note on Alternative Preparation Programs

Currently over 600,000 children receive their special education services from approximately 40,000 individuals who are not even minimally qualified under licensing standards to practice special education. Many other children receive special education services from teachers doing double duty because over 3,000 special education teaching positions remain vacant each year or school districts have assigned them caseloads that are too large.

This crisis in demand for special education teachers is fueling a good deal of interest in alternative ways to prepare special educators. Many of these alternatives hold promise and CEC actively embraces innovative approaches preparing well-qualified special educators. However, some poorly conceptualized alternative approaches appear to have sacrificed standards in attempting to place unprepared individuals in poorly supported teaching positions. The result has been an expensive revolving door through which ill-prepared individuals are rushed into classrooms only to become overwhelmed and disillusioned. These individuals leave special education in large numbers. Most significantly, a large price is extracted from the learning of children with exceptionalities.

Alternative preparation programs have historically and can continue to play a positive role in addressing the demand deficit in special education. However, decision-makers must not be seduced by "quick fixes." School districts cannot afford to waste precious dollars on recruitment and induction of unprepared individuals. Most importantly, too many children will never benefit from the promise of the Individuals with Disabilities Education Act (IDEA) unless decision-makers embrace solutions that address both quantity and quality in teacher preparation.

Regardless of whether a preparation program is traditional or alternative, campus-based or school-based, distance or face-to-face, CEC expects all programs preparing special educators to meet CEC nationally validated standards by undergoing performance-based review. As stated in the introduction, this approach provides the most reasonable assurance to the parents and the public that beginning special education teachers are prepared for their professional responsibilities.

Assuring High-Quality State Licensure

Historically, the licensing of individuals to practice has been the responsibility of states and provinces. While approaches to licensing special educators taken by jurisdictions have been variable and somewhat idiosyncratic, most states today base their licensing process on the standards of the national societies representing the various disciplines within education. Currently, over 40 states are committed to align their licensing processes with the CEC standards.

As mentioned above, most individuals are now licensed for multicategorical practice. Many states use terms such as Teaching of Students with Mild/Moderate Exceptionalities and Teaching of Students with Severe/Profound Exceptionalities to describe these multicategorical licenses. According to the latest figures from the U.S. Department of Education, over 90% percent of the titles of the special education degrees granted each year are multicategorical (U.S. Department of Education, 2003).

For those states that use a multicategorical approach, CEC has developed the Curriculum Referenced Licensing and Program Accreditation Framework. The Individualized General Education Curriculum and Individualized Independence Curriculum describe these multicategorical licenses, and reference the curricula in which the licensed teacher will primarily practice. In using multicategorical licensing approaches, it is important that states balance the need for both breadth and depth of knowledge and skills for special education teachers. On the one hand, licensing approaches that are overly broad result in teachers who are not adequately prepared for the complex challenges of students with exceptional learning needs. On the other hand, licensing approaches that are overly narrow do not prepare prospective special educators for the increasing diversity of students with exceptional learning needs that special educators serve today.

Based on the premise that the standards for national program recognition and state licensure should align, CEC organized its professional standards to explicitly align with the 10 INTASC principles for model licensing standards at the entry level and with the National Board for Professional Teaching Standards (NBPTS) at the advanced level. It is also encouraging, that the initial licensing and advanced certification approaches suggested by both INTASC and NBPTS align closely with the CEC Curriculum Referenced Licensing and Program Accreditation Framework, reflecting a strong national convergence regarding the balance of depth and spread (see Figure 2.3). This close alignment also reflects the explicit intentions of CEC, INTASC, NCATE, and the NBPTS to collaborate and coordinate with each other.

INDUCTION AND MENTORING

Even with well-designed and implemented preparation, the beginning special educator faces a myriad of challenges in applying and generalizing learned skills during their begin-

FIGURE 2.3
Comparison of Professional Frameworks

	INTASC	NBPTS
1. Individualized General Curriculum	•	•
2. Individualized Independence Curriculum	•	•
3. Deaf/Hard of Hearing	•	•
4. Blind/Vision Impaired	•	•
5. Early Childhood Special Education	•	•
6. Gifted/Talented Special Education		

ning teaching. Like other professionals, special educators who have the focused support of veteran colleagues, as mentors, become proficient more quickly, and are more likely to remain in the profession. Every new professional in special education must receive an intensive focused induction program under a mentor during the first year or so of special education practice. The mentor must be an accomplished special educator in the same or a similar role to the mentored individual who can provide expertise and support on a continuing basis throughout the induction (Mason & White, in press).

The goals of the mentorship program include

- Facilitating the application of knowledge and skills learned.
- Conveying advanced knowledge and skills.
- Acculturating into the school's learning communities.
- Reducing job stress and enhancing job satisfaction.
- Supporting professional induction.

In addition, whenever a special educator begins practice in a new area of licensure, they also should have the opportunity to work with mentors who are accomplished professionals in similar roles. The purpose of mentors is to provide expertise and support to the individual on a continuing basis for at least the first year of practice in that area of licensure. The mentorship is a professional relationship between the individual in a new area of practice and an accomplished individual in the area that supports the individual in further

developing knowledge and skills in the given area of licensure and provides the support required to sustain the individual in practice. The mentorship must be collegial rather than supervisory. It is essential that the mentor have accomplished knowledge, skills, and experience relevant to the position in order to provide the expertise and support required to practice effectively.

Mentorship can be an effective part of career ladders. Veterans of the special education profession are expected to periodically serve as mentors as part of their professional responsibility, and they must receive the resources and support necessary to carry out this responsibility effectively.

CONTINUOUS PROFESSIONAL GROWTH

Like their colleagues in general education, special educators are lifelong learners committed to developing the highest educational and quality-of-life potential of individuals with exceptionalities. The fifth principle in the CEC Code of Ethics states that special educators strive to advance their knowledge and skills regarding the education of individuals with exceptionalities.

Effective professional development programs:

- Increase mastery of content
- Demonstrate how to teach
- Are ongoing and collegial

Continuing Licensure/Certification

Both state/provincial licensure and advanced certification of individuals for professional practice in the field of special education should be for a limited period, and renewal should be based on planned, organized, and recognized professional development related to the professional's field of practice. CEC expects practicing special educators to develop and implement a Professional Development Plan (PDP). The PDP is reviewed and amended at least annually. The professional development activities in the PDP should go beyond routine job functions of the professional, and no single activity or category should make up the plan. This PDP should include participation in an average of at least 36 contact hours (or an average of 3.6 continuing education units) each year of planned, organized, and recognized professional development related to the professional's field of practice within the following categories:

- Career related academic activities.
- Conducting or supporting research.
- Participating in district and/or school-based professional development programs.
- Teaching courses.
- Delivering presentations.
- Publishing.
- Participating in mentoring or supervised collegial support activities.
- Providing service to professional association(s).
- Participating in approved educational travel.
- Other projects.

Section 3 contains resources for developing the annual Professional Development Plan.

Advanced Special Education Study

In 2001 the CEC National Clearinghouse for Professions in Special Education queried state education agencies (SEAs) regarding special education career ladders. Of the 16 states that responded, only 5 indicated that they offer an advanced special education licensure. The Bright Futures Report (Council for Exceptional Children, 2000) found that when special educators have viable career paths to pursue, retention is enhanced. Advanced licensure options are an important component of any special education career ladder program.

As special educators progress in their teaching careers, many seek to deepen their teaching skills through advanced study in specialty areas. Other special educators will pursue new roles within special education. Within the field of special education, CEC has developed advanced standards for the following roles:

- Administration
- Educational Diagnosticians
- Technology Specialists
- Transition Specialists

CEC is developing standards in other advanced role areas including a number of categorical specialty areas. CEC is developing a process through which professional development programs that have earned CEC national recognition may apply to award CEC Advanced Certificates to their program graduates.

National Board for Professional Teaching Standards (NBPTS) offers another avenue for advanced certification for teachers (see Appendix 5). CEC has had a long and fruitful relationship with the NBPTS. Through the NBPTS special educators may earn the advanced certification for teachers of exceptional needs students. The NBPTS recognizes five areas of specialization:

- Mild/Moderate Disabilities Exceptional Needs Specialist
- Severe and Multiple Exceptional Needs Specialist
- Early Childhood Exceptional Needs Specialist
- Visual Impairments Exceptional Needs Specialist
- Deaf/Hard of Hearing Exceptional Needs Specialist

Still other special educators will pursue doctoral level studies in special education. There are currently over 150 programs preparing special educators at the doctoral level. Like other preparation programs, CEC expects doctoral programs to demonstrate their quality through CEC performance-based recognition.

References

Connelly, V. J., & Rosenberg, M. S. (2003). *Developing teaching as a profession: Comparison with careers that have achieved full professional standing.* (COPSSE Document No. RS-9). Gainesville: University of Florida, Center on Personnel Studies in Special Education.

Council for Exceptional Children. (2000). *Bright futures for exceptional learners: An agenda to achieve quality conditions for teaching and learning.* Reston, VA: Author.

Darling-Hammond, L. (2000). Teacher quality and student achievement: A review of state policy evidence. *Education Policy Analysis Archives, 8*(1). Retrieved 10/21/03 from http://epaa.asu.edu/epaa/v8n1.

Mason, C., & White, M. (in press). *Guidelines for mentoring new special educators.* Arlington, VA: Council for Exceptional Children.

U.S. Department of Education. National Center for Education Statistics. (2003). *Digest of education statistics 2002.* (NCES 2003-060). Washington, DC: Author.

Notes

"Exceptional Condition" is used throughout to include both single and co-existing conditions. These may be two or more disabling conditions or exceptional gifts or talents co-existing with one or more disabling conditions.

"Special Curricula" is used throughout to denote curricular areas not routinely emphasized or addressed in general curricula; e.g., social, communication, motor, independence, self-advocacy.

As used, the phrase, "core academic subject matter content of the general curriculum," means only the content of the general curriculum including math, reading, English/language arts, science, social studies, and the arts. It does not per se include the additional specialized knowledge and skill that special educators possess in areas such as reading, writing, math, social/emotional skills, functional independent living skills, transition skills, etc.

Advanced specialty areas are those areas beyond entry-level special education teacher preparation programs. Advanced specialty area programs are preparation programs that require full special education teacher licensure as a program entrance prerequisite.

Section 3

Tools and Strategies
for Using the Standards

Section 3 contains a number of tools to help make the CEC Standards more accessible. There are forms for state education personnel to use to compare their state standards to the CEC standards. There is information to help teachers use the standards to develop a professional development plan, as well as strategies to help them advocate for appropriate inservice opportunities. Students in teacher preparation programs are provided with a self-assessment tool they can use to determine their progress in developing their professional knowledge and skills. Teacher educators will find a diagram that will help them chart their course as they develop and implement a standards-driven performance-based assessment system. Teacher educators will also find instructions and forms they can use with their students to help their students become familiar with the standards and with professional literature in their field.

A. State Licensure: Comparing CEC Standards to State Standards

In this newest set of CEC standards, CEC has rearranged its Knowledge and Skill Sets so that each explicitly aligns with the Interstate New Teacher and Assessment and Support Consortium's (INTASC) Model Standards for Teacher licensure. Each set has been reorganized into 10 domain areas that parallel the domain areas of each of the 10 INTASC Core Principles. This alignment is demonstrated in Table 3.1 (see page 13 for a complete description of this re-organization).

One of the primary purposes of this change was to support states, especially those states that use the INTASC standards as a key component of their licensure frameworks, to use the CEC Standards as they develop state standards for licensure of special education teachers.

CEC's Standards for Preparation and Licensure are written in two tiers. The foundational standards are the Knowledge and Skill Sets. These sets have been developed to meet the variety of state licensure frameworks. There are standards for both categorical and multicategorical licensure frameworks. CEC also developed a set of 10 Content Standards, based on the Knowledge and Skill Standards, one for each of the domain areas listed in Table 3.1. (See Appendix 2 for a complete description of their development.) The Content Standards are written at a more general level and are a single set—that is, they do not delineate the differences between the competencies needed by early childhood special education teachers, teachers of students with mild to moderate disabilities, teachers of students who are deaf and hard of hearing, and so forth. This level of specificity is found in the Knowledge and Skill Sets of Standards.

The following charts were designed to be helpful to states as they go through the process of determining the alignment of their state standards and the CEC standards. This could be done at the Content Standard level or the Knowledge and Skill Standards level. Figure 3.1 is a simple chart that lists the CEC Content Standards in the left column and provides a column for states to use to fill in the state standards that address the specific CEC Content Standards. Figure 3.2 is a chart created for states to use to compare their state standards for Early Childhood Special Education with the CEC Knowledge and Skill Standards. Early Childhood was used as an example; states could create a similar chart for other CEC standards that align with the state framework. All of the CEC Standards, along with electronic versions of the following forms, can be found on the CEC Web site at www.cec.sped.org.

TABLE 3.1
Alignment of INTASC Core Principles and CEC Standard Domain Areas

INTASC Core Principles	CEC Standard Domain Areas
1. Content Knowledge	1. Foundations
2. Learner Development	2. Characteristics of Learners
3. Learner Diversity	3. Individual Differences
4. Instructional Strategies	4. Instructional Strategies
5. Learning Environment	5. Learning Environments and Social Interactions
6. Communication	6. Language
7. Planning for Instruction	7. Instructional Planning
8. Assessment	8. Assessment
9. Reflective Practice and Professional Development	9. Ethics and Professional Practice
10. Community	10. Collaboration

FIGURE 3.1
Worksheet to Compare CEC Content Standards and State Content Standards

CEC Content Standards	*Corresponding State Standards*
1. Foundations Special educators understand the field as an evolving and changing discipline based on philosophies, evidence-based **principles and theories,** relevant **laws and policies,** diverse and **historical** points of view, and **human issues** that have historically influenced and continue to influence the field of special education and the education and treatment of individuals with exceptional needs both in school and society. Special educators understand how these **influence professional practice,** including assessment, instructional planning, implementation, and program evaluation. Special educators understand how **issues of human diversity** can impact families, cultures, and schools, and how these complex human issues can interact with issues in the delivery of special education services. They understand the **relationships of organizations** of **special education** to the organizations and functions of schools, school systems, and other agencies. Special educators use this knowledge as a ground upon which to construct their own personal understandings and philosophies of special education. Beginning special educators demonstrate their mastery of this standard through the mastery of the CEC Common Core Knowledge and Skills, as well as through the appropriate CEC Specialty Area(s) Knowledge and Skills for which the program is preparing candidates.	
2. Development and Characteristics of Learners Special educators know and **demonstrate respect** for their students first as unique human beings. Special educators understand the **similarities and differences in human development** and the characteristics between and among individuals with and without exceptional learning needs (ELN). Moreover, special educators understand how **exceptional conditions** can **interact** with the domains of human development and they **use this knowledge to respond to the varying abilities and behaviors of individuals** with ELN. Special educators understand how the experiences of individuals with ELN can impact families, as well as the individual's ability to learn, interact socially, and live as fulfilled contributing members of the community. Beginning special educators demonstrate their mastery of this standard through the mastery of the CEC Common Core Knowledge and Skills, as well as through the appropriate CEC Specialty Area(s) Knowledge and Skills for which the program is preparing candidates.	
3. Individual Learning Differences Special educators understand the **effects that an exceptional condition** can have **on an individual's learning** in school and throughout life. Special educators understand that the beliefs, traditions, and values across and within cultures can affect relationships among and between students, their families, and the school community. Moreover, special educators are **active and resourceful in seeking to understand how primary language, culture, and familial backgrounds interact with the individual's exceptional condition** to impact the individual's academic and social abilities, attitudes, values, interests, and career options. The understanding of these learning differences and their possible interactions **provides the foundation** upon which **special educators individualize instruction** to provide meaningful and challenging learning for individuals with ELN. Beginning special educators demonstrate their mastery of this standard through the mastery of the CEC Common Core Knowledge and Skills, as well as through the appropriate CEC Specialty Area(s) Knowledge and Skills for which the program is preparing candidates.	

continued

FIGURE 3.1 *continued*

CEC Content Standards	Corresponding State Standards
4. Instructional Strategies Special educators possess a repertoire of evidence-based **instructional strategies to individualize instruction** for individuals with ELN. Special educators select, adapt, and use these instructional strategies to promote **positive learning results in general and special curricula** and to appropriately **modify learning environments** for individuals with ELN. They enhance the **learning of critical thinking, problem-solving, and performance skills** of individuals with ELN, and increase their self-awareness, self-management, self-control, self-reliance, and self-esteem. Moreover, special educators emphasize the **development, maintenance, and generalization** of knowledge and skills across environments, settings, and the life span. Beginning special educators demonstrate their mastery of this standard through the mastery of the CEC Common Core Knowledge and Skills, as well as through the appropriate CEC Specialty Area(s) Knowledge and Skills for which the program is preparing candidates.	
5. Learning Environments and Social Interactions Special educators actively **create learning environments** for individuals with ELN that foster cultural understanding, safety and emotional well-being, positive social interactions, and **active engagement** of individuals with ELN. In addition, special educators **foster environments in which diversity is valued** and individuals are taught to live harmoniously and productively in a culturally diverse world. Special educators shape **environments to encourage the independence,** self-motivation, self-direction, personal empowerment, and self-advocacy of individuals with ELN. Special educators **help their general education colleagues integrate individuals** with ELN in general education environments and engage them in meaningful learning activities and interactions. Special educators use **direct motivational and instructional interventions** with individuals with ELN to teach them to respond effectively to current expectations. When necessary, special educators can safely **intervene with individuals with ELN in crisis.** Special educators coordinate all these efforts and **provide guidance and direction to paraeducators and others,** such as classroom volunteers and tutors. Beginning special educators demonstrate their mastery of this standard through the mastery of the CEC Common Core Knowledge and Skills, as well as through the appropriate CEC Specialty Area(s) Knowledge and Skills for which the program is preparing candidates.	
6. Language Special educators understand **typical and atypical language development** and the ways in which exceptional conditions can interact with an individual's experience with and use of language. Special educators use individualized strategies to **enhance language development** and **teach communication skills** to individuals with ELN. Special educators are familiar with **augmentative, alternative, and assistive technologies** to support and enhance communication of individuals with exceptional needs. Special educators match their communication methods to an individual's language proficiency and cultural and linguistic differences. Special educators provide **effective language models** and they use communication strategies and resources to **facilitate understanding of subject matter for individuals with ELN whose primary language is not English.** Beginning special educators demonstrate their mastery of this standard through the mastery of the CEC Common Core Knowledge and Skills, as well as through the appropriate CEC Specialty Area(s) Knowledge and Skills for which the program is preparing candidates.	

continued

FIGURE 3.1 *continued*

CEC Content Standards	Corresponding State Standards
7. Instructional Planning Individualized decision-making and instruction is at the center of special education practice. Special educators develop **long-range individualized instructional plans** anchored in both general and special education curricula. In addition, special educators systematically translate these individualized plans into carefully selected **shorter-range goals and objectives** taking into consideration an individual's abilities and needs, the learning environment, and a myriad of cultural and linguistic factors. Individualized instructional plans emphasize **explicit modeling** and **efficient guided practice** to assure acquisition and fluency through maintenance and generalization. Understanding of these factors as well as the implications of an individual's exceptional condition, guides the special educator's selection, adaptation, and creation of materials, and the use of powerful instructional variables. Instructional plans are **modified based on ongoing analysis of the individual's learning progress.** Moreover, special educators facilitate this instructional planning in a **collaborative context** including the individuals with exceptionalities, families, professional colleagues, and personnel from other agencies as appropriate. Special educators also develop a variety of **individualized transition plans,** such as transitions from preschool to elementary school and from secondary settings to a variety of postsecondary work and learning contexts. Special educators are comfortable using **appropriate technologies** to support instructional planning and individualized instruction. Beginning special educators demonstrate their mastery of this standard through the mastery of the CEC Common Core Knowledge and Skills, as well as through the appropriate CEC Specialty Area(s) Knowledge and Skills for which the program is preparing candidates.	
8. Assessment Assessment is integral to the decision-making and teaching of special educators and special educators use **multiple types of assessment information** for a variety of educational decisions. Special educators use the results of assessments to help identify exceptional learning needs and to develop and implement individualized instructional programs, as well as to adjust instruction in response to ongoing learning progress. Special educators understand the **legal policies and ethical principles of measurement and assessment** related to referral, eligibility, program planning, instruction, and placement for individuals with ELN, including those from culturally and linguistically diverse backgrounds. Special educators understand **measurement theory and practices** for addressing issues of validity, reliability, norms, bias, and interpretation of assessment results. In addition, special educators understand the appropriate **use and limitations** of various types of assessments. Special educators collaborate with families and other colleagues to assure **nonbiased, meaningful assessments and decision-making.** Special educators conduct **formal and informal assessments** of behavior, learning, achievement, and environments to design learning experiences that support the growth and development of individuals with ELN. Special educators use assessment information to **identify supports and adaptations** required for individuals with ELN to access the general curriculum and to participate in school, system, and statewide assessment programs. Special educators **regularly monitor the progress** of individuals with ELN in general and special curricula. Special educators **use appropriate technologies** to support their assessments. Beginning special educators demonstrate their mastery of this standard through the mastery of the CEC Common Core Knowledge and Skills, as well as through the appropriate CEC Specialty Area(s) Knowledge and Skills for which the program is preparing candidates.	

continued

FIGURE 3.1 *continued*

CEC Content Standards	Corresponding State Standards
9. Professional and Ethical Practice Special educators are guided by the profession's ethical and professional practice standards. Special educators practice in multiple roles and complex situations across wide age and developmental ranges. Their practice requires ongoing attention to **legal matters** along with serious professional and **ethical considerations.** Special educators engage in **professional activities** and participate in learning communities that benefit individuals with ELN, their families, colleagues, and their own professional growth. Special educators view themselves as **lifelong learners** and regularly reflect on and adjust their practice. Special educators are aware of how their own and others' attitudes, behaviors, and ways of communicating can influence their practice. Special educators understand that culture and language can interact with exceptionalities, and are **sensitive to the many aspects of diversity** of individuals with ELN and their families. Special educators actively plan and engage in activities that foster their professional growth and keep them **current with evidence-based best practices.** Special educators know their own limits of practice and practice within them. Beginning special educators demonstrate their mastery of this standard through the mastery of the CEC Common Core Knowledge and Skills, as well as through the appropriate CEC Specialty Area(s) Knowledge and Skills for which the program is preparing candidates.	
10. Collaboration Special educators routinely and effectively **collaborate with families, other educators, related service providers, and personnel from community agencies in culturally responsive ways.** This collaboration assures that the needs of individuals with ELN are addressed throughout schooling. Moreover, special educators embrace their special role as advocate for individuals with ELN. Special educators promote and advocate the learning and well-being of individuals with ELN across a wide range of settings and a range of different learning experiences. Special educators are viewed as specialists by a myriad of people who actively seek their collaboration to effectively include and teach individuals with ELN. Special educators are a **resource to their colleagues** in understanding the laws and policies relevant to individuals with ELN. Special educators use collaboration to **facilitate the successful transitions** of individuals with ELN across settings and services. Beginning special educators demonstrate their mastery of this standard through the mastery of the CEC Common Core Knowledge and Skills, as well as through the appropriate CEC Specialty Area(s) Knowledge and Skills for which the program is preparing candidates.	

Notes:

"Individual with exceptional learning needs" is used throughout to include individuals with disabilities and individuals with exceptional gifts and talents.

"Exceptional condition" is used throughout to include both single and co-existing conditions. These may be two or more disabling conditions or exceptional gifts or talents co-existing with one or more disabling conditions.

"Special curricula" is used throughout to denote curricular areas not routinely emphasized or addressed in general curricula; e.g., social, communication, motor, independence, self-advocacy.

FIGURE 3.2
Comparison of CEC Knowledge and Skill Standards
and State Standards for Early Childhood Special Education Teachers[1]

CEC Knowledge and Skill Standards		Corresponding State Standards
Standard #1: Foundations		
CC1K1	Models, theories, and philosophies that form the basis for special education practice.	
CC1K2	Laws, policies, and ethical principles regarding behavior management planning and implementation.	
CC1K3	Relationship of special education to the organization and function of educational agencies.	
CC1K4	Rights and responsibilities of students, parents, teachers, and other professionals, and schools related to exceptional learning needs.	
CC1K5	Issues in definition and identification of individuals with exceptional learning needs, including those from culturally and linguistically diverse backgrounds.	
CC1K6	Issues, assurances and due process rights related to assessment, eligibility, and placement within a continuum of services.	
CC1K7	Family systems and the role of families in the educational process.	
CC1K8	Historical points of view and contribution of culturally diverse groups.	
CC1K9	Impact of the dominant culture on shaping schools and the individuals who study and work in them.	
CC1K10	Potential impact of differences in values, languages, and customs that can exist between the home and school.	
EC1K1	Historical and philosophical foundations of services for young children both with and without exceptional learning needs.	
EC1K2	Trends and issues in early childhood education and early-childhood special education.	
EC1K3	Law and policies that affect young children, families, and programs for young children.	
CC1S1	Articulate personal philosophy of special education.	
Standard #2: Development and Characteristics of Learners		
CC2K1	Typical and atypical human growth and development.	
CC2K2	Educational implications of characteristics of various exceptionalities.	
CC2K3	Characteristics and effects of the cultural and environmental milieu of the individual with exceptional learning needs and the family.	
CC2K4	Family systems and the role of families in supporting development.	
CC2K5	Similarities and differences of individuals with and without exceptional learning needs.	
CC2K6	Similarities and differences among individuals with exceptional learning needs.	

[1]*Note On Coding:* CC in the number code indicates a Common Core item; EC indicates an Early Childhood Special Education item; K indicates a Knowledge item; S indicates a Skill item.

Note: The Early Childhood Standards are presented as an example. Forms for the other standard sets are available on the CEC web site (www.cec.sped.org).

continued

FIGURE 3.2 *continued*

CEC Knowledge and Skill Standards		Corresponding State Standards
CC2K7	Effects of various medications on individuals with exceptional learning needs.	
EC2K1	Theories of typical and atypical early childhood development.	
EC2K2	Effect of biological and environmental factors on pre-, peri-, and postnatal development.	
EC2K3	Influence of stress and trauma, protective factors and resilience, and supportive relationships on the social and emotional development of young children.	
EC2K4	Significance of sociocultural and political contexts for the development and learning of young children who are culturally and linguistically diverse.	
EC2K5	Impact of medical conditions on family concerns, resources, and priorities.	
EC2K6	Childhood illnesses and communicable diseases.	
Standard #3: Individual Learning Differences		
CC3K1	Effects an exceptional condition(s) can have on an individual's life.	
CC3K2	Impact of learners' academic and social abilities, attitudes, interests, and values on instruction and career development.	
CC3K3	Variations in beliefs, traditions, and values across and within cultures and their effects on relationships among individuals with exceptional learning needs, family, and schooling.	
CC3K4	Cultural perspectives influencing the relationships among families, schools, and communities as related to instruction.	
CC3K5	Differing ways of learning of individuals with exceptional learning needs including those from culturally diverse backgrounds and strategies for addressing these differences.	
EC3S1	Use intervention strategies with young children and their families that affirm and respect family, cultural, and linguistic diversity.	
Standard #4: Instructional Strategies		
CC4S1	Use strategies to facilitate integration into various settings.	
CC4S2	Teach individuals to use self-assessment, problem-solving, and other cognitive strategies to meet their needs.	
CC4S3	Select, adapt, and use instructional strategies and materials according to characteristics of the individual with exceptional learning needs.	
CC4S4	Use strategies to facilitate maintenance and generalization of skills across learning environments.	
CC4S5	Use procedures to increase the individual's self-awareness, self-management, self-control, self-reliance, and self-esteem.	
CC4S6	Use strategies that promote successful transitions for individuals with exceptional learning needs.	
EC4S1	Use instructional practices based on knowledge of the child, family, community, and the curriculum.	
EC4S2	Use knowledge of future educational settings to develop learning experiences and select instructional strategies for young children.	
EC4S3	Prepare young children for successful transitions.	

continued

FIGURE 3.2 *continued*

CEC Knowledge and Skill Standards		Corresponding State Standards
Standard #5: Learning Environments and Social Interactions		
CC5K1	Demands of learning environments.	
CC5K2	Basic classroom management theories and strategies for individuals with exceptional learning needs.	
CC5K3	Effective management of teaching and learning.	
CC5K4	Teacher attitudes and behaviors that influence behavior of individuals with exceptional learning needs.	
CC5K5	Social skills needed for educational and other environments.	
CC5K6	Strategies for crisis prevention and intervention.	
CC5K7	Strategies for preparing individuals to live harmoniously and productively in a culturally diverse world.	
CC5K8	Ways to create learning environments that allow individuals to retain and appreciate their own and each others' respective language and cultural heritage.	
CC5K9	Ways specific cultures are negatively stereotyped.	
CC5K10	Strategies used by diverse populations to cope with a legacy of former and continuing racism	
EC5K1	Medical care considerations for premature, low-birth-weight, and other young children with medical and health conditions.	
CC5S1	Create a safe, equitable, positive, and supportive learning environment in which diversities are valued.	
CC5S2	Identify realistic expectations for personal and social behavior in various settings.	
CC5S3	Identify supports needed for integration into various program placements.	
CC5S4	Design learning environments that encourage active participation in individual and group activities.	
CC5S5	Modify the learning environment to manage behaviors.	
CC5S6	Use performance data and information from all stakeholders to make or suggest modifications in learning environments.	
CC5S7	Establish and maintain rapport with individuals with and without exceptional learning needs.	
CC5S8	Teach self-advocacy.	
CC5S9	Create an environment that encourages self-advocacy and increased independence.	
CC5S10	Use effective and varied behavior management strategies.	
CC5S11	Use the least intensive behavior management strategy consistent with the needs of the individual with exceptional learning needs.	
CC5S12	Design and manage daily routines.	
CC5S13	Organize, develop, and sustain learning environments that support positive intracultural and intercultural experiences.	
CC5S14	Mediate controversial intercultural issues among students within the learning environment in ways that enhance any culture, group, or person.	
CC5S15	Structure, direct, and support the activities of paraeducators, volunteers, and tutors.	
CC5S16	Use universal precautions.	

continued

FIGURE 3.2 *continued*

CEC Knowledge and Skill Standards		Corresponding State Standards
EC5S1	Implement nutrition plans and feeding strategies.	
EC5S2	Use health appraisal procedures and make referrals as needed.	
EC5S3	Design, implement, and evaluate environments to assure developmental and functional appropriateness.	
EC5S4	Provide a stimuli-rich indoor and outdoor environment that employs materials, media, and technology, including adaptive and assistive technology.	
EC5S5	Maximize young children's progress in group and home settings through organization of the physical, temporal, and social environments.	
Standard #6: Language		
CC6K1	Effects of cultural and linguistic differences on growth and development.	
CC6K2	Characteristics of one's own culture and use of language and the ways in which these can differ from other cultures and uses of languages.	
CC6K3	Ways of behaving and communicating among cultures that can lead to misinterpretation and misunderstanding.	
CC6K4	Augmentative and assistive communication strategies.	
CC6S1	Use strategies to support and enhance communication skills of individuals with exceptional learning needs.	
CC6S2	Use communication strategies and resources to facilitate understanding of subject matter for students whose primary language is not the dominant language.	
EC6S1	Support and facilitate family and child interactions as primary contexts for learning and development.	
Standard #7: Instructional Planning		
CC7K1	Theories and research that form the basis of curriculum development and instructional practice.	
CC7K2	Scope and sequences of general and special curricula.	
CC7K3	National, state or provincial, and local curricula standards.	
CC7K4	Technology for planning and managing the teaching and learning environment.	
CC7K5	Roles and responsibilities of the paraeducator related to instruction, intervention, and direct service.	
CC7S1	Identify and prioritize areas of the general curriculum and accommodations for individuals with exceptional learning needs.	
CC7S2	Develop and implement comprehensive, longitudinal individualized programs in collaboration with team members.	
CC7S3	Involve the individual and family in setting instructional goals and monitoring progress.	
CC7S4	Use functional assessments to develop intervention plans.	
CC7S5	Use task analysis.	
CC7S6	Sequence, implement, and evaluate individualized learning objectives.	
CC7S7	Integrate affective, social, and life skills with academic curricula.	

continued

FIGURE 3.2 *continued*

CEC Knowledge and Skill Standards		Corresponding State Standards
CC7S8	Develop and select instructional content, resources, and strategies that respond to cultural, linguistic, and gender differences.	
CC7S9	Incorporate and implement instructional and assistive technology into the educational program.	
CC7S10	Prepare lesson plans.	
CC7S11	Prepare and organize materials to implement daily lesson plans.	
CC7S12	Use instructional time effectively.	
CC7S13	Make responsive adjustments to instruction based on continual observations.	
CC7S14	Prepare individuals to exhibit self-enhancing behavior in response to societal attitudes and actions.	
EC7S1	Implement, monitor, and evaluate individualized family service plans and individualized education plans.	
EC7S2	Plan and implement developmentally and individually appropriate curriculum.	
EC7S3	Design intervention strategies incorporating information from multiple disciplines.	
EC7S4	Implement developmentally and functionally appropriate individual and group activities including play, environmental routines, parent-mediated activities, group projects, cooperative learning, inquiry experiences, and systematic instruction.	
Standard #8: Assessment		
CC8K1	Basic terminology used in assessment.	
CC8K2	Legal provisions and ethical principles regarding assessment of individuals.	
CC8K3	Screening, prereferral, referral, and classification procedures.	
CC8K4	Use and limitations of assessment instruments.	
CC8K5	National, state or provincial, and local accommodations and modifications.	
CC8S1	Gather relevant background information.	
CC8S2	Administer nonbiased formal and informal assessments.	
CC8S3	Use technology to conduct assessments.	
CC8S4	Develop or modify individualized assessment strategies.	
CC8S5	Interpret information from formal and informal assessments.	
CC8S6	Use assessment information in making eligibility, program, and placement decisions for individuals with exceptional learning needs, including those from culturally and/or linguistically diverse backgrounds.	
CC8S7	Report assessment results to all stakeholders using effective communication skills.	
CC8S8	Evaluate instruction and monitor progress of individuals with exceptional learning needs.	
CC8S9	Create and maintain records.	
EC8S1	Assess the development and learning of young children.	
EC8S2	Select, adapt, and use specialized formal and informal assessments for infants, young children, and their families.	

continued

FIGURE 3.2 *continued*

CEC Knowledge and Skill Standards		Corresponding State Standards
EC8S3	Participate as a team member to integrate assessment results in the development and implementation of individualized family service plans and individualized education plans.	
EC8S4	Assist families in identifying their concerns, resources, and priorities.	
EC8S5	Participate and collaborate as a team member with other professionals in conducting family-centered assessments.	
EC8S6	Evaluate services with families.	
Standard #9: Professional and Ethical Practice		
CC9K1	Personal cultural biases and differences that affect one's teaching.	
CC9K2	Importance of the teacher serving as a model for individuals with exceptional learning needs.	
CC9K3	Continuum of lifelong professional development.	
CC9K4	Methods to remain current regarding research-validated practice.	
EC9K1	Organizations and publications relevant to the field of early childhood special education.	
CC9S1	Practice within the CEC Code of Ethics and other standards of the profession.	
CC9S2	Uphold high standards of competence and integrity and exercise sound judgment in the practice of the professional.	
CC9S3	Act ethically in advocating for appropriate services.	
CC9S4	Conduct professional activities in compliance with applicable laws and policies.	
CC9S5	Demonstrate commitment to developing the highest education and quality-of-life potential of individuals with exceptional learning needs.	
CC9S6	Demonstrate sensitivity for the culture, language, religion, gender, disability, socioeconomic status, and sexual orientation of individuals.	
CC9S7	Practice within one's skill limit and obtain assistance as needed.	
CC9S8	Use verbal, nonverbal, and written language effectively.	
CC9S9	Conduct self-evaluation of instruction.	
CC9S10	Access information on exceptionalities.	
CC9S11	Reflect on one's practice to improve instruction and guide professional growth.	
CC9S12	Engage in professional activities that benefit individuals with exceptional learning needs, their families, and one's colleagues.	
EC9S1	Recognize signs of child abuse and neglect in young children and follow reporting procedures.	
EC9S2	Use family theories and principles to guide professional practice.	
EC9S3	Respect family choices and goals.	
EC9S4	Apply models of team process in early childhood.	
EC9S5	Advocate for enhanced professional status and working conditions for early childhood service providers.	

continued

FIGURE 3.2 *continued*

CEC Knowledge and Skill Standards		Corresponding State Standards
EC9S6	Participate in activities of professional organizations relevant to the field of early childhood special education.	
EC9S7	Apply research and effective practices critically in early childhood settings.	
EC9S8	Develop, implement, and evaluate a professional development plan relevant to one's work with young children.	
Standard #10: Collaboration		
CC10K1	Models and strategies of consultation and collaboration.	
CC10K2	Roles of individuals with exceptional learning needs, families, and school and community personnel in planning of an individualized program.	
CC10K3	Concerns of families of individuals with exceptional learning needs and strategies to help address these concerns.	
CC10K4	Culturally responsive factors that promote effective communication and collaboration with individuals with exceptional learning needs, families, school personnel, and community members.	
EC10K1	Dynamics of team-building, problem-solving, and conflict resolution.	
CC10S1	Maintain confidential communication about individuals with exceptional learning needs.	
CC10S2	Collaborate with families and others in assessment of individuals with exceptional learning needs.	
CC10S3	Foster respectful and beneficial relationships between families and professionals.	
CC10S4	Assist individuals with exceptional learning needs and their families in becoming active participants in the educational team.	
CC10S5	Plan and conduct collaborative conferences with individuals with exceptional learning needs and their families.	
CC10S6	Collaborate with school personnel and community members in integrating individuals with exceptional learning needs into various settings.	
CC10S7	Use group problem-solving skills to develop, implement, and evaluate collaborative activities.	
CC10S8	Model techniques and coach others in the use of instructional methods and accommodations.	
CC10S9	Communicate with school personnel about the characteristics and needs of individuals with exceptional learning needs.	
CC10S10	Communicate effectively with families of individuals with exceptional learning needs from diverse backgrounds.	
CC10S11	Observe, evaluate, and provide feedback to paraeducators.	
EC10S1	Assist the family in planning for transitions.	
EC10S2	Communicate effectively with families about curriculum and their child's progress.	
EC10S3	Apply models of team process in early childhood settings.	
EC10S4	Apply various models of consultation in early childhood settings.	

continued

FIGURE 3.2 *continued*

CEC Knowledge and Skill Standards		Corresponding State Standards
EC10S5	Establish and maintain positive collaborative relationships with families.	
EC10S6	Provide consultation and instruction specific to services for children and families.	

Notes:

"Individual with exceptional learning needs" is used throughout to include individuals with disabilities and individuals with exceptional gifts and talents.

"Exceptional condition" is used throughout to include both single and co-existing conditions. These may be two or more disabling conditions or exceptional gifts or talents co-existing with one or more disabling conditions.

"Special curricula" is used throughout to denote curricular areas not routinely emphasized or addressed in general curricula; e.g., social, communication, motor, independence, self-advocacy.

B. Teachers: Developing a Professional Development Plan

CEC is the world's leader in the development of standards for special education teachers. These standards are used by hundreds of colleges and universities to develop their curricula and as a measure to assess their graduates' competence. Over half of the states use the CEC standards as models for their state licensure frameworks. But do these standards have any use or relevance for special education teachers working every day in classrooms?

The answer is a resounding Yes. There are numerous ways that practicing special educators can and should use the CEC standards to ensure that they have and maintain the knowledge and skills necessary to meet the needs of their students. The standards are an excellent yardstick that can be used by individuals to assess their own competence as well as to determine the best use of their professional development hours. Practitioners can also use the standards to evaluate their ability and proficiency as they contemplate a job change or a move to working with children with different kinds of disabilities.

The CEC standards can be a powerful tool for special educators to request and receive the professional development opportunities they need to update their current skills and learn new skills required for the challenges they face every day. The standards can be and are being used by schools and districts as the basis for helping their teachers develop professional development programs that will ensure that all teachers have the knowledge and skills they need to work successfully with children with disabilities.

HOW TO USE THE STANDARDS TO IMPROVE YOUR PRACTICE

The CEC standards can be used as a road map to help practicing teachers structure a professional development plan, to ensure that they maintain an appropriate level of expertise, and to evaluate their competence as they move into new areas. Beginning teachers can find them particularly useful as a way of measuring their developing expertise. The following steps outline a process teachers can use:

1. Select the most appropriate set of standards from the CEC Web site (http://www.cec.sped.org/ps/perf_based_stds/index.html). The standard sets are also available as Word Documents by sending a request to cecprof@cec.sped.org.
2. Rate your level of mastery on each of the individual standards. Two suggested formats for creating an evaluation form are shown in Figures 3.3 and 3.4.
3. After you have gone though the entire set, add up the number of items checked in each domain area (e.g., Characteristics of Learners, Assessment, etc.). Play closest attention to those domain areas that have the highest (or lowest) scores.
4. Choose the domain area(s) that you want to work on and plan your continuing education program or professional development plan accordingly. These could be those in the domain areas that had your highest (or lowest) rating or it could be in the domain area that would meet the greatest need you have at this particular time.

Some examples:

A beginning teacher who is working with children with mild to moderate disabilities could select the Individualized General Curriculum set of standards. This set is designed for teachers working with children with disabilities who are expected to be successful in the general curriculum and most closely aligns with a mild/moderate licensure framework. By going through the steps above, beginning teachers can determine in which areas they feel the least confident. This information can be used to help select course work required for continuing education licensure, inservice or conference sessions needed for CEUs, extra reading, and so forth.

If a teacher is considering moving into a new role or working with a new kind of student, he or she can evaluate their knowledge and skills in the same way. For example, perhaps a teacher has been asked to teach a class of students who are developmentally delayed even though all their previous years of experience have been with students with mild to moderate learning disabilities. Following the steps above, and using the CEC Mental Retardation and Developmental Disabilities set of standards, the teacher can determine which areas might be the most challenging for them. This documentation can be provided to the principal or special education coordinator as part of a request for additional training.

This process could also be used by a group of teachers. Each could complete a self-evaluation and then the group could evaluate their domain scores together to help plan or request the inservice educational opportunities that would benefit them the most. This documentation could be provided to the principal, district supervisor, or inservice director as a part of request for coverage of specific topic areas.

SUMMARY

Teaching is a life-long learning process. Men and women who leave training programs are novices entering their profession. Using the CEC standards to gauge their professional development is a way for ALL teachers to ensure that their knowledge and skills are up-to-date and sufficient to meet the needs of their students.

FIGURE 3.3
Self-Evaluation Form for Mastery of CEC Knowledge and Skill Standards for Beginning Special Education Teachers of Students in Individualized General Curriculums (most closely aligned with a Mild/Moderate licensure framework): Domain Areas 2 and 10

Domain Area #2: Development and Characteristics of Learners

		Could I improve my knowledge/skill base in this area?	If yes, what can I do to improve my mastery in this area?
GC2K1	Etiology and diagnosis related to various theoretical approaches.		
GC2K2	Impact of sensory impairments and physical and health disabilities on individuals, families, and society.		
GC2K3	Etiologies and medical aspects of conditions affecting individuals with disabilities.		
GC2K4	Psychological and social-emotional characteristics of individuals with disabilities.		
GC2K5	Common etiologies and the impact of sensory disabilities on learning and experience.		
GC2K6	Types and transmission routes of infectious disease.		

Domain Area #10: Collaboration

		Could I improve my knowledge/skill base in this area?	If yes, what can I do to improve my mastery in this area?
GC10K1	Parent education programs and behavior management guides that address severe behavior problems and facilitation communication for individuals with disabilities.		
GC10K2	Collaborative and/or consultative role of the special education teacher in the reintegration of individuals with disabilities.		
GC10K3	Roles of professional groups and referral agencies in identifying, assessing, and providing services to individuals with disabilities.		
GC10K4	Co-planning and co-teaching methods to strengthen content acquisition of individuals with learning disabilities.		
GC10S1	Use local community and state and provincial resources to assist in programming with individuals with disabilities.		
GC10S2	Select, plan, and coordinate activities of related services personnel to maximize direct instruction for individuals with disabilities.		
GC10S3	Teach parents to use appropriate behavior management and counseling techniques.		
GC10S4	Collaborate with team members to plan transition to adulthood that encourages full community participation.		

Note:

Implicit to all of the knowledge and skills standards in this section is the focus on individuals with disabilities whose education focuses on an individualized general curriculum.

FIGURE 3.4

Self-Evaluation Form for Mastery of CEC Knowledge and Skill Standards for Beginning Special Education Teachers of Students in Individualized General Curriculums (most closely aligned with a Mild/Moderate licensure framework): Domain Area 4

Domain #4:   Instructional Strategies

		What is my level of mastery of this standard?		
		Novice	Proficient	Accomplished
GC4K1	Sources of specialized materials, curricula, and resources for individuals with disabilities.			
GC4K2	Strategies to prepare for and take tests.			
GC4K3	Advantages and limitations of instructional strategies and practices for teaching individuals with disabilities.			
GC4K4	Prevention and intervention strategies for individuals at risk for a disability.			
GC4K5	Strategies for integrating student-initiated learning experiences into ongoing instruction.			
GC4K6	Methods for increasing accuracy and proficiency in math calculations and applications.			
GC4K7	Methods for guiding individuals in identifying and organizing critical content.			
GC4S1	Use research-supported methods for academic and nonacademic instruction of individuals with disabilities.			
GC4S2	Use strategies from multiple theoretical approaches for individuals with disabilities.			
GC4S3	Teach learning strategies and study skills to acquire academic content.			
GC4S4	Use reading methods appropriate to individuals with disabilities.			
GC4S5	Use methods to teach mathematics appropriate to the individuals with disabilities.			
GC4S6	Modify pace of instruction and provide organizational cures.			
GC4S7	Use appropriate adaptations and technology for all individuals with disabilities.			
GC4S8	Resources and techniques used to transition individuals with disabilities into and out of school and postschool environments.			
GC4S9	Use a variety of nonaversive techniques to control targeted behavior and maintain attention of individuals with disabilities.			
GC4S10	Identify and teach basic structures and relationships within and across curricula.			
GC4S11	Use instructional methods to strengthen and compensate for deficits in perception, comprehension, memory, and retrieval.			
GC4S12	Use responses and errors to guide instructional decisions and provide feedback to learners.			

continued

FIGURE 3.4 *continued*

		What is my level of mastery of this standard?		
		Novice	Proficient	Accomplished
GC4S13	Identify and teach essential concepts, vocabulary, and content across the general curriculum.			
GC4S14	Implement systematic instruction in teaching reading comprehension and monitoring strategies.			
GC4S15	Teach strategies for organizing and composing written products.			
GC4S16	Implement systematic instruction to teach accuracy, fluency, and comprehension in content area reading and written language.			

Note:

Implicit to all of the knowledge and skills standards in this section is the focus on individuals with disabilities whose education focuses on an individualized general curriculum.

C. Students: Do I Know What I Need to Know?

The following chart (see Figure 3.5) is a self-evaluation instrument designed to be used by students of special education to evaluate their progress in learning the knowledge and skills they will need upon graduation from the preparation program. Students can use it in a variety of ways. Students can check off each knowledge and skill competency as it is acquired; they can also include the course number, as well as the specific activity that they completed as they mastered each item.

Several colleges and universities have used a similar instrument for their students to use to self-evaluate their mastery of the CEC Stan-dards periodically throughout the preparation program, including during their first year of teaching. This has provided rich data for the preparation program that can then be used to improve the program.

The matrix included in this chart is for the Individualized General Curriculum Referenced Standards; page limitations have prevented us from including the other Area of Specialization matrices. Similar matrices for each Area of Specialization could easily be prepared using the same format. All of the CEC standards can be found on the CEC Web site at www.cec.sped.org.

FIGURE 3.5
A Self-Evaluation Tool for Students Preparing to Become
Special Education Teachers of Students in Individualized General Curriculum

Standard #1: Foundations		*Cite the course number and/or course lecture or activity in which each standard was mastered.*
CC1K1	Models, theories, and philosophies that form the basis for special education practice.	
CC1K2	Laws, policies, and ethical principles regarding behavior management planning and implementation.	
CC1K3	Relationship of special education to the organization and function of educational agencies.	
CC1K4	Rights and responsibilities of students, parents, teachers, and other professionals, and schools related to exceptional learning needs.	
CC1K5	Issues in definition and identification of individuals with exceptional learning needs, including those from culturally and linguistically diverse backgrounds.	
CC1K6	Issues, assurances, and due process rights related to assessment, eligibility, and placement within a continuum of services.	
CC1K7	Family systems and the role of families in the educational process.	
CC1K8	Historical points of view and contribution of culturally diverse groups.	
CC1K9	Impact of the dominant culture on shaping schools and the individuals who study and work in them.	
CC1K10	Potential impact of differences in values, languages, and customs that can exist between the home and school.	
CC1S1	Articulate personal philosophy of special education.	
GC1K1	Definitions and issues related to the identification of individuals with disabilities.	
GC1K2	Models and theories of deviance and behavior problems.	
GC1K3	Historical foundations, classic studies, major contributors, major legislation, and current issues related to knowledge and practice.	
GC1K4	The legal, judicial, and educational systems to assist individuals with disabilities.	
GC1K5	Continuum of placement and services available for individuals with disabilities.	
GC1K6	Laws and policies related to provision of specialized health care in educational settings.	
GC1K7	Factors that influence the over-representation of culturally/linguistically diverse students in programs for individuals with disabilities.	
GC1K8	Principles of normalization and concept of least restrictive environment.	
GC1K9	Theory of reinforcement techniques in serving individuals with disabilities.	

continued

FIGURE 3.5 *continued*

Standard #2: Development and Characteristics of Learners		Cite the course number and/or course lecture or activity in which each standard was mastered.
CC2K1	Typical and atypical human growth and development.	
CC2K2	Educational implications of characteristics of various exceptionalities.	
CC2K3	Characteristics and effects of the cultural and environmental milieu of the individual with exceptional learning needs and the family.	
CC2K4	Family systems and the role of families in supporting development.	
CC2K5	Similarities and differences of individuals with and without exceptional learning needs.	
CC2K6	Similarities and differences among individuals with exceptional learning needs.	
CC2K7	Effects of various medications on individuals with exceptional learning needs.	
GC2K1	Etiology and diagnosis related to various theoretical approaches.	
GC2K2	Impact of sensory impairments, physical and health disabilities on individuals, families, and society.	
GC2K3	Etiologies and medical aspects of conditions affecting individuals with disabilities.	
GC2K4	Psychological and social-emotional characteristics of individuals with disabilities.	
GC2K5	Common etiologies and the impact of sensory disabilities on learning and experience.	
GC2K6	Types and transmission routes of infectious disease.	

Standard #3: Individual Learning Differences		Cite the course number and/or course lecture or activity in which each standard was mastered.
CC3K1	Effects an exceptional condition(s) can have on an individual's life.	
CC3K2	Impact of learners' academic and social abilities, attitudes, interests, and values on instruction and career development.	
CC3K3	Variations in beliefs, traditions, and values across and within cultures and their effects on relationships among individuals with exceptional learning needs, family, and schooling.	
CC3K4	Cultural perspectives influencing the relationships among families, schools, and communities as related to instruction.	
CC3K5	Differing ways of learning of individuals with exceptional learning needs including those from culturally diverse back-grounds and strategies for addressing these differences.	
GC3K1	Impact of disabilities on auditory and information processing skills.	
GC3S1	Relate levels of support to the needs of the individual.	

continued

FIGURE 3.5 *continued*

Standard #4: Instructional Strategies		*Cite the course number and/or course lecture or activity in which each standard was mastered.*
GC4K1	Sources of specialized materials, curricula, and resources for individuals with disabilities.	
GC4K2	Strategies to prepare for and take tests.	
GC4K3	Advantages and limitations of instructional strategies and practices for teaching individuals with disabilities.	
GC4K4	Prevention and intervention strategies for individuals at risk for a disability.	
GC4K5	Strategies for integrating student-initiated learning experiences into ongoing instruction.	
GC4K6	Methods for increasing accuracy and proficiency in math calculations and applications.	
GC4K7	Methods for guiding individuals in identifying and organizing critical content.	
CC4S1	Use strategies to facilitate integration into various settings.	
CC4S2	Teach individuals to use self-assessment, problem-solving, and other cognitive strategies to meet their needs.	
CC4S3	Select, adapt, and use instructional strategies and materials according to characteristics of the individual with exceptional learning needs.	
CC4S4	Use strategies to facilitate maintenance and generalization of skills across learning environments.	
CC4S5	Use procedures to increase the individual's self-awareness, self-management, self-control, self-reliance, and self-esteem.	
CC4S6	Use strategies that promote successful transitions for individuals with exceptional learning needs.	
GC4S1	Use research-supported methods for academic and non-academic instruction of individuals with disabilities.	
GC4S2	Use strategies from multiple theoretical approaches for individuals with disabilities.	
GC4S3	Teach learning strategies and study skills to acquire academic content.	
GC4S4	Use reading methods appropriate to individuals with disabilities.	
GC4S5	Use methods to teach mathematics appropriate to the individuals with disabilities.	
GC4S6	Modify pace of instruction and provide organizational cures.	
GC4S7	Use appropriate adaptations and technology for all individuals with disabilities.	
GC4S8	Resources and techniques used to transition individuals with disabilities into and out of school and postschool environments.	
GC4S9	Use a variety of nonaversive techniques to control targeted behavior and maintain attention of individuals with disabilities.	
GC4S10	Identify and teach basic structures and relationships within and across curricula.	

continued

FIGURE 3.5 *continued*

		Cite the course number and/or course lecture or activity in which each standard was mastered.
GC4S11	Use instructional methods to strengthen and compensate for deficits in perception, comprehension, memory, and retrieval.	
GC4S12	Use responses and errors to guide instructional decisions and provide feedback to learners.	
GC4S13	Identify and teach essential concepts, vocabulary, and content across the general curriculum.	
GC4S14	Implement systematic instruction in teaching reading comprehension and monitoring strategies.	
GC4S15	Teach strategies for organizing and composing written products.	

Standard #5: Learning Environments and Social Interactions		Cite the course number and/or course lecture or activity in which each standard was mastered.
CC5K1	Demands of learning environments.	
CC5K2	Basic classroom management theories and strategies for individuals with exceptional learning needs.	
CC5K3	Effective management of teaching and learning.	
CC5K4	Teacher attitudes and behaviors that influence behavior of individuals with exceptional learning needs.	
CC5K5	Social skills needed for educational and other environments.	
CC5K6	Strategies for crisis prevention and intervention.	
CC5K7	Strategies for preparing individuals to live harmoniously and productively in a culturally diverse world.	
CC5K8	Ways to create learning environments that allow individuals to retain and appreciate their own and each others' respective language and cultural heritage.	
CC5K9	Ways specific cultures are negatively stereotyped.	
CC5K10	Strategies used by diverse populations to cope with a legacy of former and continuing racism.	
GC5K1	Barriers to accessibility and acceptance of individuals with disabilities.	
GC5K2	Adaptation of the physical environment to provide optimal learning opportunities for individuals with disabilities.	
GC5K3	Methods for ensuring individual academic success in one-to-one, small-group, and large-group settings.	
CC5S1	Create a safe, equitable, positive, and supportive learning environment in which diversities are valued.	
CC5S2	Identify realistic expectations for personal and social behavior in various settings.	
CC5S3	Identify supports needed for integration into various program placements.	
CC5S4	Design learning environments that encourage active participation in individual and group activities.	
CC5S5	Modify the learning environment to manage behaviors.	

continued

FIGURE 3.5 *continued*

		Cite the course number and/or course lecture or activity in which each standard was mastered.
CC5S6	Use performance data and information from all stakeholders to make or suggest modifications in learning environments.	
CC5S7	Establish and maintain rapport with individuals with and without exceptional learning needs.	
CC5S8	Teach self-advocacy.	
CC5S9	Create an environment that encourages self-advocacy and increased independence.	
CC5S10	Use effective and varied behavior management strategies.	
CC5S11	Use the least intensive behavior management strategy consistent with the needs of the individual with exceptional learning needs.	
CC5S12	Design and manage daily routines.	
CC5S13	Organize, develop, and sustain learning environments that support positive intracultural and intercultural experiences.	
CC5S14	Mediate controversial intercultural issues among students within the learning environment in ways that enhance any culture, group, or person.	
CC5S15	Structure, direct, and support the activities of paraeducators, volunteers, and tutors.	
CC5S16	Use universal precautions.	
GC5S1	Provide instruction in community-based settings.	
GC5S2	Use and maintain assistive technologies.	
GC5S3	Plan instruction in a variety of educational settings.	
GC5S4	Teach individuals with disabilities to give and receive meaningful feedback from peers and adults.	
GC5S5	Use skills in problem-solving and conflict resolution.	
GC5S6	Establish a consistent classroom routine for individuals with disabilities.	

Standard #6: Language		Cite the course number and/or course lecture or activity in which each standard was mastered.
CC6K1	Effects of cultural and linguistic differences on growth and development.	
CC6K2	Characteristics of one's own culture and use of language and the ways in which these can differ from other cultures and uses of languages.	
CC6K3	Ways of behaving and communicating among cultures that can lead to misinterpretation and misunderstanding.	
CC6K4	Augmentative and assistive communication strategies.	
GC6K1	Impact of language development and listening comprehension on academic and nonacademic learning of individuals with disabilities.	
GC6K2	Communication and social interaction alternatives for individuals who are nonspeaking.	

continued

FIGURE 3.5 *continued*

		Cite the course number and/or course lecture or activity in which each standard was mastered.
GC6K3	Typical language development and how that may differ for individuals with learning disabilities.	
GC6S1	Enhance vocabulary development.	
GC6S2	Teach strategies for spelling accuracy and generalization.	
GC6S3	Teach individuals with disabilities to monitor for errors in oral and written language.	
GC6S4	Teach methods and strategies for producing legible documents.	
GC6S5	Plan instruction on the use of alternative and augmentative communication systems.	

Standard #7: Instructional Planning		*Cite the course number and/or course lecture or activity in which each standard was mastered.*
CC7K1	Theories and research that form the basis of curriculum development and instructional practice.	
CC7K2	Scope and sequences of general and special curricula.	
CC7K3	National, state or provincial, and local curricula standards.	
CC7K4	Technology for planning and managing the teaching and learning environment.	
CC7K5	Roles and responsibilities of the paraeducator related to instruction, intervention, and direct service.	
GC7K1	Integrate academic instruction and behavior management for individuals and groups with disabilities.	
GC7K2	Model career, vocational, and transition programs for individuals with disabilities.	
GC7K3	Interventions and services for children who may be at risk for learning disabilities.	
GC7K4	Relationships among disabilities and reading instruction.	
CC7S1	Identify and prioritize areas of the general curriculum and accommodations for individuals with exceptional learning needs.	
CC7S2	Develop and implement comprehensive, longitudinal individualized programs in collaboration with team members.	
CC7S3	Involve the individual and family in setting instructional goals and monitoring progress.	
CC7S4	Use functional assessments to develop intervention plans.	
CC7S5	Use task analysis.	
CC7S6	Sequence, implement, and evaluate individualized learning objectives.	
CC7S7	Integrate affective, social, and life skills with academic curricula.	
CC7S8	Develop and select instructional content, resources, and strategies that respond to cultural, linguistic, and gender differences.	

continued

FIGURE 3.5 *continued*

		Cite the course number and/or course lecture or activity in which each standard was mastered.
CC7S9	Incorporate and implement instructional and assistive technology into the educational program.	
CC7S10	Prepare lesson plans.	
CC7S11	Prepare and organize materials to implement daily lesson plans.	
CC7S12	Use instructional time effectively.	
CC7S13	Make responsive adjustments to instruction based on continual observations.	
CC7S14	Prepare individuals to exhibit self-enhancing behavior in response to societal attitudes and actions.	
GC7S1	Plan and implement individualized reinforcement systems and environmental modifications at levels equal to the intensity of the behavior.	
GC7S2	Select and use specialized instructional strategies appropriate to the abilities and needs of the individual.	
GC7S3	Plan and implement age- and ability-appropriate instruction for individuals with disabilities.	
GC7S4	Select, design, and use technology, materials, and resources required to educate individuals whose disabilities interfere with communication.	
GC7S5	Interpret sensory, mobility, reflex, and perceptual information to create or adapt appropriate learning plans.	
GC7S6	Design and implement instructional programs that address independent living and career education for individuals.	
GC7S7	Design and implement curriculum and instructional strategies for medical self-management procedures.	
GC7S8	Design, implement, and evaluate instructional programs that enhance social participation across environments.	

Standard #8: Assessment		Cite the course number and/or course lecture or activity in which each standard was mastered.
CC8K1	Basic terminology used in assessment.	
CC8K2	Legal provisions and ethical principles regarding assessment of individuals.	
CC8K3	Screening, prereferral, referral, and classification procedures.	
CC8K4	Use and limitations of assessment instruments.	
CC8K5	National, state or provincial, and local accommodations and modifications.	
GC8K1	Specialized terminology used in the assessment of individuals with disabilities.	
GC8K2	Laws and policies regarding referral and placement procedures for individuals with disabilities.	
GC8K3	Types and importance of information concerning individuals with disabilities available from families and public agencies.	

continued

FIGURE 3.5 *continued*

		Cite the course number and/or course lecture or activity in which each standard was mastered.
GC8K4	Procedures for early identification of young children who may be at risk for disabilities.	
CC8S1	Gather relevant background information.	
CC8S2	Administer nonbiased formal and informal assessments.	
CC8S3	Use technology to conduct assessments.	
CC8S4	Develop or modify individualized assessment strategies.	
CC8S5	Interpret information from formal and informal assessments.	
CC8S6	Use assessment information in making eligibility, program, and placement decisions for individuals with exceptional learning needs, including those from culturally and/or linguistically diverse backgrounds.	
CC8S7	Report assessment results to all stakeholders using effective communication skills.	
CC8S8	Evaluate instruction and monitor progress of individuals with exceptional learning needs.	
CC8S9	Develop or modify individualized assessment strategies.	
CC8S10	Create and maintain records.	
GC8S1	Implement procedures for assessing and reporting both appropriate and problematic social behaviors of individuals with disabilities.	
GC8S2	Use exceptionality-specific assessment instruments with individuals with disabilities.	
GC8S3	Select, adapt, and modify assessments to accommodate the unique abilities and needs of individuals with disabilities.	
GC8S4	Assess reliable methods of response of individuals who lack typical communication and performance abilities.	
GC8S5	Monitor intragroup behavior changes across subjects and activities.	

Standard #9: Professional and Ethical Practice		Cite the course number and/or course lecture or activity in which each standard was mastered.
CC9K1	Personal cultural biases and differences that affect one's teaching.	
CC9K2	Importance of the teacher serving as a model for individuals with exceptional learning needs.	
CC9K3	Continuum of lifelong professional development.	
CC9K4	Methods to remain current regarding research-validated practice.	
GC9K1	Sources of unique services, networks, and organizations for individuals with disabilities.	
GC9K2	Organizations and publications relevant to individuals with disabilities.	
CC9S1	Practice within the CEC Code of Ethics and other standards of the profession.	

continued

FIGURE 3.5 *continued*

		Cite the course number and/or course lecture or activity in which each standard was mastered.
CC9S2	Uphold high standards of competence and integrity and exercise sound judgment in the practice of the professional.	
CC9S3	Act ethically in advocating for appropriate services.	
CC9S4	Conduct professional activities in compliance with applicable laws and policies.	
CC9S5	Demonstrate commitment to developing the highest education and quality-of-life potential of individuals with exceptional learning needs.	
CC9S6	Demonstrate sensitivity for the culture, language, religion, gender, disability, socio-economic status, and sexual orientation of individuals.	
CC9S7	Practice within one's skill limit and obtain assistance as needed.	
CC9S8	Use verbal, nonverbal, and written language effectively.	
CC9S9	Conduct self-evaluation of instruction.	
CC9S10	Access information on exceptionalities.	
CC9S11	Reflect on one's practice to improve instruction and guide professional growth.	
CC9S12	Engage in professional activities that benefit individuals with exceptional learning needs, their families, and one's colleagues.	
GC9S1	Participate in the activities of professional organizations relevant to individuals with disabilities.	
GC9S2	Ethical responsibility to advocate for appropriate services for individuals with disabilities.	

Standard #10: Collaboration		Cite the course number and/or course lecture or activity in which each standard was mastered.
CC10K1	Models and strategies of consultation and collaboration.	
CC10K2	Roles of individuals with exceptional learning needs, families, and school and community personnel in planning of an individualized program.	
CC10K3	Concerns of families of individuals with exceptional learning needs and strategies to help address these concerns.	
CC10K4	Culturally responsive factors that promote effective communication and collaboration with individuals with exceptional learning needs, families, school personnel, and community members.	
GC10K1	Parent education programs and behavior management guides that address severe behavior problems and facilitation communication for individuals with disabilities.	
GC10K2	Collaborative and/or consultative role of the special education teacher in the reintegration of individuals with disabilities.	
GC10K3	Roles of professional groups and referral agencies in identifying, assessing, and providing services to individuals with disabilities.	

continued

FIGURE 3.5 *continued*

		Cite the course number and/or course lecture or activity in which each standard was mastered.
GC10K4	Co-planning and co-teaching methods to strengthen content acquisition of individuals with learning disabilities.	
GC10S1	Maintain confidential communication about individuals with exceptional learning needs.	
CC10S2	Collaborate with families and others in assessment of individuals with exceptional learning needs.	
CC10S3	Foster respectful and beneficial relationships between families and professionals.	
CC10S4	Assist individuals with exceptional learning needs and their families in becoming active participants in the educational team.	
CC10S5	Plan and conduct collaborative conferences with individuals with exceptional learning needs and their families.	
CC10S6	Collaborate with school personnel and community members in integrating individuals with exceptional learning needs into various settings.	
CC10S7	Use group problem-solving skills to develop, implement, and evaluate collaborative activities.	
CC10S8	Model techniques and coach others in the use of instructional methods and accommodations.	
CC10S9	Communicate with school personnel about the characteristics and needs of individuals with exceptional learning needs.	
CC10S10	Communicate effectively with families of individuals with exceptional learning needs from diverse backgrounds.	
CC10S11	Observe, evaluate, and provide feedback to paraeducators.	
GC10S1	Use local community, and state and provincial resources to assist in programming with individuals with disabilities.	
GC10S2	Select, plan, and coordinate activities of related services personnel to maximize direct instruction for individuals with disabilities.	
GC10S3	Teach parents to use appropriate behavior management and counseling techniques.	
GC10S4	Collaborate with team members to plan transition to adulthood that encourages full community participation	

Note:

Implicit to all of the knowledge and skills standards in this section is the focus on individuals with disabilities whose education focuses on an individualized general curriculum.

D. Teacher Preparation Programs:
Developing a Performance-Based Assessment System

Karen E. Santos
James Madison University

Planning and implementing a performance-based candidate assessment system is a multi-step process. Each step is important and, in most cases, a prerequisite for accomplishing successive steps. Programs may be in various developmental stages along this continuum. The chart on the next page (see Figure 3.6) can be used to identify completed steps and target activities yet to be accomplished.

It is important that the process be accomplished collaboratively with faculty and other stakeholders in order to gain varied perspectives at each step but also to assure consensus among all stakeholders. All faculty must understand their roles and it is essential for candidates to understand the assessment system.

While the entire process takes time and is at times cumbersome, the end result is a well-articulated program with accountability for candidate performance and ownership by relevant stakeholders.

FIGURE 3.6
Steps in Designing an Assessment System

1 Curriculum Alignment	2 Program Sequence	3 Assessment Points	4 Key Assessments	5 Assessment Criteria and Rubrics	6 Curriculum and Assessment Implementation	7 Data Collection and Aggregation	8 Data Analysis Process	9 Data Usage to Inform Candidates	10 Data Usage to Improve Program
Determine which sets of standards are relevant to initial versus advanced programs. → While considering the Unit Conceptual Framework, simultaneously align various sets of standards with courses and field experiences. Revise program as needed. The specific CEC Knowledge and Skills for the Common Core and Specialty Areas should be aligned with program.	Sequence courses and field experiences. → Determine important knowledge, skills, and dispositions to assess.	Identify logical important assessment points for the program. These should include entry, during, exit, and follow-up.	Identify all performance-based assessments related to knowledge, skills, and dispositions in courses and field experiences. → Determine 8–15 key performance assessments and at which points they occur. → Link each performance assessment to one or more CEC Content Standards. Ensure all standards are addressed.	For each of the key assessments, determine specific evaluation criteria and/or candidate performance levels and develop rubrics, scoring guides, etc., as appropriate.	Communicate assessment system to candidates. → Assure courses and/or field experiences actually implement the assigned standards and performance assessments as previously determined. (This requires informing all faculty, including part-time/adjunct. Consider developing syllabi templates identifying standards and key assessments for each course/field experience.)	Design feasible system for collecting, aggregating, and recording data. (Must have adequate support to sustain this data collection system over time.) → Collect performance data for key assessments. → Aggregate data. → Record data.	Identify process and procedures for regularly analyzing aggregated performance data.	At appropriate decision points, use data to inform individual teacher candidates regarding performance. Determine if each candidate meets or does not meet expectations. Inform candidate if eligible to continue or not continue in the program and implement remediation plan as appropriate.	Analyze data and systematically use data to improve program.

Note: The purpose of this process is to use assessment data to determine individual teacher candidate performance and systematically improve the program. Key stakeholders need to be involved at various stages.

E. Faculty: A Teacher Education Activity to Explore CEC Beginning Teacher Standards and *TEC*

Carol A. Long
Winona State University

This project was developed to help candidates become familiar with the CEC standards and with CEC's publication *TEACHING Exceptional Children (TEC)*. Preservice teachers in the Special Education program at Winona State University piloted this project and found it to be highly valuable in several ways. First, it brought home to them that they are part of a larger profession, and that this profession has defined what beginning special educators should know and the skills they should be able to demonstrate. Second, it introduced them to *TEACHING Exceptional Children (TEC)*, a publication they should use as a resource throughout their teaching career. Third, students learned practical strategies for working with students with disabilities from the articles they analyzed. And, finally, it required them to practice collaboration and strategies for arriving at consensus.

PROJECT

Teams of students read and evaluated several articles in a single issue of *TEC*. For each article they selected the CEC Area of Specialization Standards (e.g., General Curriculum, Early Childhood, etc.) that most applied to the article. They then selected which domain areas (e.g., Characteristics of Learners, Instructional Strategies, etc.) are addressed in the article and then which specific standards from each domain area are addressed. They provided a rationale for each specific knowledge and skill they selected.

PROCESS

The students were divided into teams of two and each team was assigned an issue of *TEC*. The students were given the entire set of standards and Forms 1 and 2 (see Figures 3.7 and 3.8) in an orientation session. The purpose of the project, the process to use, and an overview of the standards were presented. They were told to individually complete the forms for each article in their issue and then as a team come to consensus and fill out a final set of forms. Thus each article was analyzed three times, by both members of the team individually and again as a collaborative effort.

The instructor collected all three forms for each article, reviewed the final form for accuracy, and had each student reflect on her or his learning using the report form provided. Students were also asked to give feedback on the overall project.

Student feedback made it clear that faculty should provide a thorough introduction to the standards prior to initiating this activity.

FIGURE 3.7
Form 1: *TEC* Article and Evaluation: Domain Area and Standards Addressed

Student Name(s) _____ Date Submitted _____

Issue Volume _____, Number _____, Month _____, Year _____, Pages ___through ___

Title _____

Author(s) _____

Decide which area(s) such as Early Childhood or Learning Disabilities applies and check. Then check which sets listed under each area apply. Use Form 2 to record specific standards and corresponding rationales.

Individualized General Curriculum		*Individualized Independence Curriculum*		*Deaf or Hard of Hearing*		*Early Childhood*		*Emotional and Behavioral Disorders*	
Foundations		Foundations		Foundations		Foundations		Foundations	
Development & Characteristics of Learners		Development & Characteristics of Learners		Development & Characteristics of Learners		Development & Characteristics of Learners		Development & Characteristics of Learners	
Individual Learning Differences		Individual Learning Differences		Individual Learning Differences		Individual Learning Differences		Individual Learning Differences	
Instructional Strategies		Instructional Strategies		Instructional Strategies		Instructional Strategies		Instructional Strategies	
Learning Environments & Social Interactions		Learning Environments & Social Interactions		Learning Environments & Social Interactions		Learning Environments & Social Interactions		Learning Environments & Social Interactions	
Language		Language		Language		Language		Language	
Instructional Planning		Instructional Planning		Instructional Planning		Instructional Planning		Instructional Planning	
Assessment		Assessment		Assessment		Assessment		Assessment	
Professional & Ethical Practice		Professional & Ethical Practice		Professional & Ethical Practice		Professional & Ethical Practice		Professional & Ethical Practice	
Collaboration		Collaboration		Collaboration		Collaboration		Collaboration	

continued

FIGURE 3.7 *continued*

Gifts and Talents	Learning Disabilities	Mental Retardation/ Developmental Disabilities	Physical and Health Disabilities	Visual Impairments	
Foundations	Foundations	Foundations	Foundations	Foundations	
Development & Characteristics of Learners	Development & Characteristics of Learners	Development & Characteristics of Learners	Development & Characteristics of Learners	Development & Characteristics of Learners	
Individual Learning Differences	Individual Learning Differences	Individual Learning Differences	Individual Learning Differences	Individual Learning Differences	
Instructional Strategies	Instructional Strategies	Instructional Strategies	Instructional Strategies	Instructional Strategies	
Learning Environments & Social Interactions	Learning Environments & Social Interactions	Learning Environments & Social Interactions	Learning Environments & Social Interactions	Learning Environments & Social Interactions	
Language	Language	Language	Language	Language	
Instructional Planning	Instructional Planning	Instructional Planning	Instructional Planning	Instructional Planning	
Assessment	Assessment	Assessment	Assessment	Assessment	
Professional & Ethical Practice	Professional & Ethical Practice	Professional & Ethical Practice	Professional & Ethical Practice	Professional & Ethical Practice	
Collaboration	Collaboration	Collaboration	Collaboration	Collaboration	

FIGURE 3.8
Form 2: *TEC* Article Evaluation: Standards Addressed and Rationale

Student Name(s) _____   Date Submitted _____

Issue Volume _____, Number _____, Month _____, Year _____, Pages ___through ___

Title _____

Author(s) _____

Note: Will need to consider Common Core Standards under each area.

Standard	Rationale

Attach to Form 1

FIGURE 3.8 *continued*

Standard	Rationale

Attach to Form

Section 4

The CEC Standards

Section 4 is divided into four parts. The first part (A) includes all of the knowledge and skill standards for the preparation of special education teachers entering special education practice for the first time. The Common Core and Area of Specialization Knowledge and Skills have been combined throughout the respective sets to make clear that the Common Core is never a stand-alone set of standards. The second part (B) includes the standards for preparation programs seeking accreditation through NCATE and CEC. Please note that information to help faculty prepare for CEC and NCATE accreditation is not included in this section. In order to ensure that faculty receive the most up-to-date guidance, all information on preparing the program review materials has been placed on the CEC web site (www.cec. sped.org). Part (C) provides information to states on CEC's recommendations for state licensure standards. Finally, part (D) includes the CEC Mentoring and Continuing Education Standards.

A. CEC Knowledge and Skill Standards

CEC Knowledge and Skill Base for All Entry-Level Special Education Teachers of Students with Exceptionalities in Individualized General Curriculums[1]

(most closely aligns with a Mild/Moderate licensure framework)

Standard #1: Foundations	
CC1K1	Models, theories, and philosophies that form the basis for special education practice.
CC1K2	Laws, policies, and ethical principles regarding behavior management planning and implementation.
CC1K3	Relationship of special education to the organization and function of educational agencies.
CC1K4	Rights and responsibilities of students, parents, teachers, and other professionals, and schools related to exceptional learning needs.
CC1K5	Issues in definition and identification of individuals with exceptional learning needs, including those from culturally and linguistically diverse backgrounds.
CC1K6	Issues, assurances, and due process rights related to assessment, eligibility, and placement within a continuum of services.
CC1K7	Family systems and the role of families in the educational process.
CC1K8	Historical points of view and contribution of culturally diverse groups.
CC1K9	Impact of the dominant culture on shaping schools and the individuals who study and work in them.
CC1K10	Potential impact of differences in values, languages, and customs that can exist between the home and school.
GC1K1	Definitions and issues related to the identification of individuals with disabilities.
GC1K2	Models and theories of deviance and behavior problems.
GC1K3	Historical foundations, classic studies, major contributors, major legislation, and current issues related to knowledge and practice.
GC1K4	The legal, judicial, and educational systems to assist individuals with disabilities.
GC1K5	Continuum of placement and services available for individuals with disabilities.
GC1K6	Laws and policies related to provision of specialized health care in educational settings.
GC1K7	Factors that influence the overrepresentation of culturally/linguistically diverse students in programs for individuals with disabilities.
GC1K8	Principles of normalization and concept of least restrictive environment.
GC1K9	Theory of reinforcement techniques in serving individuals with disabilities.
CC1S1	Articulate personal philosophy of special education.
Standard #2: Development and Characteristics of Learners	
CC2K1	Typical and atypical human growth and development.
CC2K2	Educational implications of characteristics of various exceptionalities.
CC2K3	Characteristics and effects of the cultural and environmental milieu of the individual with exceptional learning needs and the family.
CC2K4	Family systems and the role of families in supporting development.
CC2K5	Similarities and differences of individuals with and without exceptional learning needs.
CC2K6	Similarities and differences among individuals with exceptional learning needs.
CC2K7	Effects of various medications on individuals with exceptional learning needs.
GC2K1	Etiology and diagnosis related to various theoretical approaches.

[1]*Note On Coding:* CC in the number code indicates a Common Core item; EC indicates an Early Childhood Special Education item; K indicates a Knowledge item; S indicates a Skill item.

GC2K2	Impact of sensory impairments, physical and health disabilities on individuals, families, and society.
GC2K3	Etiologies and medical aspects of conditions affecting individuals with disabilities.
GC2K4	Psychological and social-emotional characteristics of individuals with disabilities.
GC2K5	Common etiologies and the impact of sensory disabilities on learning and experience.
GC2K6	Types and transmission routes of infectious disease.

Standard #3: Individual Learning Differences

CC3K1	Effects an exceptional condition(s) can have on an individual's life.
CC3K2	Impact of learners' academic and social abilities, attitudes, interests, and values on instruction and career development.
CC3K3	Variations in beliefs, traditions, and values across and within cultures and their effects on relationships among individuals with exceptional learning needs, family, and schooling.
CC3K4	Cultural perspectives influencing the relationships among families, schools, and communities as related to instruction.
CC3K5	Differing ways of learning of individuals with exceptional learning needs including those from culturally diverse backgrounds and strategies for addressing these differences.
GC3K1	Impact of disabilities on auditory and information processing skills.
GC3S1	Relate levels of support to the needs of the individual.

Standard #4: Instructional Strategies

GC4K1	Sources of specialized materials, curricula, and resources for individuals with disabilities.
GC4K2	Strategies to prepare for and take tests.
GC4K3	Advantages and limitations of instructional strategies and practices for teaching individuals with disabilities.
GC4K4	Prevention and intervention strategies for individuals at risk for a disability.
GC4K5	Strategies for integrating student-initiated learning experiences into ongoing instruction.
GC4K6	Methods for increasing accuracy and proficiency in math calculations and applications.
GC4K7	Methods for guiding individuals in identifying and organizing critical content.
CC4S1	Use strategies to facilitate integration into various settings.
CC4S2	Teach individuals to use self-assessment, problem-solving, and other cognitive strategies to meet their needs.
CC4S3	Select, adapt, and use instructional strategies and materials according to characteristics of the individual with exceptional learning needs.
CC4S4	Use strategies to facilitate maintenance and generalization of skills across learning environments.
CC4S5	Use procedures to increase the individual's self-awareness, self-management, self-control, self-reliance, and self-esteem.
CC4S6	Use strategies that promote successful transitions for individuals with exceptional learning needs.
GC4S1	Use research-supported methods for academic and nonacademic instruction of individuals with disabilities.
GC4S2	Use strategies from multiple theoretical approaches for individuals with disabilities.
GC4S3	Teach learning strategies and study skills to acquire academic content.
GC4S4	Use reading methods appropriate to individuals with disabilities.
GC4S5	Use methods to teach mathematics appropriate to the individuals with disabilities.
GC4S6	Modify pace of instruction and provide organizational cures.
GC4S7	Use appropriate adaptations and technology for all individuals with disabilities.
GC4S8	Resources and techniques used to transition individuals with disabilities into and out of school and postschool environments.
GC4S9	Use a variety of nonaversive techniques to control targeted behavior and maintain attention of individuals with disabilities.
GC4S10	Identify and teach basic structures and relationships within and across curricula.

GC4S11	Use instructional methods to strengthen and compensate for deficits in perception, comprehension, memory, and retrieval.
GC4S12	Use responses and errors to guide instructional decisions and provide feedback to learners.
GC4S13	Identify and teach essential concepts, vocabulary, and content across the general curriculum.
GC4S14	Implement systematic instruction in teaching reading comprehension and monitoring strategies.
GC4S15	Teach strategies for organizing and composing written products.
GC4S16	Implement systematic instruction to teach accuracy, fluency, and comprehension in content area reading and written language.

Standard #5: Learning Environments and Social Interactions

CC5K1	Demands of learning environments.
CC5K2	Basic classroom management theories and strategies for individuals with exceptional learning needs.
CC5K3	Effective management of teaching and learning.
CC5K4	Teacher attitudes and behaviors that influence behavior of individuals with exceptional learning needs.
CC5K5	Social skills needed for educational and other environments.
CC5K6	Strategies for crisis prevention and intervention.
CC5K7	Strategies for preparing individuals to live harmoniously and productively in a culturally diverse world.
CC5K8	Ways to create learning environments that allow individuals to retain and appreciate their own and each others' respective language and cultural heritage.
CC5K9	Ways specific cultures are negatively stereotyped.
CC5K10	Strategies used by diverse populations to cope with a legacy of former and continuing racism.
GC5K1	Barriers to accessibility and acceptance of individuals with disabilities.
GC5K2	Adaptation of the physical environment to provide optimal learning opportunities for individuals with disabilities.
GC5K3	Methods for ensuring individual academic success in one-to-one, small-group, and large-group settings.
CC5S1	Create a safe, equitable, positive, and supportive learning environment in which diversities are valued.
CC5S2	Identify realistic expectations for personal and social behavior in various settings.
CC5S3	Identify supports needed for integration into various program placements.
CC5S4	Design learning environments that encourage active participation in individual and group activities.
CC5S5	Modify the learning environment to manage behaviors.
CC5S6	Use performance data and information from all stakeholders to make or suggest modifications in learning environments.
CC5S7	Establish and maintain rapport with individuals with and without exceptional learning needs.
CC5S8	Teach self-advocacy.
CC5S9	Create an environment that encourages self-advocacy and increased independence.
CC5S10	Use effective and varied behavior management strategies.
CC5S11	Use the least intensive behavior management strategy consistent with the needs of the individual with exceptional learning needs.
CC5S12	Design and manage daily routines.
CC5S13	Organize, develop, and sustain learning environments that support positive intracultural and intercultural experiences.
CC5S14	Mediate controversial intercultural issues among students within the learning environment in ways that enhance any culture, group, or person.
CC5S15	Structure, direct, and support the activities of paraeducators, volunteers, and tutors.
CC5S16	Use universal precautions.
GC5S1	Provide instruction in community-based settings.

GC5S2	Use and maintain assistive technologies.
GC5S3	Plan instruction in a variety of educational settings.
GC5S4	Teach individuals with disabilities to give and receive meaningful feedback from peers and adults.
GC5S5	Use skills in problem-solving and conflict resolution.
GC5S6	Establish a consistent classroom routine for individuals with disabilities.

Standard #6: Language

CC6K1	Effects of cultural and linguistic differences on growth and development.
CC6K2	Characteristics of one's own culture and use of language and the ways in which these can differ from other cultures and uses of languages.
CC6K3	Ways of behaving and communicating among cultures that can lead to misinterpretation and misunderstanding.
CC6K4	Augmentative and assistive communication strategies.
GC6K1	Impact of language development and listening comprehension on academic and nonacademic learning of individuals with disabilities.
GC6K2	Communication and social interaction alternatives for individuals who are nonspeaking.
GC6K3	Typical language development and how that may differ for individuals with learning disabilities.
CC6S1	Use strategies to support and enhance communication skills of individuals with exceptional learning needs.
CC6S2	Use communication strategies and resources to facilitate understanding of subject matter for students whose primary language is not the dominant language.
GC6S1	Enhance vocabulary development.
GC6S2	Teach strategies for spelling accuracy and generalization.
GC6S3	Teach individuals with disabilities to monitor for errors in oral and written language.
GC6S4	Teach methods and strategies for producing legible documents.
GC6S5	Plan instruction on the use of alternative and augmentative communication systems.

Standard #7: Instructional Planning

CC7K1	Theories and research that form the basis of curriculum development and instructional practice.
CC7K2	Scope and sequences of general and special curricula.
CC7K3	National, state or provincial, and local curricula standards.
CC7K4	Technology for planning and managing the teaching and learning environment.
CC7K5	Roles and responsibilities of the paraeducator related to instruction, intervention, and direct service.
GC7K1	Integrate academic instruction and behavior management for individuals and groups with disabilities.
GC7K2	Model career, vocational, and transition programs for individuals with disabilities.
GC7K3	Interventions and services for children who may be at risk for learning disabilities.
GC7K4	Relationships among disabilities and reading instruction.
CC7S1	Identify and prioritize areas of the general curriculum and accommodations for individuals with exceptional learning needs.
CC7S2	Develop and implement comprehensive, longitudinal individualized programs in collaboration with team members.
CC7S3	Involve the individual and family in setting instructional goals and monitoring progress.
CC7S4	Use functional assessments to develop intervention plans.
CC7S5	Use task analysis.
CC7S6	Sequence, implement, and evaluate individualized learning objectives.
CC7S7	Integrate affective, social, and life skills with academic curricula.
CC7S8	Develop and select instructional content, resources, and strategies that respond to cultural, linguistic, and gender differences.
CC7S9	Incorporate and implement instructional and assistive technology into the educational program.

CC7S10	Prepare lesson plans.
CC7S11	Prepare and organize materials to implement daily lesson plans.
CC7S12	Use instructional time effectively.
CC7S13	Make responsive adjustments to instruction based on continual observations.
CC7S14	Prepare individuals to exhibit self-enhancing behavior in response to societal attitudes and actions.
GC7S1	Plan and implement individualized reinforcement systems and environmental modifications at levels equal to the intensity of the behavior.
GC7S2	Select and use specialized instructional strategies appropriate to the abilities and needs of the individual.
GC7S3	Plan and implement age- and ability-appropriate instruction for individuals with disabilities.
GC7S4	Select, design, and use technology, materials, and resources required to educate individuals whose disabilities interfere with communication.
GC7S5	Interpret sensory, mobility, reflex, and perceptual information to create or adapt appropriate learning plans.
GC7S6	Design and implement instructional programs that address independent living and career education for individuals.
GC7S7	Design and implement curriculum and instructional strategies for medical self-management procedures.
GC7S8	Design, implement, and evaluate instructional programs that enhance social participation across environments.

Standard #8: Assessment

CC8K1	Basic terminology used in assessment.
CC8K2	Legal provisions and ethical principles regarding assessment of individuals.
CC8K3	Screening, prereferral, referral, and classification procedures.
CC8K4	Use and limitations of assessment instruments.
CC8K5	National, state or provincial, and local accommodations and modifications.
GC8K1	Specialized terminology used in the assessment of individuals with disabilities.
GC8K2	Laws and policies regarding referral and placement procedures for individuals with disabilities.
GC8K3	Types and importance of information concerning individuals with disabilities available from families and public agencies.
GC8K4	Procedures for early identification of young children who may be at risk for disabilities.
CC8S1	Gather relevant background information.
CC8S2	Administer nonbiased formal and informal assessments.
CC8S3	Use technology to conduct assessments.
CC8S4	Develop or modify individualized assessment strategies.
CC8S5	Interpret information from formal and informal assessments.
CC8S6	Use assessment information in making eligibility, program, and placement decisions for individuals with exceptional learning needs, including those from culturally and/or linguistically diverse backgrounds.
CC8S7	Report assessment results to all stakeholders using effective communication skills.
CC8S8	Evaluate instruction and monitor progress of individuals with exceptional learning needs.
CC8S9	Develop or modify individualized assessment strategies.
CC8S10	Create and maintain records.
GC8S1	Implement procedures for assessing and reporting both appropriate and problematic social behaviors of individuals with disabilities.
GC8S2	Use exceptionality-specific assessment instruments with individuals with disabilities.
GC8S3	Select, adapt and modify assessments to accommodate the unique abilities and needs of individuals with disabilities.

GC8S4	Assess reliable methods of response of individuals who lack typical communication and performance abilities.
GC8S5	Monitor intragroup behavior changes across subjects and activities.

Standard #9: Professional and Ethical Practice

CC9K1	Personal cultural biases and differences that affect one's teaching.
CC9K2	Importance of the teacher serving as a model for individuals with exceptional learning needs.
CC9K3	Continuum of lifelong professional development.
CC9K4	Methods to remain current regarding research-validated practice.
GC9K1	Sources of unique services, networks, and organizations for individuals with disabilities.
GC9K2	Organizations and publications relevant to individuals with disabilities.
CC9S1	Practice within the CEC Code of Ethics and other standards of the profession.
CC9S2	Uphold high standards of competence and integrity and exercise sound judgment in the practice of the professional.
CC9S3	Act ethically in advocating for appropriate services.
CC9S4	Conduct professional activities in compliance with applicable laws and policies.
CC9S5	Demonstrate commitment to developing the highest education and quality-of-life potential of individuals with exceptional learning needs.
CC9S6	Demonstrate sensitivity for the culture, language, religion, gender, disability, socioeconomic status, and sexual orientation of individuals.
CC9S7	Practice within one's skill limit and obtain assistance as needed.
CC9S8	Use verbal, nonverbal, and written language effectively.
CC9S9	Conduct self-evaluation of instruction.
CC9S10	Access information on exceptionalities.
CC9S11	Reflect on one's practice to improve instruction and guide professional growth.
CC9S12	Engage in professional activities that benefit individuals with exceptional learning needs, their families, and one's colleagues.
GC9S1	Participate in the activities of professional organizations relevant to individuals with disabilities.
GC9S2	Ethical responsibility to advocate for appropriate services for individuals with disabilities.

Standard #10: Collaboration

CC10K1	Models and strategies of consultation and collaboration.
CC10K2	Roles of individuals with exceptional learning needs, families, and school and community personnel in planning of an individualized program.
CC10K3	Concerns of families of individuals with exceptional learning needs and strategies to help address these concerns.
CC10K4	Culturally responsive factors that promote effective communication and collaboration with individuals with exceptional learning needs, families, school personnel, and community members.
GC10K1	Parent education programs and behavior management guides that address severe behavior problems and facilitation communication for individuals with disabilities.
GC10K2	Collaborative and/or consultative role of the special education teacher in the reintegration of individuals with disabilities.
GC10K3	Roles of professional groups and referral agencies in identifying, assessing, and providing services to individuals with disabilities.
GC10K4	Co-planning and co-teaching methods to strengthen content acquisition of individuals with learning disabilities.
CC10S1	Maintain confidential communication about individuals with exceptional learning needs.
CC10S2	Collaborate with families and others in assessment of individuals with exceptional learning needs.
CC10S3	Foster respectful and beneficial relationships between families and professionals.
CC10S4	Assist individuals with exceptional learning needs and their families in becoming active participants in the educational team.

CC10S5	Plan and conduct collaborative conferences with individuals with exceptional learning needs and their families.
CC10S6	Collaborate with school personnel and community members in integrating individuals with exceptional learning needs into various settings.
CC10S7	Use group problem-solving skills to develop, implement, and evaluate collaborative activities.
CC10S8	Model techniques and coach others in the use of instructional methods and accommodations.
CC10S9	Communicate with school personnel about the characteristics and needs of individuals with exceptional learning needs.
CC10S10	Communicate effectively with families of individuals with exceptional learning needs from diverse backgrounds.
CC10S11	Observe, evaluate, and provide feedback to paraeducators.
GC10S1	Use local community, and state and provincial resources to assist in programming with individuals with disabilities.
GC10S2	Select, plan, and coordinate activities of related services personnel to maximize direct instruction for individuals with disabilities.
GC10S3	Teach parents to use appropriate behavior management and counseling techniques.
GC10S4	Collaborate with team members to plan transition to adulthood that encourages full community participation.

Notes:

Implicit to all of the knowledge and skills standards in this section is the focus on individuals with disabilities whose education focuses on an individualized general curriculum.

"Individual with exceptional learning needs" is used throughout to include individuals with disabilities and individuals with exceptional gifts and talents.

"Exceptional condition" is used throughout to include both single and co-existing conditions. These may be two or more disabling conditions or exceptional gifts or talents co-existing with one or more disabling conditions.

"Special curricula" is used throughout to denote curricular areas not routinely emphasized or addressed in general curricula; e.g., social, communication, motor, independence, self-advocacy.

CEC Knowledge and Skill Base for All Entry-Level Special Education Teachers of Students with Exceptionalities in Individualized Independence Curriculums[1]

(most closely aligns with a Severe/Profound licensure framework)

	Standard #1: Foundations
CC1K1	Models, theories, and philosophies that form the basis for special education practice.
CC1K2	Laws, policies, and ethical principles regarding behavior management planning and implementation.
CC1K3	Relationship of special education to the organization and function of educational agencies.
CC1K4	Rights and responsibilities of students, parents, teachers, and other professionals, and schools related to exceptional learning needs.
CC1K5	Issues in definition and identification of individuals with exceptional learning needs, including those from culturally and linguistically diverse backgrounds.
CC1K6	Issues, assurances, and due process rights related to assessment, eligibility, and placement within a continuum of services.
CC1K7	Family systems and the role of families in the educational process.
CC1K8	Historical points of view and contribution of culturally diverse groups.
CC1K9	Impact of the dominant culture on shaping schools and the individuals who study and work in them.
CC1K10	Potential impact of differences in values, languages, and customs that can exist between the home and school.
IC1K1	Definitions and issues related to the identification of individuals with disabilities.
IC1K2	Historical foundations, classic studies, major contributors, major legislation, and current issues related to knowledge and practice.
IC1K3	The legal, judicial, and educational systems to assist individuals with disabilities.
IC1K4	Continuum of placement and services available for individuals with disabilities.
IC1K5	Laws and policies related to provision of specialized health care in educational settings.
IC1K6	Principles of normalization and concept of least restrictive environment.
IC1K7	Theory of reinforcement techniques in serving individuals with disabilities.
IC1K8	Theories of behavior problems of individuals with disabilities.
CC1S1	Articulate personal philosophy of special education.
	Standard #2: Development and Characteristics of Learners
CC2K1	Typical and atypical human growth and development.
CC2K2	Educational implications of characteristics of various exceptionalities.
CC2K3	Characteristics and effects of the cultural and environmental milieu of the individual with exceptional learning needs and the family.
CC2K4	Family systems and the role of families in supporting development.
CC2K5	Similarities and differences of individuals with and without exceptional learning needs.
CC2K6	Similarities and differences among individuals with exceptional learning needs.
CC2K7	Effects of various medications on individuals with exceptional learning needs.
IC2K1	Etiology and diagnosis related to various theoretical approaches.
IC2K2	Impact of sensory impairments, physical and health disabilities on individuals, families, and society.
IC2K3	Etiologies and medical aspects of conditions affecting individuals with disabilities.
IC2K4	Psychological and social-emotional characteristics of individuals with disabilities.
IC2K5	Types and transmission routes of infectious disease.

[1]*Note On Coding:* CC in the number code indicates a Common Core item; EC indicates an Early Childhood Special Education item; K indicates a Knowledge item; S indicates a Skill item.

Standard #3: Individual Learning Differences

CC3K1	Effects an exceptional condition(s) can have on an individual's life.
CC3K2	Impact of learners' academic and social abilities, attitudes, interests, and values on instruction and career development.
CC3K3	Variations in beliefs, traditions, and values across and within cultures and their effects on relationships among individuals with exceptional learning needs, family, and schooling.
CC3K4	Cultural perspectives influencing the relationships among families, schools, and communities as related to instruction.
CC3K5	Differing ways of learning of individuals with exceptional learning needs including those from culturally diverse backgrounds and strategies for addressing these differences.
IC3K1	Complications and implications of medical support services.
IC3K2	Impact disabilities may have on auditory and information processing skills.
IC3K3	Impact of multiple disabilities on behavior.
IC3S1	Relate levels of support to the needs of the individual.

Standard #4: Instructional Strategies

IC4K1	Specialized materials for individuals with disabilities.
IC4K2	Prevention and intervention strategies for individuals with disabilities.
IC4K3	Strategies for integrating student-initiated learning experiences into ongoing instruction.
IC4K4	Resources, and techniques used to transition individuals with disabilities into and out of school and postschool environments.
CC4S1	Use strategies to facilitate integration into various settings.
CC4S2	Teach individuals to use self-assessment, problem-solving, and other cognitive strategies to meet their needs.
CC4S3	Select, adapt, and use instructional strategies and materials according to characteristics of the individual with exceptional learning needs.
CC4S4	Use strategies to facilitate maintenance and generalization of skills across learning environments.
CC4S5	Use procedures to increase the individual's self-awareness, self-management, self-control, self-reliance, and self-esteem.
CC4S6	Use strategies that promote successful transitions for individuals with exceptional learning needs.
IC4S1	Use research-supported instructional strategies and practices.
IC4S2	Use appropriate adaptations and assistive technology for all individuals with disabilities.
IC4S3	Use a variety of nonaversive techniques to control targeted behavior and maintain attention of individuals with disabilities.
IC4S4	Identify and teach basic structures and relationships within and across curricula.
IC4S5	Use instructional methods to strengthen and compensate for deficits in perception, comprehension, memory, and retrieval.
IC4S6	Use responses and errors to guide instructional decisions and provide feedback to learners.

Standard #5: Learning Environments and Social Interactions

CC5K1	Demands of learning environments.
CC5K2	Basic classroom management theories and strategies for individuals with exceptional learning needs.
CC5K3	Effective management of teaching and learning.
CC5K4	Teacher attitudes and behaviors that influence behavior of individuals with exceptional learning needs.
CC5K5	Social skills needed for educational and other environments.
CC5K6	Strategies for crisis prevention and intervention.
CC5K7	Strategies for preparing individuals to live harmoniously and productively in a culturally diverse world.

CC5K8	Ways to create learning environments that allow individuals to retain and appreciate their own and each others' respective language and cultural heritage.
CC5K9	Ways specific cultures are negatively stereotyped.
CC5K10	Strategies used by diverse populations to cope with a legacy of former and continuing racism.
IC5K1	Specialized health care interventions for individuals with physical and health disabilities in educational settings.
IC5K2	Barriers to accessibility and acceptance of individuals with disabilities.
IC5K3	Adaptation of the physical environment to provide optimal learning opportunities for individuals with disabilities.
IC5K4	Methods for ensuring individual academic success in one-to-one, small-group, and large-group settings.
IC5K5	Advantages and disadvantages of placement options and programs on the continuum of services for individuals with disabilities.
CC5S1	Create a safe, equitable, positive, and supportive learning environment in which diversities are valued.
CC5S2	Identify realistic expectations for personal and social behavior in various settings.
CC5S3	Identify supports needed for integration into various program placements.
CC5S4	Design learning environments that encourage active participation in individual and group activities.
CC5S5	Modify the learning environment to manage behaviors.
CC5S6	Use performance data and information from all stakeholders to make or suggest modifications in learning environments.
CC5S7	Establish and maintain rapport with individuals with and without exceptional learning needs.
CC5S8	Teach self-advocacy.
CC5S9	Create an environment that encourages self-advocacy and increased independence.
CC5S10	Use effective and varied behavior management strategies.
CC5S11	Use the least intensive behavior management strategy consistent with the needs of the individual with exceptional learning needs.
CC5S12	Design and manage daily routines.
CC5S13	Organize, develop, and sustain learning environments that support positive intracultural and intercultural experiences.
CC5S14	Mediate controversial intercultural issues among students within the learning environment in ways that enhance any culture, group, or person.
CC5S15	Structure, direct, and support the activities of paraeducators, volunteers, and tutors.
CC5S16	Use universal precautions.
IC5S1	Provide instruction in community-based settings.
IC5S2	Use and maintain assistive technologies.
IC5S3	Structure the educational environment to provide optimal learning opportunities for individuals with disabilities.
IC5S4	Plan instruction in a variety of educational settings.
IC5S5	Teach individuals with disabilities to give and receive meaningful feedback from peers and adults.
IC5S6	Design learning environments that are multisensory and that facilitate active participation, self-advocacy, and independence of individuals with disabilities in a variety of group and individual learning activities.
IC5S7	Use techniques of physical positioning and management of individuals with disabilities to ensure participation in academic and social environments.
IC5S8	Demonstrate appropriate body mechanics to ensure student and teacher safety in transfer, lifting, positioning, and seating.
IC5S9	Use positioning techniques that decrease inappropriate tone and facilitate appropriate postural reactions to enhance participation.
IC5S10	Use skills in problem-solving and conflict resolution.

IC5S11	Design and implement sensory stimulation programs.
IC5S12	Plan instruction for independent functional life skills relevant to the community, personal living, sexuality, and employment.

Standard #6: Language

CC6K1	Effects of cultural and linguistic differences on growth and development.
CC6K2	Characteristics of one's own culture and use of language and the ways in which these can differ from other cultures and uses of languages.
CC6K3	Ways of behaving and communicating among cultures that can lead to misinterpretation and misunderstanding.
CC6K4	Augmentative and assistive communication strategies.
IC6K1	Impact of language development and listening comprehension on academic and nonacademic learning of individuals with disabilities.
IC6K2	Communication and social interaction alternatives for individuals who are nonspeaking.
CC6S1	Use strategies to support and enhance communication skills of individuals with exceptional learning needs.
CC6S2	Use communication strategies and resources to facilitate understanding of subject matter for students whose primary language is not the dominant language.
IC6S1	Teach individuals with disabilities to monitor for errors in oral and written language.
IC6S2	Teach methods and strategies for producing legible documents.
IC6S3	Plan instruction on the use of alternative and augmentative communication systems.

Standard #7: Instructional Planning

CC7K1	Theories and research that form the basis of curriculum development and instructional practice.
CC7K2	Scope and sequences of general and special curricula.
CC7K3	National, state or provincial, and local curricula standards.
CC7K4	Technology for planning and managing the teaching and learning environment.
CC7K5	Roles and responsibilities of the paraeducator related to instruction, intervention, and direct service.
IC7K1	Model career, vocational, and transition programs for individuals with disabilities.
CC7S1	Identify and prioritize areas of the general curriculum and accommodations for individuals with exceptional learning needs.
CC7S2	Develop and implement comprehensive, longitudinal individualized programs in collaboration with team members.
CC7S3	Involve the individual and family in setting instructional goals and monitoring progress.
CC7S4	Use functional assessments to develop intervention plans.
CC7S5	Use task analysis.
CC7S6	Sequence, implement, and evaluate individualized learning objectives.
CC7S7	Integrate affective, social, and life skills with academic curricula.
CC7S8	Develop and select instructional content, resources, and strategies that respond to cultural, linguistic, and gender differences.
CC7S9	Incorporate and implement instructional and assistive technology into the educational program.
CC7S10	Prepare lesson plans.
CC7S11	Prepare and organize materials to implement daily lesson plans.
CC7S12	Use instructional time effectively.
CC7S13	Make responsive adjustments to instruction based on continual observations.
CC7S14	Prepare individuals to exhibit self-enhancing behavior in response to societal attitudes and actions.
IC7S1	Plan and implement individualized reinforcement systems and environmental modifications.
IC7S2	Plan and implement age- and ability-appropriate instruction for individuals with disabilities.
IC7S3	Select and plan for integration of related services into the instructional program.

IC7S4	Select, design, and use medical materials and resources required to educate individuals whose disabilities interfere with communications.
IC7S5	Interpret sensory and physical information to create or adapt appropriate learning plans.
IC7S6	Design and implement instructional programs that address independent living and career education.
IC7S7	Design and implement curriculum strategies for medical self-management procedures.
IC7S8	Design, implement, and evaluate instructional programs that enhance social participation across environments.

Standard #8: Assessment

CC8K1	Basic terminology used in assessment.
CC8K2	Legal provisions and ethical principles regarding assessment of individuals.
CC8K3	Screening, prereferral, referral, and classification procedures.
CC8K4	Use and limitations of assessment instruments.
CC8K5	National, state or provincial, and local accommodations and modifications.
IC8K1	Specialized terminology used in the assessment of individuals with disabilities.
IC8K2	Laws and policies regarding referral and placement procedures for individuals with disabilities.
IC8K3	Types and importance of information concerning individuals with disabilities available from families and public agencies.
CC8S1	Gather relevant background information.
CC8S2	Administer nonbiased formal and informal assessments.
CC8S3	Use technology to conduct assessments.
CC8S4	Develop or modify individualized assessment strategies.
CC8S5	Interpret information from formal and informal assessments.
CC8S6	Use assessment information in making eligibility, program, and placement decisions for individuals with exceptional learning needs, including those from culturally and/or linguistically diverse backgrounds.
CC8S7	Report assessment results to all stakeholders using effective communication skills.
CC8S8	Evaluate instruction and monitor progress of individuals with exceptional learning needs.
CC8S9	Develop or modify individualized assessment strategies.
CC8S10	Create and maintain records.
IC8S1	Implement procedures for assessing and reporting both appropriate and problematic social behaviors of individuals with disabilities.
IC8S2	Use exceptionality-specific assessment instruments with individuals with disabilities.
IC8S3	Select, adapt, and modify assessments to accommodate the unique abilities and needs of individuals with disabilities.
IC8S4	Adapt and modify assessments to accommodate the unique abilities and needs of individuals with disabilities.
IC8S5	Develop and use a technology plan based on adaptive technology assessment.
IC8S6	Assess reliable method(s) of response of individuals who lack typical communication and performance abilities.
IC8S7	Monitor intragroup behavior changes across subjects and activities.

Standard #9: Professional and Ethical Practice

CC9K1	Personal cultural biases and differences that affect one's teaching.
CC9K2	Importance of the teacher serving as a model for individuals with exceptional learning needs.
CC9K3	Continuum of lifelong professional development.
CC9K4	Methods to remain current regarding research-validated practice.
IC9K1	Sources of unique services, networks, and organizations for individuals with disabilities.
IC9K2	Organizations and publications relevant to individuals with disabilities.
CC9S1	Practice within the CEC Code of Ethics and other standards of the profession.

CC9S2	Uphold high standards of competence and integrity and exercise sound judgment in the practice of the professional.
CC9S3	Act ethically in advocating for appropriate services.
CC9S4	Conduct professional activities in compliance with applicable laws and policies.
CC9S5	Demonstrate commitment to developing the highest education and quality-of-life potential of individuals with exceptional learning needs.
CC9S6	Demonstrate sensitivity for the culture, language, religion, gender, disability, socioeconomic status, and sexual orientation of individuals.
CC9S7	Practice within one's skill limit and obtain assistance as needed.
CC9S8	Use verbal, nonverbal, and written language effectively.
CC9S9	Conduct self-evaluation of instruction.
CC9S10	Access information on exceptionalities.
CC9S11	Reflect on one's practice to improve instruction and guide professional growth.
CC9S12	Engage in professional activities that benefit individuals with exceptional learning needs, their families, and one's colleagues.
IC9S1	Participate in the activities of professional organizations relevant to individuals with disabilities.
IC9S2	Ethical responsibility to advocate for appropriate services for individuals with disabilities.
IC9S3	Seek information regarding protocols, procedural guidelines, and policies designed to assist individuals with disabilities as they participate in school and community-based activities.

Standard #10: Collaboration

CC10K1	Models and strategies of consultation and collaboration.
CC10K2	Roles of individuals with exceptional learning needs, families, and school and community personnel in planning of an individualized program.
CC10K3	Concerns of families of individuals with exceptional learning needs and strategies to help address these concerns.
CC10K4	Culturally responsive factors that promote effective communication and collaboration with individuals with exceptional learning needs, families, school personnel, and community members.
CC10S1	Maintain confidential communication about individuals with exceptional learning needs.
CC10S2	Collaborate with families and others in assessment of individuals with exceptional learning needs.
CC10S3	Foster respectful and beneficial relationships between families and professionals.
CC10S4	Assist individuals with exceptional learning needs and their families in becoming active participants in the educational team.
CC10S5	Plan and conduct collaborative conferences with individuals with exceptional learning needs and their families.
CC10S6	Collaborate with school personnel and community members in integrating individuals with exceptional learning needs into various settings.
CC10S7	Use group problem-solving skills to develop, implement, and evaluate collaborative activities.
CC10S8	Model techniques and coach others in the use of instructional methods and accommodations.
CC10S9	Communicate with school personnel about the characteristics and needs of individuals with exceptional learning needs.
CC10S10	Communicate effectively with families of individuals with exceptional learning needs from diverse backgrounds.
CC10S11	Observe, evaluate, and provide feedback to paraeducators.
IC10K1	Parent education programs and behavior management guides that address severe behavior problems and facilitation communication for individuals with disabilities.
IC10K2	Collaborative and/or consultative role of the special education teacher in the reintegration of individuals with disabilities.
IC10K3	Roles of professional groups and referral agencies in identifying, assessing, and providing services to individuals with disabilities.

IC10S1	Participate in the selection and implementation of augmentative or alternative communication systems.
IC10S2	Use local community, and state and provincial resources to assist in programming with individuals with disabilities.
IC10S3	Select, plan, and coordinate activities of related services personnel to maximize direct instruction for individuals with disabilities.
IC10S4	Collaborate with team members to plan transition to adulthood that encourages full community participation.
IC10S5	Collaborate with families of and service providers to individuals who are chronically or terminally ill.

Notes:

Implicit to all of the knowledge and skills standards in this section is the focus on individuals with disabilities whose education focuses on an individualized general curriculum.

"Individual with exceptional learning needs" is used throughout to include individuals with disabilities and individuals with exceptional gifts and talents.

"Exceptional condition" is used throughout to include both single and co-existing conditions. These may be two or more disabling conditions or exceptional gifts or talents co-existing with one or more disabling conditions.

"Special curricula" is used throughout to denote curricular areas not routinely emphasized or addressed in general curricula; e.g., social, communication, motor, independence, self-advocacy.

CEC Knowledge and Skill Base for All Entry-Level Special Education Teachers of Students Who Are Deaf and Hard of Hearing[1]

Standard #1: Foundations	
CC1K1	Models, theories, and philosophies that form the basis for special education practice.
CC1K2	Laws, policies, and ethical principles regarding behavior management planning and implementation.
CC1K3	Relationship of special education to the organization and function of educational agencies.
CC1K4	Rights and responsibilities of students, parents, teachers, and other professionals, and schools related to exceptional learning needs.
CC1K5	Issues in definition and identification of individuals with exceptional learning needs, including those from culturally and linguistically diverse backgrounds.
CC1K6	Issues, assurances, and due process rights related to assessment, eligibility, and placement within a continuum of services.
CC1K7	Family systems and the role of families in the educational process.
CC1K8	Historical points of view and contribution of culturally diverse groups.
CC1K9	Impact of the dominant culture on shaping schools and the individuals who study and work in them.
CC1K10	Potential impact of differences in values, languages, and customs that can exist between the home and school.
DH1K1	Educational definitions, identification criteria, labeling issues, and incidence and prevalence figures for individuals who are deaf or hard of hearing.
DH1K2	Models, theories, and philosophies that provide the basis for educational practice for individuals who are deaf or hard of hearing.
DH1K3	Etiologies of hearing loss that can result in additional sensory, motor, and/or learning differences.
DH1K4	Issues and trends in the field of education of individuals who are deaf or hard of hearing.
DH1K5	Major contributors to the field of education of individuals who are deaf or hard of hearing.
CC1S1	Articulate personal philosophy of special education.
DH1S1	Apply theories, philosophies, and models of practice to the education of individuals who are deaf or hard of hearing.
Standard #2: Development and Characteristics of Learners	
CC2K1	Typical and atypical human growth and development.
CC2K2	Educational implications of characteristics of various exceptionalities.
CC2K3	Characteristics and effects of the cultural and environmental milieu of the individual with exceptional learning needs and the family.
CC2K4	Family systems and the role of families in supporting development.
CC2K5	Similarities and differences of individuals with and without exceptional learning needs.
CC2K6	Similarities and differences among individuals with exceptional learning needs.
CC2K7	Effects of various medications on individuals with exceptional learning needs.
DH2K1	Cognitive development of individuals who are deaf or hard of hearing.
DH2K2	Impact of the onset of hearing loss, age of identification, and provision of services on the development of the individual who is deaf or hard of hearing.
Standard #3: Individual Learning Differences	
CC3K1	Effects an exceptional condition(s) can have on an individual's life.
CC3K2	Impact of learners' academic and social abilities, attitudes, interests, and values on instruction and career development.
CC3K3	Variations in beliefs, traditions, and values across and within cultures and their effects on relationships among individuals with exceptional learning needs, family, and schooling.

[1]*Note On Coding:* CC in the number code indicates a Common Core item; EC indicates an Early Childhood Special Education item; K indicates a Knowledge item; S indicates a Skill item.

CC3K4	Cultural perspectives influencing the relationships among families, schools, and communities as related to instruction.
CC3K5	Differing ways of learning of individuals with exceptional learning needs including those from culturally diverse backgrounds and strategies for addressing these differences.
DH3K1	Impact of educational placement options with regard to cultural identity and linguistic, academic, and social-emotional development.
DH3K2	Cultural dimensions of hearing loss that may impact the individual.
DH3K3	Influence of families on the overall development of the individual who is deaf or hard of hearing.
DH3K4	Impact of hearing loss on learning and experience.

Standard #4: Instructional Strategies

DH4K1	Sources of specialized materials for individuals who are deaf or hard of hearing.
DH4K2	Required procedures and technologies consistent with program philosophy required to educate individuals who are deaf or hard of hearing.
DH4K3	Instructional strategies for teaching individuals who are deaf or hard of hearing.
CC4S1	Use strategies to facilitate integration into various settings.
CC4S2	Teach individuals to use self-assessment, problem-solving, and other cognitive strategies to meet their needs.
CC4S3	Select, adapt, and use instructional strategies and materials according to characteristics of the individual with exceptional learning needs.
CC4S4	Use strategies to facilitate maintenance and generalization of skills across learning environments.
CC4S5	Use procedures to increase the individual's self-awareness, self-management, self-control, self-reliance, and self-esteem.
CC4S6	Use strategies that promote successful transitions for individuals with exceptional learning needs.
DH4S1	Proficiency in the languages used to teach individuals who are deaf or hard of hearing.
DH4S2	Provide activities to promote literacy in English and/or ASL.
DH4S3	Prepare individuals who are deaf or hard of hearing in the use of interpreters.
DH4S4	Apply first and second language teaching strategies to the needs of the individual.

Standard #5: Learning Environments and Social Interactions

CC5K1	Demands of learning environments.
CC5K2	Basic classroom management theories and strategies for individuals with exceptional learning needs.
CC5K3	Effective management of teaching and learning.
CC5K4	Teacher attitudes and behaviors that influence behavior of individuals with exceptional learning needs.
CC5K5	Social skills needed for educational and other environments.
CC5K6	Strategies for crisis prevention and intervention.
CC5K7	Strategies for preparing individuals to live harmoniously and productively in a culturally diverse world.
CC5K8	Ways to create learning environments that allow individuals to retain and appreciate their own and each others' respective language and cultural heritage.
CC5K9	Ways specific cultures are negatively stereotyped.
CC5K10	Strategies used by diverse populations to cope with a legacy of former and continuing racism.
DH5K1	Processes for establishing ongoing interactions of individuals who are deaf or hard of hearing with peers and role models who are deaf or hard of hearing.
DH5K2	Learner opportunities for interaction with communities of individuals who are deaf or hard of hearing on local, state, and national levels.
CC5S1	Create a safe, equitable, positive, and supportive learning environment in which diversities are valued.
CC5S2	Identify realistic expectations for personal and social behavior in various settings.
CC5S3	Identify supports needed for integration into various program placements.

CC5S4	Design learning environments that encourage active participation in individual and group activities.
CC5S5	Modify the learning environment to manage behaviors.
CC5S6	Use performance data and information from all stakeholders to make or suggest modifications in learning environments.
CC5S7	Establish and maintain rapport with individuals with and without exceptional learning needs.
CC5S8	Teach self-advocacy.
CC5S9	Create an environment that encourages self-advocacy and increased independence.
CC5S10	Use effective and varied behavior management strategies.
CC5S11	Use the least intensive behavior management strategy consistent with the needs of the individual with exceptional learning needs.
CC5S12	Design and manage daily routines.
CC5S13	Organize, develop, and sustain learning environments that support positive intracultural and intercultural experiences.
CC5S14	Mediate controversial intercultural issues among students within the learning environment in ways that enhance any culture, group, or person.
CC5S15	Structure, direct, and support the activities of paraeducators, volunteers, and tutors.
CC5S16	Use universal precautions.
DH5S1	Modify the instructional environment to meet the physical, cognitive, cultural, and communication needs of the individual who is deaf or hard of hearing.
DH5S2	Modify incidental language experiences to fit the visual and other sensory needs of individuals who are deaf or hard of hearing.
DH5S3	Manage assistive/augmentative technology for individuals who are deaf or hard of hearing.
DH5S4	Select, adapt, and implement classroom management strategies considering deaf cultural factors.
DH5S5	Design a classroom environment that maximizes opportunities for visual and/or auditory learning for individuals who are deaf or hard of hearing.

Standard #6: Language

CC6K1	Effects of cultural and linguistic differences on growth and development.
CC6K2	Characteristics of one's own culture and use of language and the ways in which these can differ from other cultures and uses of languages.
CC6K3	Ways of behaving and communicating among cultures that can lead to misinterpretation and misunderstanding.
CC6K4	Augmentative and assistive communication strategies.
DH6K1	Communication features salient to the individual who is deaf or hard of hearing that are necessary to enhance cognitive, emotional, and social development.
DH6K2	Impact of early communication on the development of the individual who is deaf or hard of hearing.
DH6K3	Effects of sensory input on the development of language and cognition.
DH6K4	Components of nonlinguistic and linguistic communication used by individuals who are deaf or hard of hearing.
DH6K5	Communication modes used by and with individuals who are deaf or hard of hearing.
DH6K6	Current theories of language development in individuals who are hearing and those who are deaf or hard of hearing.
DH6K7	Strategies to facilitate cognitive and communicative development in individuals who are deaf or hard of hearing.
DH6K8	Strategies for stimulating and using residual hearing.
CC6S1	Use strategies to support and enhance communication skills of individuals with exceptional learning needs.
CC6S2	Use communication strategies and resources to facilitate understanding of subject matter for students whose primary language is not the dominant language.
DH6S1	Gather and analyze verbal and nonverbal communication samples.

DH6S2	Facilitate independent communication.
DH6S3	Facilitate communication between the individual who is deaf or hard of hearing and the primary caregivers.

Standard #7: Instructional Planning

CC7K1	Theories and research that form the basis of curriculum development and instructional practice.
CC7K2	Scope and sequences of general and special curricula.
CC7K3	National, state or provincial, and local curricula standards.
CC7K4	Technology for planning and managing the teaching and learning environment.
CC7K5	Roles and responsibilities of the paraeducator related to instruction, intervention, and direct service.
DH7K1	Model programs, including career/vocational and transition, for individuals who are deaf or hard of hearing.
CC7S1	Identify and prioritize areas of the general curriculum and accommodations for individuals with exceptional learning needs.
CC7S2	Develop and implement comprehensive, longitudinal individualized programs in collaboration with team members.
CC7S3	Involve the individual and family in setting instructional goals and monitoring progress.
CC7S4	Use functional assessments to develop intervention plans.
CC7S5	Use task analysis.
CC7S6	Sequence, implement, and evaluate individualized learning objectives.
CC7S7	Integrate affective, social, and life skills with academic curricula.
CC7S8	Develop and select instructional content, resources, and strategies that respond to cultural, linguistic, and gender differences.
CC7S9	Incorporate and implement instructional and assistive technology into the educational program.
CC7S10	Prepare lesson plans.
CC7S11	Prepare and organize materials to implement daily lesson plans.
CC7S12	Use instructional time effectively.
CC7S13	Make responsive adjustments to instruction based on continual observations.
CC7S14	Prepare individuals to exhibit self-enhancing behavior in response to societal attitudes and actions.
DH7S1	Select, design, and use technology, materials, and resources required to educate individuals who are deaf or hard of hearing.
DH7S2	Integrate speech skills as consistent with educational philosophy into academic areas.
DH7S3	Plan and implement instruction for individuals who are deaf or hard of hearing and who have multiple disabilities and special needs.

Standard #8: Assessment

CC8K1	Basic terminology used in assessment.
CC8K2	Legal provisions and ethical principles regarding assessment of individuals.
CC8K3	Screening, prereferral, referral, and classification procedures.
CC8K4	Use and limitations of assessment instruments.
CC8K5	National, state or provincial, and local accommodations and modifications.
DH8K1	Specialized terminology used in assessing individuals who are deaf or hard of hearing.
DH8K2	Specialized procedures for evaluation, eligibility, placement, and program planning for individuals who are deaf or hard of hearing.
DH8K3	Specialized policies on referral and placement procedures for individuals who are deaf or hard of hearing.
CC8S1	Gather relevant background information.
CC8S2	Administer nonbiased formal and informal assessments.
CC8S3	Use technology to conduct assessments.
CC8S4	Develop or modify individualized assessment strategies.

CC8S5	Interpret information from formal and informal assessments.
CC8S6	Use assessment information in making eligibility, program, and placement decisions for individuals with exceptional learning needs, including those from culturally and/or linguistically diverse backgrounds.
CC8S7	Report assessment results to all stakeholders using effective communication skills.
CC8S8	Evaluate instruction and monitor progress of individuals with exceptional learning needs.
CC8S9	Develop or modify individualized assessment strategies.
CC8S10	Create and maintain records.
DH8S1	Administer assessment tools using the natural/native/preferred language of the individual who is deaf or hard of hearing.
DH8S2	Use disability-specific assessment instruments.

Standard #9: Professional and Ethical Practice

CC9K1	Personal cultural biases and differences that affect one's teaching.
CC9K2	Importance of the teacher serving as a model for individuals with exceptional learning needs.
CC9K3	Continuum of lifelong professional development.
CC9K4	Methods to remain current regarding research-validated practice.
DH9K1	Roles and responsibilities of teachers and support personnel in educational practice for individuals who are deaf or hard of hearing.
DH9K2	Professional development to acquire knowledge of philosophies and skills in communication modes.
DH9K3	Organizations and publications relevant to the field of education of individuals who are deaf or hard of hearing.
CC9S1	Practice within the CEC Code of Ethics and other standards of the profession.
CC9S2	Uphold high standards of competence and integrity and exercise sound judgment in the practice of the professional.
CC9S3	Act ethically in advocating for appropriate services.
CC9S4	Conduct professional activities in compliance with applicable laws and policies.
CC9S5	Demonstrate commitment to developing the highest education and quality-of-life potential of individuals with exceptional learning needs.
CC9S6	Demonstrate sensitivity for the culture, language, religion, gender, disability, socioeconomic status, and sexual orientation of individuals.
CC9S7	Practice within one's skill limit and obtain assistance as needed.
CC9S8	Use verbal, nonverbal, and written language effectively.
CC9S9	Conduct self-evaluation of instruction.
CC9S10	Access information on exceptionalities.
CC9S11	Reflect on one's practice to improve instruction and guide professional growth.
CC9S12	Engage in professional activities that benefit individuals with exceptional learning needs, their families, and one's colleagues.
DH9S1	Interact with a variety of individuals who are deaf or hard of hearing on an adult-to-adult level.
DH9S2	Participate in the activities of professional organizations in the field of hearing impairment.

Standard #10: Collaboration

CC10K1	Models and strategies of consultation and collaboration.
CC10K2	Roles of individuals with exceptional learning needs, families, and school and community personnel in planning of an individualized program.
CC10K3	Concerns of families of individuals with exceptional learning needs and strategies to help address these concerns.
CC10K4	Culturally responsive factors that promote effective communication and collaboration with individuals with exceptional learning needs, families, school personnel, and community members.
DH10K1	Effects of communication on the development of family relationships.

DH10K2	Services and networks for and organizations of individuals who are deaf or hard of hearing.
CC10S1	Maintain confidential communication about individuals with exceptional learning needs.
CC10S2	Collaborate with families and others in assessment of individuals with exceptional learning needs.
CC10S3	Foster respectful and beneficial relationships between families and professionals.
CC10S4	Assist individuals with exceptional learning needs and their families in becoming active participants in the educational team.
CC10S5	Plan and conduct collaborative conferences with individuals with exceptional learning needs and their families.
CC10S6	Collaborate with school personnel and community members in integrating individuals with exceptional learning needs into various settings.
CC10S7	Use group problem-solving skills to develop, implement, and evaluate collaborative activities.
CC10S8	Model techniques and coach others in the use of instructional methods and accommodations.
CC10S9	Communicate with school personnel about the characteristics and needs of individuals with exceptional learning needs.
CC10S10	Communicate effectively with families of individuals with exceptional learning needs from diverse backgrounds.
CC10S11	Observe, evaluate, and provide feedback to paraeducators.
DH10S1	Coordinate support personnel to meet the diverse communication needs of the individual who is deaf or hard of hearing and the primary caregivers.
DH10S2	Provide families with knowledge, skills, and support to make choices regarding communication modes/philosophies and educational options across the lifespan.

Notes:

"Individual with exceptional learning needs" is used throughout to include individuals with disabilities and individuals with exceptional gifts and talents.

"Exceptional condition" is used throughout to include both single and co-existing conditions. These may be two or more disabling conditions or exceptional gifts or talents co-existing with one or more disabling conditions.

"Special curricula" is used throughout to denote curricular areas not routinely emphasized or addressed in general curricula; e.g., social, communication, motor, independence, self-advocacy.

CEC Knowledge and Skill Base for All Entry-Level Special Education Teachers of Students in Early Childhood[1]

Standard #1: Foundations	
CC1K1	Models, theories, and philosophies that form the basis for special education practice.
CC1K2	Laws, policies, and ethical principles regarding behavior management planning and implementation.
CC1K3	Relationship of special education to the organization and function of educational agencies.
CC1K4	Rights and responsibilities of students, parents, teachers, and other professionals, and schools related to exceptional learning needs.
CC1K5	Issues in definition and identification of individuals with exceptional learning needs, including those from culturally and linguistically diverse backgrounds.
CC1K6	Issues, assurances, and due process rights related to assessment, eligibility, and placement within a continuum of services.
CC1K7	Family systems and the role of families in the educational process.
CC1K8	Historical points of view and contribution of culturally diverse groups.
CC1K9	Impact of the dominant culture on shaping schools and the individuals who study and work in them.
CC1K10	Potential impact of differences in values, languages, and customs that can exist between the home and school.
EC1K1	Historical and philosophical foundations of services for young children both with and without exceptional learning needs.
EC1K2	Trends and issues in early childhood education and early childhood special education.
EC1K3	Law and policies that affect young children, families, and programs for young children.
CC1S1	Articulate personal philosophy of special education.
Standard #2: Development and Characteristics of Learners	
CC2K1	Typical and atypical human growth and development.
CC2K2	Educational implications of characteristics of various exceptionalities.
CC2K3	Characteristics and effects of the cultural and environmental milieu of the individual with exceptional learning needs and the family.
CC2K4	Family systems and the role of families in supporting development.
CC2K5	Similarities and differences of individuals with and without exceptional learning needs.
CC2K6	Similarities and differences among individuals with exceptional learning needs.
CC2K7	Effects of various medications on individuals with exceptional learning needs.
EC2K1	Theories of typical and atypical early childhood development.
EC2K2	Effect of biological and environmental factors on pre-, peri-, and post-natal development.
EC2K3	Influence of stress and trauma, protective factors and resilience, and supportive relationships on the social and emotional development of young children.
EC2K4	Significance of sociocultural and political contexts for the development and learning of young children who are culturally and linguistically diverse.
EC2K5	Impact of medical conditions on family concerns, resources, and priorities.
EC2K6	Childhood illnesses and communicable diseases
Standard #3: Individual Learning Differences	
CC3K1	Effects an exceptional condition(s) can have on an individual's life.
CC3K2	Impact of learners' academic and social abilities, attitudes, interests, and values on instruction and career development.

[1]*Note On Coding:* CC in the number code indicates a Common Core item; EC indicates an Early Childhood Special Education item; K indicates a Knowledge item; S indicates a Skill item.

CC3K3	Variations in beliefs, traditions, and values across and within cultures and their effects on relationships among individuals with exceptional learning needs, family, and schooling.
CC3K4	Cultural perspectives influencing the relationships among families, schools, and communities as related to instruction.
CC3K5	Differing ways of learning of individuals with exceptional learning needs including those from culturally diverse backgrounds and strategies for addressing these differences.
EC3S1	Use intervention strategies with young children and their families that affirm and respect family, cultural, and linguistic diversity.

Standard #4: Instructional Strategies

CC4S1	Use strategies to facilitate integration into various settings.
CC4S2	Teach individuals to use self-assessment, problem-solving, and other cognitive strategies to meet their needs.
CC4S3	Select, adapt, and use instructional strategies and materials according to characteristics of the individual with exceptional learning needs.
CC4S4	Use strategies to facilitate maintenance and generalization of skills across learning environments.
CC4S5	Use procedures to increase the individual's self-awareness, self-management, self-control, self-reliance, and self-esteem.
CC4S6	Use strategies that promote successful transitions for individuals with exceptional learning needs.
EC4S1	Use instructional practices based on knowledge of the child, family, community, and the curriculum.
EC4S2	Use knowledge of future educational settings to develop learning experiences and select instructional strategies for young children.
EC4S3	Prepare young children for successful transitions.

Standard #5: Learning Environments and Social Interactions

CC5K1	Demands of learning environments.
CC5K2	Basic classroom management theories and strategies for individuals with exceptional learning needs.
CC5K3	Effective management of teaching and learning.
CC5K4	Teacher attitudes and behaviors that influence behavior of individuals with exceptional learning needs.
CC5K5	Social skills needed for educational and other environments.
CC5K6	Strategies for crisis prevention and intervention.
CC5K7	Strategies for preparing individuals to live harmoniously and productively in a culturally diverse world.
CC5K8	Ways to create learning environments that allow individuals to retain and appreciate their own and each others' respective language and cultural heritage.
CC5K9	Ways specific cultures are negatively stereotyped.
CC5K10	Strategies used by diverse populations to cope with a legacy of former and continuing racism.
EC5K1	Medical care considerations for premature, low-birth-weight, and other young children with medical and health conditions.
CC5S1	Create a safe, equitable, positive, and supportive learning environment in which diversities are valued.
CC5S2	Identify realistic expectations for personal and social behavior in various settings.
CC5S3	Identify supports needed for integration into various program placements.
CC5S4	Design learning environments that encourage active participation in individual and group activities.
CC5S5	Modify the learning environment to manage behaviors.
CC5S6	Use performance data and information from all stakeholders to make or suggest modifications in learning environments.
CC5S7	Establish and maintain rapport with individuals with and without exceptional learning needs.
CC5S8	Teach self-advocacy.
CC5S9	Create an environment that encourages self-advocacy and increased independence.

CC5S10	Use effective and varied behavior management strategies.
CC5S11	Use the least intensive behavior management strategy consistent with the needs of the individual with exceptional learning needs.
CC5S12	Design and manage daily routines.
CC5S13	Organize, develop, and sustain learning environments that support positive intracultural and intercultural experiences.
CC5S14	Mediate controversial intercultural issues among students within the learning environment in ways that enhance any culture, group, or person.
CC5S15	Structure, direct, and support the activities of paraeducators, volunteers, and tutors.
CC5S16	Use universal precautions.
EC5S1	Implement nutrition plans and feeding strategies.
EC5S2	Use health appraisal procedures and make referrals as needed.
EC5S3	Design, implement, and evaluate environments to assure developmental and functional appropriateness.
EC5S4	Provide a stimuli-rich indoor and outdoor environment that employs materials, media, and technology, including adaptive and assistive technology.
EC5S5	Maximize young children's progress in group and home settings through organization of the physical, temporal, and social environments.

Standard #6: Language

CC6K1	Effects of cultural and linguistic differences on growth and development.
CC6K2	Characteristics of one's own culture and use of language and the ways in which these can differ from other cultures and uses of languages.
CC6K3	Ways of behaving and communicating among cultures that can lead to misinterpretation and misunderstanding.
CC6K4	Augmentative and assistive communication strategies.
CC6S1	Use strategies to support and enhance communication skills of individuals with exceptional learning needs.
CC6S2	Use communication strategies and resources to facilitate understanding of subject matter for students whose primary language is not the dominant language.
EC6S1	Support and facilitate family and child interactions as primary contexts for learning and development.

Standard #7: Instructional Planning

CC7K1	Theories and research that form the basis of curriculum development and instructional practice.
CC7K2	Scope and sequences of general and special curricula.
CC7K3	National, state or provincial, and local curricula standards.
CC7K4	Technology for planning and managing the teaching and learning environment.
CC7K5	Roles and responsibilities of the paraeducator related to instruction, intervention, and direct service.
CC7S1	Identify and prioritize areas of the general curriculum and accommodations for individuals with exceptional learning needs.
CC7S2	Develop and implement comprehensive, longitudinal individualized programs in collaboration with team members.
CC7S3	Involve the individual and family in setting instructional goals and monitoring progress.
CC7S4	Use functional assessments to develop intervention plans.
CC7S5	Use task analysis.
CC7S6	Sequence, implement, and evaluate individualized learning objectives.
CC7S7	Integrate affective, social, and life skills with academic curricula.
CC7S8	Develop and select instructional content, resources, and strategies that respond to cultural, linguistic, and gender differences.
CC7S9	Incorporate and implement instructional and assistive technology into the educational program.

CC7S10	Prepare lesson plans.
CC7S11	Prepare and organize materials to implement daily lesson plans.
CC7S12	Use instructional time effectively.
CC7S13	Make responsive adjustments to instruction based on continual observations.
CC7S14	Prepare individuals to exhibit self-enhancing behavior in response to societal attitudes and actions.
EC7S1	Implement, monitor, and evaluate individualized family service plans and individualized education programs.
EC7S2	Plan and implement developmentally and individually appropriate curriculum.
EC7S3	Design intervention strategies incorporating information from multiple disciplines.
EC7S4	Implement developmentally and functionally appropriate individual and group activities including play, environmental routines, parent-mediated activities, group projects, cooperative learning, inquiry experiences, and systematic instruction.

Standard #8: Assessment

CC8K1	Basic terminology used in assessment.
CC8K2	Legal provisions and ethical principles regarding assessment of individuals.
CC8K3	Screening, prereferral, referral, and classification procedures.
CC8K4	Use and limitations of assessment instruments.
CC8K5	National, state or provincial, and local accommodations and modifications.
CC8S1	Gather relevant background information.
CC8S2	Administer nonbiased formal and informal assessments.
CC8S3	Use technology to conduct assessments.
CC8S4	Develop or modify individualized assessment strategies.
CC8S5	Interpret information from formal and informal assessments.
CC8S6	Use assessment information in making eligibility, program, and placement decisions for individuals with exceptional learning needs, including those from culturally and/or linguistically diverse backgrounds.
CC8S7	Report assessment results to all stakeholders using effective communication skills.
CC8S8	Evaluate instruction and monitor progress of individuals with exceptional learning needs.
CC8S9	Create and maintain records.
EC8S1	Assess the development and learning of young children.
EC8S2	Select, adapt, and use specialized formal and informal assessments for infants, young children, and their families.
EC8S3	Participate as a team member to integrate assessment results in the development and implementation of individualized family service plans and individualized education programs.
EC8S4	Assist families in identifying their concerns, resources, and priorities.
EC8S5	Participate and collaborate as a team member with other professionals in conducting family-centered assessments.
EC8S6	Evaluate services with families.

Standard #9: Professional and Ethical Practice

CC9K1	Personal cultural biases and differences that affect one's teaching.
CC9K2	Importance of the teacher serving as a model for individuals with exceptional learning needs.
CC9K3	Continuum of lifelong professional development.
CC9K4	Methods to remain current regarding research-validated practice.
EC9K1	Organizations and publications relevant to the field of early childhood special education.
CC9S1	Practice within the CEC Code of Ethics and other standards of the profession.
CC9S2	Uphold high standards of competence and integrity and exercise sound judgment in the practice of the professional.
CC9S3	Act ethically in advocating for appropriate services.

CC9S4	Conduct professional activities in compliance with applicable laws and policies.
CC9S5	Demonstrate commitment to developing the highest education and quality-of-life potential of individuals with exceptional learning needs.
CC9S6	Demonstrate sensitivity for the culture, language, religion, gender, disability, socioeconomic status, and sexual orientation of individuals.
CC9S7	Practice within one's skill limit and obtain assistance as needed.
CC9S8	Use verbal, nonverbal, and written language effectively.
CC9S9	Conduct self-evaluation of instruction.
CC9S10	Access information on exceptionalities.
CC9S11	Reflect on one's practice to improve instruction and guide professional growth.
CC9S12	Engage in professional activities that benefit individuals with exceptional learning needs, their families, and one's colleagues.
EC9S1	Recognize signs of child abuse and neglect in young children and follow reporting procedures.
EC9S2	Use family theories and principles to guide professional practice.
EC9S3	Respect family choices and goals.
EC9S4	Apply models of team process in early childhood.
EC9S5	Advocate for enhanced professional status and working conditions for early childhood service providers.
EC9S6	Participate in activities of professional organizations relevant to the field of early childhood special education.
EC9S7	Apply research and effective practices critically in early childhood settings.
EC9S8	Develop, implement, and evaluate a professional development plan relevant to one's work with young children.

Standard #10: Collaboration

CC10K1	Models and strategies of consultation and collaboration.
CC10K2	Roles of individuals with exceptional learning needs, families, and school and community personnel in planning of an individualized program.
CC10K3	Concerns of families of individuals with exceptional learning needs and strategies to help address these concerns.
CC10K4	Culturally responsive factors that promote effective communication and collaboration with individuals with exceptional learning needs, families, school personnel, and community members.
EC10K1	Dynamics of team-building, problem-solving, and conflict resolution.
CC10S1	Maintain confidential communication about individuals with exceptional learning needs.
CC10S2	Collaborate with families and others in assessment of individuals with exceptional learning needs.
CC10S3	Foster respectful and beneficial relationships between families and professionals.
CC10S4	Assist individuals with exceptional learning needs and their families in becoming active participants in the educational team.
CC10S5	Plan and conduct collaborative conferences with individuals with exceptional learning needs and their families.
CC10S6	Collaborate with school personnel and community members in integrating individuals with exceptional learning needs into various settings.
CC10S7	Use group problem-solving skills to develop, implement, and evaluate collaborative activities.
CC10S8	Model techniques and coach others in the use of instructional methods and accommodations.
CC10S9	Communicate with school personnel about the characteristics and needs of individuals with exceptional learning needs.
CC10S10	Communicate effectively with families of individuals with exceptional learning needs from diverse backgrounds.
CC10S11	Observe, evaluate, and provide feedback to paraeducators.
EC10S1	Assist the family in planning for transitions.

EC10S2	Communicate effectively with families about curriculum and their child's progress.
EC10S3	Apply models of team process in early childhood settings.
EC10S4	Apply various models of consultation in early childhood settings.
EC10S5	Establish and maintain positive collaborative relationships with families.
EC10S6	Provide consultation and instruction specific to services for children and families.

Notes:

"Individual with exceptional learning needs" is used throughout to include individuals with disabilities and individuals with exceptional gifts and talents.

"Exceptional condition" is used throughout to include both single and co-existing conditions. These may be two or more disabling conditions or exceptional gifts or talents co-existing with one or more disabling conditions.

"Special curricula" is used throughout to denote curricular areas not routinely emphasized or addressed in general curricula; e.g., social, communication, motor, independence, self-advocacy.

CEC Knowledge and Skill Base for All Entry-Level Special Education Teachers of Students with Emotional and Behavioral Disorders[1]

Standard #1: Foundations	
CC1K1	Models, theories, and philosophies that form the basis for special education practice.
CC1K2	Laws, policies, and ethical principles regarding behavior management planning and implementation.
CC1K3	Relationship of special education to the organization and function of educational agencies.
CC1K4	Rights and responsibilities of students, parents, teachers, and other professionals, and schools related to exceptional learning needs.
CC1K5	Issues in definition and identification of individuals with exceptional learning needs, including those from culturally and linguistically diverse backgrounds.
CC1K6	Issues, assurances, and due process rights related to assessment, eligibility, and placement within a continuum of services.
CC1K7	Family systems and the role of families in the educational process.
CC1K8	Historical points of view and contribution of culturally diverse groups.
CC1K9	Impact of the dominant culture on shaping schools and the individuals who study and work in them.
CC1K10	Potential impact of differences in values, languages, and customs that can exist between the home and school.
BD1K1	Educational terminology and definitions of individuals with emotional/behavioral disorders.
BD1K2	Models that describe deviance.
BD1K3	Foundations and issues related to knowledge and practice in emotional/behavioral disorders.
BD1K4	The legal, judicial, and educational systems serving individuals with emotional/behavioral disorders.
BD1K5	Theory of reinforcement techniques in serving individuals with emotional/behavioral disorders.
BD1K6	Principles of normalization and concept of least restrictive environment for individuals with emotional/behavioral disorders in programs.
CC1S1	Articulate personal philosophy of special education.
Standard #2: Development and Characteristics of Learners	
CC2K1	Typical and atypical human growth and development.
CC2K2	Educational implications of characteristics of various exceptionalities.
CC2K3	Characteristics and effects of the cultural and environmental milieu of the individual with exceptional learning needs and the family.
CC2K4	Family systems and the role of families in supporting development.
CC2K5	Similarities and differences of individuals with and without exceptional learning needs.
CC2K6	Similarities and differences among individuals with exceptional learning needs.
CC2K7	Effects of various medications on individuals with exceptional learning needs.
BD2K1	Etiology and diagnosis related to various theoretical approaches in the field of emotional/behavioral disorders.
BD2K2	Physical development, disability, and health impairments related to individuals with emotional/behavioral disorders.
BD2K3	Social characteristics of individuals with emotional/behavioral disorders.
BD2K4	Factors that influence overrepresentation of diverse individuals in programs for individuals with emotional/behavior disorders.
Standard #3: Individual Learning Differences	
CC3K1	Effects an exceptional condition(s) can have on an individual's life.

[1]*Note On Coding:* CC in the number code indicates a Common Core item; EC indicates an Early Childhood Special Education item; K indicates a Knowledge item; S indicates a Skill item.

CC3K2	Impact of learners' academic and social abilities, attitudes, interests, and values on instruction and career development.
CC3K3	Variations in beliefs, traditions, and values across and within cultures and their effects on relationships among individuals with exceptional learning needs, family, and schooling.
CC3K4	Cultural perspectives influencing the relationships among families, schools, and communities as related to instruction.
CC3K5	Differing ways of learning of individuals with exceptional learning needs including those from culturally diverse backgrounds and strategies for addressing these differences.

Standard #4: Instructional Strategies

BD4K1	Sources of specialized materials for individuals with emotional/behavioral disorders.
BD4K2	Advantages and limitations of instructional strategies and practices for teaching individuals with emotional/behavioral disorders.
BD4K3	Resources and techniques used to transition individuals with emotional/behavioral disorders into and out of school and postschool environments.
BD4K4	Prevention and intervention strategies for individuals at risk of emotional/behavioral disorders.
BD4K5	Strategies for integrating student-initiated learning experiences into ongoing instruction for individuals with emotional/behavioral disorders.
CC4S1	Use strategies to facilitate integration into various settings.
CC4S2	Teach individuals to use self-assessment, problem-solving, and other cognitive strategies to meet their needs.
CC4S3	Select, adapt, and use instructional strategies and materials according to characteristics of the individual with exceptional learning needs.
CC4S4	Use strategies to facilitate maintenance and generalization of skills across learning environments.
CC4S5	Use procedures to increase the individual's self-awareness, self-management, self-control, self-reliance, and self-esteem.
CC4S6	Use strategies that promote successful transitions for individuals with exceptional learning needs.
BD4S1	Use strategies from multiple theoretical approaches for individuals with emotional/behavioral disorders.
BD4S2	Use a variety of nonaversive techniques to control targeted behavior and maintain attention of individuals with emotional/behavioral disorders.

Standard #5: Learning Environments and Social Interactions

CC5K1	Demands of learning environments.
CC5K2	Basic classroom management theories and strategies for individuals with exceptional learning needs.
CC5K3	Effective management of teaching and learning.
CC5K4	Teacher attitudes and behaviors that influence behavior of individuals with exceptional learning needs.
CC5K5	Social skills needed for educational and other environments.
CC5K6	Strategies for crisis prevention and intervention.
CC5K7	Strategies for preparing individuals to live harmoniously and productively in a culturally diverse world.
CC5K8	Ways to create learning environments that allow individuals to retain and appreciate their own and each others' respective language and cultural heritage.
CC5K9	Ways specific cultures are negatively stereotyped.
CC5K10	Strategies used by diverse populations to cope with a legacy of former and continuing racism.
BD5K1	Advantages and disadvantages of placement options and the continuum of services for individuals with emotional/behavioral disorders.
BD5K2	Functional classroom designs for individuals with emotional/behavioral disorders.
CC5S1	Create a safe, equitable, positive, and supportive learning environment in which diversities are valued.

CC5S2	Identify realistic expectations for personal and social behavior in various settings.
CC5S3	Identify supports needed for integration into various program placements.
CC5S4	Design learning environments that encourage active participation in individual and group activities.
CC5S5	Modify the learning environment to manage behaviors.
CC5S6	Use performance data and information from all stakeholders to make or suggest modifications in learning environments.
CC5S7	Establish and maintain rapport with individuals with and without exceptional learning needs.
CC5S8	Teach self-advocacy.
CC5S9	Create an environment that encourages self-advocacy and increased independence.
CC5S10	Use effective and varied behavior management strategies.
CC5S11	Use the least intensive behavior management strategy consistent with the needs of the individual with exceptional learning needs.
CC5S12	Design and manage daily routines.
CC5S13	Organize, develop, and sustain learning environments that support positive intracultural and intercultural experiences.
CC5S14	Mediate controversial intercultural issues among students within the learning environment in ways that enhance any culture, group, or person.
CC5S15	Structure, direct, and support the activities of paraeducators, volunteers, and tutors.
CC5S16	Use universal precautions.
BD5S1	Establish a consistent classroom routine for individuals with emotional/behavioral disorders.
BD5S2	Use skills in problem-solving and conflict resolution.

Standard #6: Language

CC6K1	Effects of cultural and linguistic differences on growth and development.
CC6K2	Characteristics of one's own culture and use of language and the ways in which these can differ from other cultures and uses of languages.
CC6K3	Ways of behaving and communicating among cultures that can lead to misinterpretation and misunderstanding.
CC6K4	Augmentative and assistive communication strategies.
CC6S1	Use strategies to support and enhance communication skills of individuals with exceptional learning needs.
CC6S2	Use communication strategies and resources to facilitate understanding of subject matter for students whose primary language is not the dominant language.

Standard #7: Instructional Planning

CC7K1	Theories and research that form the basis of curriculum development and instructional practice.
CC7K2	Scope and sequences of general and special curricula.
CC7K3	National, state or provincial, and local curricula standards.
CC7K4	Technology for planning and managing the teaching and learning environment.
CC7K5	Roles and responsibilities of the paraeducator related to instruction, intervention, and direct service.
BD7K1	Model programs that have been effective for individuals with emotional/behavioral disorders across the age range.
CC7S1	Identify and prioritize areas of the general curriculum and accommodations for individuals with exceptional learning needs.
CC7S2	Develop and implement comprehensive, longitudinal individualized programs in collaboration with team members.
CC7S3	Involve the individual and family in setting instructional goals and monitoring progress.
CC7S4	Use functional assessments to develop intervention plans.
CC7S5	Use task analysis.
CC7S6	Sequence, implement, and evaluate individualized learning objectives.

CC7S7	Integrate affective, social, and life skills with academic curricula.
CC7S8	Develop and select instructional content, resources, and strategies that respond to cultural, linguistic, and gender differences.
CC7S9	Incorporate and implement instructional and assistive technology into the educational program.
CC7S10	Prepare lesson plans.
CC7S11	Prepare and organize materials to implement daily lesson plans.
CC7S12	Use instructional time effectively.
CC7S13	Make responsive adjustments to instruction based on continual observations.
CC7S14	Prepare individuals to exhibit self-enhancing behavior in response to societal attitudes and actions.
BD7S1	Plan and implement individualized reinforcement systems and environmental modifications at levels equal to the intensity of the behavior.
BD7S2	Integrate academic instruction, affective education, and behavior management for individuals and groups with emotional/behavioral disorders.

Standard #8: Assessment

CC8K1	Basic terminology used in assessment.
CC8K2	Legal provisions and ethical principles regarding assessment of individuals.
CC8K3	Screening, prereferral, referral, and classification procedures.
CC8K4	Use and limitations of assessment instruments.
CC8K5	National, state or provincial, and local accommodations and modifications.
BD8K1	Characteristics of behavioral rating scales.
BD8K2	Policies and procedures involved in the screening, diagnosis, and placement of individuals with emotional/behavioral disorders including academic and social behaviors.
BD8K3	Types and importance of information concerning individuals with emotional/behavioral disorders available from families and public agencies.
CC8S1	Gather relevant background information.
CC8S2	Administer nonbiased formal and informal assessments.
CC8S3	Use technology to conduct assessments.
CC8S4	Develop or modify individualized assessment strategies.
CC8S5	Interpret information from formal and informal assessments.
CC8S6	Use assessment information in making eligibility, program, and placement decisions for individuals with exceptional learning needs, including those from culturally and/or linguistically diverse backgrounds.
CC8S7	Report assessment results to all stakeholders using effective communication skills.
CC8S8	Evaluate instruction and monitor progress of individuals with exceptional learning needs.
CC8S9	Create and maintain records.
BD8S1	Prepare assessment reports on individuals with emotional/behavioral disorders based on behavioral-ecological information.
BD8S2	Assess appropriate and problematic social behaviors of individuals with emotional/behavioral disorders.
BD8S3	Monitor intragroup behavior changes from subject to subject and activity to activity applicable to individuals with emotional/behavior disorders.

Standard #9: Professional and Ethical Practice

CC9K1	Personal cultural biases and differences that affect one's teaching.
CC9K2	Importance of the teacher serving as a model for individuals with exceptional learning needs.
CC9K3	Continuum of lifelong professional development.
CC9K4	Methods to remain current regarding research-validated practice.
BD9K1	Organizations and publications relevant to the field of emotional/behavioral disorders.
CC9S1	Practice within the CEC Code of Ethics and other standards of the profession.

CC9S2	Uphold high standards of competence and integrity and exercise sound judgment in the practice of the profession.
CC9S3	Act ethically in advocating for appropriate services.
CC9S4	Conduct professional activities in compliance with applicable laws and policies.
CC9S5	Demonstrate commitment to developing the highest education and quality-of-life potential of individuals with exceptional learning needs.
CC9S6	Demonstrate sensitivity for the culture, language, religion, gender, disability, socioeconomic status, and sexual orientation of individuals.
CC9S7	Practice within one's skills limit and obtain assistance as needed.
CC9S8	Use verbal, nonverbal, and written language effectively.
CC9S9	Conduct self-evaluation of instruction.
CC9S10	Access information on exceptionalities.
CC9S11	Reflect on one's practice to improve instruction and guide professional growth.
CC9S12	Engage in professional activities that benefit individuals with exceptional learning needs, their families, and one's colleagues.
BD9S1	Participate in activities of professional organizations relevant to the field of emotional/behavioral disorders.

Standard #10: Collaboration

CC10K1	Models and strategies of consultation and collaboration.
CC10K2	Roles of individuals with exceptional learning needs, families, and school and community personnel in planning of an individualized program.
CC10K3	Concerns of families of individuals with exceptional learning needs and strategies to help address these concerns.
CC10K4	Culturally responsive factors that promote effective communication and collaboration with individuals with exceptional learning needs, families, school personnel, and community members.
BD10K1	Services, networks, and organizations for individuals with emotional/behavioral disorders.
BD10K2	Parent education programs and behavior management guides that address severe behavioral problems and facilitate communication for individuals with emotional/behavioral disorders.
BD10K3	Collaborative and consultative roles of the special education teacher in the reintegration of individuals with emotional/behavioral disorders.
BD10K4	Role of professional groups and referral agencies in identifying, assessing, and providing services to individuals with emotional/behavioral disorders.
CC10S1	Maintain confidential communication about individuals with exceptional learning needs.
CC10S2	Collaborate with families and others in assessment of individuals with exceptional learning needs.
CC10S3	Foster respectful and beneficial relationships between families and professionals.
CC10S4	Assist individuals with exceptional learning needs and their families in becoming active participants in the educational team.
CC10S5	Plan and conduct collaborative conferences with individuals with exceptional learning needs and their families.
CC10S6	Collaborate with school personnel and community members in integrating individuals with exceptional learning needs into various settings.
CC10S7	Use group problem-solving skills to develop, implement, and evaluate collaborative activities.
CC10S8	Model techniques and coach others in the use of instructional methods and accommodations.
CC10S9	Communicate with school personnel about the characteristics and needs of individuals with exceptional learning needs.
CC10S10	Communicate effectively with families of individuals with exceptional learning needs from diverse backgrounds.
CC10S11	Observe, evaluate, and provide feedback to paraeducators.
BD10S1	Teach parents to use appropriate behavior management and counseling techniques.

Notes:

"Individual with exceptional learning needs" is used throughout to include individuals with disabilities and individuals with exceptional gifts and talents.

"Exceptional condition" is used throughout to include both single and co-existing conditions. These may be two or more disabling conditions or exceptional gifts or talents co-existing with one or more disabling conditions.

"Special curricula" is used throughout to denote curricular areas not routinely emphasized or addressed in general curricula; e.g., social, communication, motor, independence, self-advocacy.

CEC Knowledge and Skill Base for All Entry-Level
Special Education Teachers of Students with Gifts and Talents[1]

Standard #1: Foundations	
GT1K1	Historical foundations of gifted and talented education.
GT1K2	Models, theories, and philosophies that form the basis for gifted education.
GT1K3	Laws and policies related to gifted and talented education.
GT1K4	Relationship of gifted education to the organization and function of educational agencies.
GT1K5	Issues in definition and identification of individuals with gifts and talents, including those from culturally and linguistically diverse backgrounds.
GT1K6	Incidence and prevalence of individuals with gifts and talents.
GT1K7	Issues, assurances and due process rights related to assessment, eligibility, and placement within a continuum of services.
GT1K8	Impact of labeling individuals with gifts and talents.
GT1K9	Potential impact of differences in values, languages, and customs that can exist between the home and school.
GT1K10	Impact of the dominant culture on shaping schools and the individuals who study and work in them.
GT1K11	Rights and responsibilities of students, parents, teachers and other professionals, and schools related to exceptional learning needs.
GT1K12	Issues and trends in gifted education and related fields.
GT1K13	Laws, policies, and ethical principles regarding behavior management planning and implementation.
GT1K14	Teacher attitudes and behaviors that influence behavior of individuals with gifts and talents.
GT1K15	Historical points of view and contributions of culturally diverse groups.
Standard #2: Development and Characteristics of Learners	
GT2K1	Typical and atypical human growth and development.
GT2K2	Similarities and differences of individuals with and without gifts and talents and the general population of learners.
GT2K3	Similarities and differences among individuals with gifts and talents.
GT2K4	Educational implications of various gifts and talents.
GT2K5	Characteristics and effects of the cultural and environmental milieu of the child and the family.
GT2K6	Effects of medications on individuals with gifts and talents.
GT2K7	Cognitive characteristics of individuals with gifts and talents in intellectual, academic, creative, leadership, and artistic domains.
GT2K8	Affective characteristics of individuals with gifts and talents in intellectual, academic, creative, leadership, and artistic domains.
GT2K9	Effects of families on the development of individuals with gifts and talents.
GT2K10	Family systems and the role of families in supporting development and educational progress for students with gifts and talents.
Standard #3: Individual Learning Differences	
GT3K1	Impact of diversity on educational placement options for individuals with gifts and talents.
GT3K2	Variations in beliefs, traditions, and values across and within cultures and their effects on relationships among individuals with gifts and talents, family, and schooling.
GT3K3	Impact gifts and talents can have on an individual's life.
GT3K4	Academic characteristic of individuals with gifts and talents, and disabilities.
GT3K5	Affective characteristics of individuals with gifts and talents, and disabilities.

[1]*Note On Coding:* CC in the number code indicates a Common Core item; EC indicates an Early Childhood Special Education item; K indicates a Knowledge item; S indicates a Skill item.

GT3K6	Impact of multiple exceptionalities that may result in sensory, motor, or learning needs.
GT3K7	Differing learning styles of individuals with gifts and talents including those from culturally diverse backgrounds and strategies for addressing these styles.
GT3K8	Impact of learners' academic and social abilities, attitudes, interests, and values on instruction and career development.
GT3K9	Cultural perspectives influencing the relationship among families, schools, and communities as related to effective instruction.

Standard #4: Instructional Strategies

GT4K1	Sources of differentiated materials for individuals with gifts and talents.
GT4K2	Technology for planning and managing the teaching and learning environment.
GT4S1	Select, adapt, and use instructional strategies and materials according to characteristics of individuals with gifts and talents.
GT4S2	Use instructional time effectively.
GT4S3	Teach individuals to use self-assessment, problem-solving, and other cognitive strategies to meet their needs.
GT4S4	Choose and use technologies to modify the instructional process.
GT4S5	Use strategies to facilitate effective integration into various settings.
GT4S6	Integrate social skills into the curriculum.
GT4S7	Use procedures to increase the individual's self-awareness, self-management, self-control, self-reliance, self-esteem, and self-advocacy.

Standard #5: Learning Environments and Social Interactions

GT5K1	Ways specific cultures are negatively stereotyped.
GT5K2	Strategies used by diverse populations to cope with a legacy of former and continuing racism.
GT5K3	Effective management of teaching and learning for students with gifts and talents.
GT5K4	Acceleration, enrichment, and counseling within a continuum of service options for individuals with gifts and talents.
GT5K5	Grouping practices that support differentiated learning environments.
GT5K6	Ways to create learning environments that allow individuals to retain and appreciate their own and each others' respective language and cultural heritage.
GT5K7	Strategies for crisis prevention and intervention.
GT5K8	Strategies for preparing individuals to live harmoniously and productively in a culturally diverse world.
GT5S1	Establish and maintain rapport with individuals with gifts and talents.
GT5S2	Structure, direct, and supervise the activities of paraeducators, volunteers, and tutors.
GT5S3	Create a safe, equitable, positive, and supportive learning environment in which diversities are valued.
GT5S4	Design learning environments that encourage active participation in individual and group activities.
GT5S5	Create an environment that encourages self-advocacy and increased independence.
GT5S6	Teach self-advocacy.
GT5S7	Prepare and organize materials to implement daily lesson plans.
GT5S8	Design and manage daily routines.
GT5S9	Direct activities of classroom volunteers.
GT5S10	Use universal precautions.
GT5S11	Organize, develop, and sustain learning environments that support positive intracultural and intercultural experiences.
GT5S12	Use communication strategies and resources to facilitate understanding of the subject matter for students whose primary language is not the dominant language.
GT5S13	Prepare individuals to exhibit self-enhancing behavior in response to societal attitudes and actions.

GT5S14	Mediate controversial intercultural issues among students within the learning environment in ways that enhance any culture, group, or person.

Standard #6: Language

GT6K1	Effects of cultural and linguistic differences on growth and development.
GT6K2	Characteristics of one's own culture and use of language and the ways in which these can differ from other cultures and uses of language.
GT6K3	Importance of the teacher serving as a model for individuals with gifts and talents.
GT6K4	Ways of behaving and communicating among cultures that can lead to misinterpretation and misunderstanding.

Standard #7: Instructional Planning

GT7K1	National, state or provincial, and local curricula standards.
GT7K2	Scopes and sequences of general and special curricula.
GT7K3	Theories and research that form the basis of curriculum development and instructional practice.
GT7K4	Identify and prioritize areas of the general curriculum and accommodations for an individual with exceptional learning needs.
GT7K5	General and differentiated curricula for individuals with gifts and talents.
GT7K6	Differential curriculum needs of individuals with gifts and talents.
GT7K7	Community-based and service learning opportunities for individuals with gifts and talents.
GT7S1	Prepare lesson plans for individuals with gifts and talents.
GT7S2	Design cognitively complex learning experiences for individuals with gifts and talents.
GT7S3	Plan instruction using cognitive, affective, and ethical taxonomies.
GT7S4	Sequence, implement, and evaluate individualized learning objectives.
GT7S5	Integrate affective, social, and career skills with academic curricula.
GT7S6	Develop and select instructional content, resources, and strategies that respond to cultural, linguistic, and gender differences.
GT7S7	Develop and implement comprehensive, longitudinal individualized programs in collaboration with team members.
GT7S8	Make responsive adjustments to instruction based on continual observations of gifted students.
GT7S9	Select instructional models to differentiate specific content areas.
GT7S10	Involve the individual and family in setting instructional goals and monitoring progress.
GT7S11	Identify realistic expectations for personal and social behavior in various settings.

Standard #8: Assessment

GT8K1	Basic terminology used in assessment.
GT8K2	Legal provisions and ethical principles regarding assessment of individuals.
GT8K3	National, state or provincial, and local assessment, accommodations, and modifications.
GT8K4	Screening, prereferral, referral, and identification procedures for individuals with gifts and talents.
GT8K5	Use and limitations of assessment instruments for students with gifts and talents.
GT8S1	Gather relevant background information.
GT8S2	Use formal and informal assessments.
GT8S3	Interpret information from formal and informal assessments.
GT8S4	Develop and administer nonbiased, informal assessment procedures.
GT8S5	Use assessment information in making eligibility, program, and placement decisions for individuals with gifts and talents, including those from culturally and/or linguistically diverse backgrounds.
GT8S6	Identify supports needed for integration into various program placements.
GT8S7	Develop or modify individualized assessment strategies.
GT8S8	Evaluate instruction and monitor progress for individuals with gifts and talents.

GT8S9	Use performance data and information from all stakeholders to make or suggest modifications in learning environments.
GT8S10	Evaluate learner products and portfolios.
GT8S11	Report assessment results to all stakeholders using effective communication skills.
GT8S12	Create and maintain records.
GT8S13	Use technology to conduct assessments.

Standard #9: Professional and Ethical Practice

GT9K1	Personal cultural biases and differences that affect one's teaching.
GT9K2	Organizations and publications relevant to the field of gifted education.
GT9K3	Continuum of lifelong professional development.
GT9S1	Articulate personal philosophy of gifted education.
GT9S2	Access information on meeting the needs of students with gifts and talents.
GT9S3	Conduct self-evaluation of instruction.
GT9S4	Evaluate program activities for continued improvement.
GT9S5	Maintain confidential communication about individuals with gifts and talents.
GT9S6	Use verbal, nonverbal, and written language effectively.
GT9S7	Demonstrate commitment to developing the highest educational potential of individuals with gifts and talents.
GT9S8	Demonstrate sensitivity for the culture, language, religion, gender, disability, socioeconomic status, and sexual orientation of individual students.
GT9S9	Uphold high standards of competence and integrity and exercise sound judgment in the practice of the profession.
GT9S10	Engage in professional activities that benefit individuals with exceptional learning needs, their families, and colleagues.
GT9S11	Conduct professional activities in compliance with applicable laws and policies.
GT9S12	Practice within one's skills limit and obtain assistance when needed.
GT9S13	Practice within the CEC Code of Ethics and other standards of the profession.
GT9S14	Maintain knowledge of research and literature in special and gifted education.
GT9S15	Participate in the activities of professional organizations related to gifted and talented education.
GT9S16	Reflect on one's practice to improve instruction and guide professional growth.
GT9S17	Act ethically in advocating for appropriate services.

Standard #10: Collaboration

GT10K1	Culturally responsive factors that promote effective communication and collaboration with individuals, families, school personnel, and community members.
GT10K2	Concerns of families of individuals with gifts and talents and strategies to help address these concerns.
GT10K3	Services, networks, and organizations for individuals with gifts and talents.
GT10K4	Models and strategies for consultation and collaboration.
GT10S1	Collaborate with families and others in assessment of individuals with gifts and talents.
GT10S2	Foster respectful and beneficial relationships between families and professionals.
GT10S3	Assist individuals with gifts and talents and their families in becoming active participants in the educational team.
GT10S4	Plan and conduct collaborative conferences with individuals with gifts and talents and their families.
GT10S5	Use group problem-solving skills to develop, implement, and evaluate collaborative activities.
GT10S6	Communicate with school personnel about the characteristics and needs of individuals with gifts and talents.
GT10S7	Communicate effectively with families of individuals with gifts and talents from diverse backgrounds.
GT10S8	Model techniques and coach others in the use of instructional methods and accommodations.

Notes:

"Individual with exceptional learning needs" is used throughout to include individuals with disabilities and individuals with exceptional gifts and talents.

"Exceptional condition" is used throughout to include both single and co-existing conditions. These may be two or more disabling conditions or exceptional gifts or talents co-existing with one or more disabling conditions.

"Special curricula" is used throughout to denote curricular areas not routinely emphasized or addressed in general curricula; e.g., social, communication, motor, independence, self-advocacy.

CEC Knowledge and Skill Base for All Entry-Level Special Education Teachers of Students with Learning Disabilities[1]

Standard #1: Foundations	
CC1K1	Models, theories, and philosophies that form the basis for special education practice.
CC1K2	Laws, policies, and ethical principles regarding behavior management planning and implementation.
CC1K3	Relationship of special education to the organization and function of educational agencies.
CC1K4	Rights and responsibilities of students, parents, teachers, and other professionals, and schools related to exceptional learning needs.
CC1K5	Issues in definition and identification of individuals with exceptional learning needs, including those from culturally and linguistically diverse backgrounds.
CC1K6	Issues, assurances, and due process rights related to assessment, eligibility, and placement within a continuum of services.
CC1K7	Family systems and the role of families in the educational process.
CC1K8	Historical points of view and contribution of culturally diverse groups.
CC1K9	Impact of the dominant culture on shaping schools and the individuals who study and work in them.
CC1K10	Potential impact of differences in values, languages, and customs that can exist between the home and school.
LD1K1	Historical foundations, classical studies, and major contributors in the field of learning disabilities.
LD1K2	Philosophies, theories, models, and issues related to individuals with learning disabilities.
LD1K3	Impact of legislation on the education of individuals with learning disabilities.
LD1K4	Laws and policies regarding prereferral, referral, and placement procedures for individuals who may have learning disabilities.
LD1K5	Current definitions and issues related to the identification of individuals with learning disabilities.
CC1S1	Articulate personal philosophy of special education.
Standard #2: Development and Characteristics of Learners	
CC2K1	Typical and atypical human growth and development.
CC2K2	Educational implications of characteristics of various exceptionalities.
CC2K3	Characteristics and effects of the cultural and environmental milieu of the individual with exceptional learning needs and the family.
CC2K4	Family systems and the role of families in supporting development.
CC2K5	Similarities and differences of individuals with and without exceptional learning needs.
CC2K6	Similarities and differences among individuals with exceptional learning needs.
CC2K7	Effects of various medications on individuals with exceptional learning needs.
LD2K1	Etiologies of learning disabilities.
LD2K2	Neurobiological and medical factors that may impact the learning of individuals with learning disabilities.
LD2K3	Psychological, social, and emotional characteristics of individuals with learning disabilities.
Standard #3: Individual Learning Differences	
CC3K1	Effects an exceptional condition(s) can have on an individual's life.
CC3K2	Impact of learners' academic and social abilities, attitudes, interests, and values on instruction and career development.
CC3K3	Variations in beliefs, traditions, and values across and within cultures and their effects on relationships among individuals with exceptional learning needs, family, and schooling.

[1]*Note On Coding:* CC in the number code indicates a Common Core item; EC indicates an Early Childhood Special Education item; K indicates a Knowledge item; S indicates a Skill item.

CC3K4	Cultural perspectives influencing the relationships among families, schools, and communities as related to instruction.
CC3K5	Differing ways of learning of individuals with exceptional learning needs including those from culturally diverse backgrounds and strategies for addressing these differences.
LD3K1	Impact of co-existing conditions and exceptionalities on individuals with learning disabilities.
LD3K2	Effects of phonological awareness on the reading abilities of individuals with learning disabilities.
LD3K3	Impact learning disabilities may have on auditory and information processing skills.

Standard #4: Instructional Strategies

LD4K1	Strategies to prepare for and take tests.
LD4K2	Methods for ensuring individual academic success in one-to-one, small-group, and large-group settings.
LD4K3	Methods for increasing accuracy and proficiency in math calculations and applications.
LD4K4	Methods for teaching individuals to independently use cognitive processing to solve problems.
LD4K5	Methods for guiding individuals in identifying and organizing critical content.
CC4S1	Use strategies to facilitate integration into various settings.
CC4S2	Teach individuals to use self-assessment, problem-solving, and other cognitive strategies to meet their needs.
CC4S3	Select, adapt, and use instructional strategies and materials according to characteristics of the individual with exceptional learning needs.
CC4S4	Use strategies to facilitate maintenance and generalization of skills across learning environments.
CC4S5	Use procedures to increase the individual's self-awareness, self-management, self-control, self-reliance, and self-esteem.
CC4S6	Use strategies that promote successful transitions for individuals with exceptional learning needs.
LD4S1	Use research-supported methods for academic and nonacademic instruction of individuals with learning disabilities.
LD4S2	Use specialized methods for teaching basic skills.
LD4S3	Modify the pace of instruction and provide organizational cues.
LD4S4	Identify and teach basic structures and relationships within and across curricula.
LD4S5	Use instructional methods to strengthen and compensate for deficits in perception, comprehension, memory, and retrieval.
LD4S6	Use responses and errors to guide instructional decisions and provide feedback to learners.
LD4S7	Identify and teach essential concepts, vocabulary, and content across the general curriculum.
LD4S8	Use reading methods appropriate to the individual with learning disabilities.
LD4S9	Implement systematic instruction in teaching reading comprehension and monitoring strategies.
LD4S10	Teach strategies for organizing and composing written products.
LD4S11	Implement systematic instruction to teach accuracy, fluency, and comprehension in content area reading and written language.
LD4S12	Use methods to teach mathematics appropriate to the individual with learning disabilities.
LD4S13	Teach learning strategies and study skills to acquire academic content.

Standard #5: Learning Environments and Social Interactions

CC5K1	Demands of learning environments.
CC5K2	Basic classroom management theories and strategies for individuals with exceptional learning needs.
CC5K3	Effective management of teaching and learning.
CC5K4	Teacher attitudes and behaviors that influence behavior of individuals with exceptional learning needs.
CC5K5	Social skills needed for educational and other environments.
CC5K6	Strategies for crisis prevention and intervention.

CC5K7	Strategies for preparing individuals to live harmoniously and productively in a culturally diverse world.
CC5K8	Ways to create learning environments that allow individuals to retain and appreciate their own and each others' respective language and cultural heritage.
CC5K9	Ways specific cultures are negatively stereotyped.
CC5K10	Strategies used by diverse populations to cope with a legacy of former and continuing racism.
CC5S1	Create a safe, equitable, positive, and supportive learning environment in which diversities are valued.
CC5S2	Identify realistic expectations for personal and social behavior in various settings.
CC5S3	Identify supports needed for integration into various program placements.
CC5S4	Design learning environments that encourage active participation in individual and group activities.
CC5S5	Modify the learning environment to manage behaviors.
CC5S6	Use performance data and information from all stakeholders to make or suggest modifications in learning environments.
CC5S7	Establish and maintain rapport with individuals with and without exceptional learning needs.
CC5S8	Teach self-advocacy.
CC5S9	Create an environment that encourages self-advocacy and increased independence.
CC5S10	Use effective and varied behavior management strategies.
CC5S11	Use the least intensive behavior management strategy consistent with the needs of the individual with exceptional learning needs.
CC5S12	Design and manage daily routines.
CC5S13	Organize, develop, and sustain learning environments that support positive intracultural and intercultural experiences.
CC5S14	Mediate controversial intercultural issues among students within the learning environment in ways that enhance any culture, group, or person.
CC5S15	Structure, direct, and support the activities of paraeducators, volunteers, and tutors.
CC5S16	Use universal precautions.
LD5S1	Teach individuals with learning disabilities to give and receive meaningful feedback from peers and adults.

Standard #6: Language

CC6K1	Effects of cultural and linguistic differences on growth and development.
CC6K2	Characteristics of one's own culture and use of language and the ways in which these can differ from other cultures and uses of languages.
CC6K3	Ways of behaving and communicating among cultures that can lead to misinterpretation and misunderstanding.
CC6K4	Augmentative and assistive communication strategies.
LD6K1	Typical language development and how that may differ for individuals with learning disabilities.
LD6K2	Impact of language development and listening comprehension on academic and nonacademic learning of individuals with learning disabilities.
CC6S1	Use strategies to support and enhance communication skills of individuals with exceptional learning needs.
CC6S2	Use communication strategies and resources to facilitate understanding of subject matter for students whose primary language is not the dominant language.
LDS1	Enhance vocabulary development.
LDS2	Teach strategies for spelling accuracy and generalization.
LDS3	Teach methods and strategies for producing legible documents.
LDS4	Teach individuals with learning disabilities to monitor for errors in oral and written communications.

Standard #7: Instructional Planning	
CC7K1	Theories and research that form the basis of curriculum development and instructional practice.
CC7K2	Scope and sequences of general and special curricula.
CC7K3	National, state or provincial, and local curricula standards.
CC7K4	Technology for planning and managing the teaching and learning environment.
CC7K5	Roles and responsibilities of the paraeducator related to instruction, intervention, and direct service.
LD7K1	Relationships among reading instruction methods and learning disabilities.
LD7K2	Sources of specialized curricula, materials, and resources for individuals with learning disabilities.
LD7K3	Interventions and services for children who may be at risk for learning disabilities.
CC7S1	Identify and prioritize areas of the general curriculum and accommodations for individuals with exceptional learning needs.
CC7S2	Develop and implement comprehensive, longitudinal individualized programs in collaboration with team members.
CC7S3	Involve the individual and family in setting instructional goals and monitoring progress.
CC7S4	Use functional assessments to develop intervention plans.
CC7S5	Use task analysis.
CC7S6	Sequence, implement, and evaluate individualized learning objectives.
CC7S7	Integrate affective, social, and life skills with academic curricula.
CC7S8	Develop and select instructional content, resources, and strategies that respond to cultural, linguistic, and gender differences.
CC7S9	Incorporate and implement instructional and assistive technology into the educational program.
CC7S10	Prepare lesson plans.
CC7S11	Prepare and organize materials to implement daily lesson plans.
CC7S12	Use instructional time effectively.
CC7S13	Make responsive adjustments to instruction based on continual observations.
CC7S14	Prepare individuals to exhibit self-enhancing behavior in response to societal attitudes and actions.
Standard #8: Assessment	
CC8K1	Basic terminology used in assessment.
CC8K2	Legal provisions and ethical principles regarding assessment of individuals.
CC8K3	Screening, prereferral, referral, and classification procedures.
CC8K4	Use and limitations of assessment instruments.
CC8K5	National, state or provincial, and local accommodations and modifications.
LD8K1	Terminology and procedures used in the assessment of individuals with learning disabilities.
LD8K2	Factors that could lead to misidentification of individuals as having learning disabilities.
LD8K3	Procedures to identify young children who may be at risk for learning disabilities.
CC8S1	Gather relevant background information.
CC8S2	Administer nonbiased formal and informal assessments.
CC8S3	Use technology to conduct assessments.
CC8S4	Develop or modify individualized assessment strategies.
CC8S5	Interpret information from formal and informal assessments.
CC8S6	Use assessment information in making eligibility, program, and placement decisions for individuals with exceptional learning needs, including those from culturally and/or linguistically diverse backgrounds.
CC8S7	Report assessment results to all stakeholders using effective communication skills.
CC8S8	Evaluate instruction and monitor progress of individuals with exceptional learning needs.
CC8S9	Develop or modify individualized assessment strategies.
CC8S10	Create and maintain records.

| LD8S1 | Choose and administer assessment instruments appropriate to the individual with learning disabilities. |

Standard #9: Professional and Ethical Practice

CC9K1	Personal cultural biases and differences that affect one's teaching.
CC9K2	Importance of the teacher serving as a model for individuals with exceptional learning needs.
CC9K3	Continuum of lifelong professional development.
CC9K4	Methods to remain current regarding research-validated practice.
LD9K1	Ethical responsibility to advocate for appropriate services for individuals with learning disabilities.
LD9K2	Professional organizations and sources of information relevant to the field of learning disabilities.
CC9S1	Practice within the CEC Code of Ethics and other standards of the profession.
CC9S2	Uphold high standards of competence and integrity and exercise sound judgment in the practice of the profession.
CC9S3	Act ethically in advocating for appropriate services.
CC9S4	Conduct professional activities in compliance with applicable laws and policies.
CC9S5	Demonstrate commitment to developing the highest education and quality-of-life potential of individuals with exceptional learning needs.
CC9S6	Demonstrate sensitivity for the culture, language, religion, gender, disability, socioeconomic status, and sexual orientation of individuals.
CC9S7	Practice within one's skills limit and obtain assistance as needed.
CC9S8	Use verbal, nonverbal, and written language effectively.
CC9S9	Conduct self-evaluation of instruction.
CC9S10	Access information on exceptionalities.
CC9S11	Reflect on one's practice to improve instruction and guide professional growth.
CC9S12	Engage in professional activities that benefit individuals with exceptional learning needs, their families, and one's colleagues.
LD9S1	Participate in activities of professional organizations relevant to the field of learning disabilities.
LD9S2	Use research findings and theories to guide practice.

Standard #10: Collaboration

CC10K1	Models and strategies of consultation and collaboration.
CC10K2	Roles of individuals with exceptional learning needs, families, and school and community personnel in planning of an individualized program.
CC10K3	Concerns of families of individuals with exceptional learning needs and strategies to help address these concerns.
CC10K4	Culturally responsive factors that promote effective communication and collaboration with individuals with exceptional learning needs, families, school personnel, and community members.
LD10K1	Co-planning and co-teaching methods to strengthen content acquisition of individuals with learning disabilities.
LD10K2	Services, networks, and organizations that provide support across the life span for individuals with learning disabilities.
CC10S1	Maintain confidential communication about individuals with exceptional learning needs.
CC10S2	Collaborate with families and others in assessment of individuals with exceptional learning needs.
CC10S3	Foster respectful and beneficial relationships between families and professionals.
CC10S4	Assist individuals with exceptional learning needs and their families in becoming active participants in the educational team.
CC10S5	Plan and conduct collaborative conferences with individuals with exceptional learning needs and their families.
CC10S6	Collaborate with school personnel and community members in integrating individuals with exceptional learning needs into various settings.
CC10S7	Use group problem-solving skills to develop, implement, and evaluate collaborative activities.

CC10S8	Model techniques and coach others in the use of instructional methods and accommodations.
CC10S9	Communicate with school personnel about the characteristics and needs of individuals with exceptional learning needs.
CC10S10	Communicate effectively with families of individuals with exceptional learning needs from diverse backgrounds.
CC10S11	Observe, evaluate, and provide feedback to paraeducators.

Notes:

"Individual with exceptional learning needs" is used throughout to include individuals with disabilities and individuals with exceptional gifts and talents.

"Exceptional condition" is used throughout to include both single and co-existing conditions. These may be two or more disabling conditions or exceptional gifts or talents co-existing with one or more disabling conditions.

"Special curricula" is used throughout to denote curricular areas not routinely emphasized or addressed in general curricula; e.g., social, communication, motor, independence, self-advocacy.

CEC Knowledge and Skill Base for All Entry-Level Special Education Teachers of Students with Mental Retardation/Developmental Disabilities[1]

Standard #1: Foundations

CC1K1	Models, theories, and philosophies that form the basis for special education practice.
CC1K2	Laws, policies, and ethical principles regarding behavior management planning and implementation.
CC1K3	Relationship of special education to the organization and function of educational agencies.
CC1K4	Rights and responsibilities of students, parents, teachers, and other professionals, and schools related to exceptional learning needs.
CC1K5	Issues in definition and identification of individuals with exceptional learning needs, including those from culturally and linguistically diverse backgrounds.
CC1K6	Issues, assurances, and due process rights related to assessment, eligibility, and placement within a continuum of services.
CC1K7	Family systems and the role of families in the educational process.
CC1K8	Historical points of view and contribution of culturally diverse groups.
CC1K9	Impact of the dominant culture on shaping schools and the individuals who study and work in them.
CC1K10	Potential impact of differences in values, languages, and customs that can exist between the home and school.
MR1K1	Definitions and issues related to the identification of individuals with mental retardation/developmental disabilities.
MR1K2	Factors that influence overrepresentation of culturally/linguistically diverse individuals.
MR1K3	Continuum of placement and services available for individuals with mental retardation/developmental disabilities.
MR1K4	Historical foundations and classic studies of mental retardation/developmental disabilities.
MR1K5	Trends and practices in the field of mental retardation/developmental disabilities.
MR1K6	Theories of behavior problems of individuals with mental retardation/developmental disabilities.
CC1S1	Articulate personal philosophy of special education.

Standard #2: Development and Characteristics of Learners

CC2K1	Typical and atypical human growth and development.
CC2K2	Educational implications of characteristics of various exceptionalities.
CC2K3	Characteristics and effects of the cultural and environmental milieu of the individual with exceptional learning needs and the family.
CC2K4	Family systems and the role of families in supporting development.
CC2K5	Similarities and differences of individuals with and without exceptional learning needs.
CC2K6	Similarities and differences among individuals with exceptional learning needs.
CC2K7	Effects of various medications on individuals with exceptional learning needs.
MR2K1	Causes and theories of intellectual disabilities and implications for prevention.
MR2K2	Medical aspects of intellectual disabilities and their implications for learning.
MR2K3	Psychological, social/emotional, and motor characteristics of individuals with mental retardation/developmental disabilities.

Standard #3: Individual Learning Differences

CC3K1	Effects an exceptional condition(s) can have on an individual's life.
CC3K2	Impact of learners' academic and social abilities, attitudes, interests, and values on instruction and career development.
CC3K3	Variations in beliefs, traditions, and values across and within cultures and their effects on relationships among individuals with exceptional learning needs, family, and schooling.

[1]*Note On Coding:* CC in the number code indicates a Common Core item; EC indicates an Early Childhood Special Education item; K indicates a Knowledge item; S indicates a Skill item.

CC3K4	Cultural perspectives influencing the relationships among families, schools, and communities as related to instruction.
CC3K5	Differing ways of learning of individuals with exceptional learning needs including those from culturally diverse backgrounds and strategies for addressing these differences.
MR3K1	Impact of multiple disabilities on behavior.
MR3K2	Complications and implications of medical support services.
MR3S1	Relate levels of support to the needs of the individual.

Standard #4: Instructional Strategies

MR4K1	Specialized materials for individuals with mental retardation/developmental disabilities.
CC4S1	Use strategies to facilitate integration into various settings.
CC4S2	Teach individuals to use self-assessment, problem-solving, and other cognitive strategies to meet their needs.
CC4S3	Select, adapt, and use instructional strategies and materials according to characteristics of the individual with exceptional learning needs.
CC4S4	Use strategies to facilitate maintenance and generalization of skills across learning environments.
CC4S5	Use procedures to increase the individual's self-awareness, self-management, self-control, self-reliance, and self-esteem.
CC4S6	Use strategies that promote successful transitions for individuals with exceptional learning needs.

Standard #5: Learning Environments and Social Interactions

CC5K1	Demands of learning environments.
CC5K2	Basic classroom management theories and strategies for individuals with exceptional learning needs.
CC5K3	Effective management of teaching and learning.
CC5K4	Teacher attitudes and behaviors that influence behavior of individuals with exceptional learning needs.
CC5K5	Social skills needed for educational and other environments.
CC5K6	Strategies for crisis prevention and intervention.
CC5K7	Strategies for preparing individuals to live harmoniously and productively in a culturally diverse world.
CC5K8	Ways to create learning environments that allow individuals to retain and appreciate their own and each others' respective language and cultural heritage.
CC5K9	Ways specific cultures are negatively stereotyped.
CC5K10	Strategies used by diverse populations to cope with a legacy of former and continuing racism.
MR5K1	Approaches to create positive learning environments for individuals with mental retardation/ developmental disabilities.
CC5S1	Create a safe, equitable, positive, and supportive learning environment in which diversities are valued.
CC5S2	Identify realistic expectations for personal and social behavior in various settings.
CC5S3	Identify supports needed for integration into various program placements.
CC5S4	Design learning environments that encourage active participation in individual and group activities.
CC5S5	Modify the learning environment to manage behaviors.
CC5S6	Use performance data and information from all stakeholders to make or suggest modifications in learning environments.
CC5S7	Establish and maintain rapport with individuals with and without exceptional learning needs.
CC5S8	Teach self-advocacy.
CC5S9	Create an environment that encourages self-advocacy and increased independence.
CC5S10	Use effective and varied behavior management strategies.
CC5S11	Use the least intensive behavior management strategy consistent with the needs of the individual with exceptional learning needs.
CC5S12	Design and manage daily routines.
CC5S13	Organize, develop, and sustain learning environments that support positive intracultural and intercultural experiences.

CC5S14	Mediate controversial intercultural issues among students within the learning environment in ways that enhance any culture, group, or person.
CC5S15	Structure, direct, and support the activities of paraeducators, volunteers, and tutors.
CC5S16	Use universal precautions.
MR5S1	Provide instruction in community-based settings.
MR5S2	Demonstrate transfer, lifting, and positioning techniques.
MR5S3	Use and maintain assistive technologies.
MR5S4	Structure the physical environment to provide optimal learning for individuals with mental retardation/developmental disabilities.
MR5S5	Plan instruction for individuals with mental retardation/developmental disabilities in a variety of placement settings.

Standard #6: Language

CC6K1	Effects of cultural and linguistic differences on growth and development.
CC6K2	Characteristics of one's own culture and use of language and the ways in which these can differ from other cultures and uses of languages.
CC6K3	Ways of behaving and communicating among cultures that can lead to misinterpretation and misunderstanding.
CC6K4	Augmentative and assistive communication strategies.
CC6S1	Use strategies to support and enhance communication skills of individuals with exceptional learning needs.
CC6S2	Use communication strategies and resources to facilitate understanding of subject matter for students whose primary language is not the dominant language.
MR6S1	Plan instruction on the use of alternative and augmentative communication systems.

Standard #7: Instructional Planning

CC7K1	Theories and research that form the basis of curriculum development and instructional practice.
CC7K2	Scope and sequences of general and special curricula.
CC7K3	National, state or provincial, and local curricula standards.
CC7K4	Technology for planning and managing the teaching and learning environment.
CC7K5	Roles and responsibilities of the paraeducator related to instruction, intervention, and direct service.
MR7K1	Model programs for individuals with mental retardation/developmental disabilities including career/vocational transition.
CC7S1	Identify and prioritize areas of the general curriculum and accommodations for individuals with exceptional learning needs.
CC7S2	Develop and implement comprehensive, longitudinal individualized programs in collaboration with team members.
CC7S3	Involve the individual and family in setting instructional goals and monitoring progress.
CC7S4	Use functional assessments to develop intervention plans.
CC7S5	Use task analysis.
CC7S6	Sequence, implement, and evaluate individualized learning objectives.
CC7S7	Integrate affective, social, and life skills with academic curricula.
CC7S8	Develop and select instructional content, resources, and strategies that respond to cultural, linguistic, and gender differences.
CC7S9	Incorporate and implement instructional and assistive technology into the educational program.
CC7S10	Prepare lesson plans.
CC7S11	Prepare and organize materials to implement daily lesson plans.
CC7S12	Use instructional time effectively.
CC7S13	Make responsive adjustments to instruction based on continual observations.
CC7S14	Prepare individuals to exhibit self-enhancing behavior in response to societal attitudes and actions.

MR7S1	Select and use specialized instructional strategies appropriate to individuals with mental retardation/developmental disabilities.
MR7S2	Design and implement sensory stimulation programs for individuals with mental retardation/developmental disabilities.
MR7S3	Plan instruction for independent functional life skills relevant to the community, personal living, sexuality, and employment.
MR7S4	Plan and implement age and ability-appropriate instruction for individuals with mental retardation/developmental disabilities.
MR7S5	Select and plan for integration of related services into the instructional program for individuals with mental retardation/developmental disabilities.
MR7S6	Design, implement, and evaluate instructional programs that enhance social participation across environments.

Standard #8: Assessment

CC8K1	Basic terminology used in assessment.
CC8K2	Legal provisions and ethical principles regarding assessment of individuals.
CC8K3	Screening, prereferral, referral, and classification procedures.
CC8K4	Use and limitations of assessment instruments.
CC8K5	National, state or provincial, and local accommodations and modifications.
MR8K1	Specialized terminology used in the assessment of individuals with mental retardation/developmental disabilities.
MR8K2	Environmental assessment conditions that promote maximum performance of individuals with mental retardation/developmental disabilities.
MR8K3	Adaptive behavior assessment.
MR8K4	Laws and policies regarding referral and placement procedures for individuals with mental retardation/developmental disabilities.
CC8S1	Gather relevant background information.
CC8S2	Administer nonbiased formal and informal assessments.
CC8S3	Use technology to conduct assessments.
CC8S4	Develop or modify individualized assessment strategies.
CC8S5	Interpret information from formal and informal assessments.
CC8S6	Use assessment information in making eligibility, program, and placement decisions for individuals with exceptional learning needs, including those from culturally and/or linguistically diverse backgrounds.
CC8S7	Report assessment results to all stakeholders using effective communication skills.
CC8S8	Evaluate instruction and monitor progress of individuals with exceptional learning needs.
CC8S9	Develop or modify individualized assessment strategies.
CC8S10	Create and maintain records.
MR8S1	Select, adapt, and use instructional assessment tools and methods to accommodate the abilities and needs of individuals with mental retardation/developmental disabilities.

Standard #9: Professional and Ethical Practice

CC9K1	Personal cultural biases and differences that affect one's teaching.
CC9K2	Importance of the teacher serving as a model for individuals with exceptional learning needs.
CC9K3	Continuum of lifelong professional development.
CC9K4	Methods to remain current regarding research-validated practice.
MR9K1	Organizations and publications in the field of mental retardation/developmental disabilities.
CC9S1	Practice within the CEC Code of Ethics and other standards of the profession.
CC9S2	Uphold high standards of competence and integrity and exercise sound judgment in the practice of the profession.
CC9S3	Act ethically in advocating for appropriate services.

CC9S4	Conduct professional activities in compliance with applicable laws and policies.
CC9S5	Demonstrate commitment to developing the highest education and quality-of-life potential of individuals with exceptional learning needs.
CC9S6	Demonstrate sensitivity for the culture, language, religion, gender, disability, socioeconomic status, and sexual orientation of individuals.
CC9S7	Practice within one's skills limit and obtain assistance as needed.
CC9S8	Use verbal, nonverbal, and written language effectively.
CC9S9	Conduct self-evaluation of instruction.
CC9S10	Access information on exceptionalities.
CC9S11	Reflect on one's practice to improve instruction and guide professional growth.
CC9S12	Engage in professional activities that benefit individuals with exceptional learning needs, their families, and one's colleagues.
MR9S1	Participate in the activities of professional organizations in the field of mental retardation/ developmental disabilities.

Standard #10: Collaboration

CC10K1	Models and strategies of consultation and collaboration.
CC10K2	Roles of individuals with exceptional learning needs, families, and school and community personnel in planning of an individualized program.
CC10K3	Concerns of families of individuals with exceptional learning needs and strategies to help address these concerns.
CC10K4	Culturally responsive factors that promote effective communication and collaboration with individuals with exceptional learning needs, families, school personnel, and community members.
MR10K1	Services, networks, and organizations for individuals with mental retardation/developmental disabilities.
CC10S1	Maintain confidential communication about individuals with exceptional learning needs.
CC10S2	Collaborate with families and others in assessment of individuals with exceptional learning needs.
CC10S3	Foster respectful and beneficial relationships between families and professionals.
CC10S4	Assist individuals with exceptional learning needs and their families in becoming active participants in the educational team.
CC10S5	Plan and conduct collaborative conferences with individuals with exceptional learning needs and their families.
CC10S6	Collaborate with school personnel and community members in integrating individuals with exceptional learning needs into various settings.
CC10S7	Use group problem-solving skills to develop, implement, and evaluate collaborative activities.
CC10S8	Model techniques and coach others in the use of instructional methods and accommodations.
CC10S9	Communicate with school personnel about the characteristics and needs of individuals with exceptional learning needs.
CC10S10	Communicate effectively with families of individuals with exceptional learning needs from diverse backgrounds.
CC10S11	Observe, evaluate, and provide feedback to paraeducators.
MR10S1	Collaborate with team members to plan transition to adulthood that encourages full community participation.

Notes:

"Individual with exceptional learning needs" is used throughout to include individuals with disabilities and individuals with exceptional gifts and talents.

"Exceptional condition" is used throughout to include both single and co-existing conditions. These may be two or more disabling conditions or exceptional gifts or talents co-existing with one or more disabling conditions.

"Special curricula" is used throughout to denote curricular areas not routinely emphasized or addressed in general curricula; e.g., social, communication, motor, independence, self-advocacy.

CEC Knowledge and Skill Base for All Entry-Level Special Education Teachers of Students with Physical and Health Disabilities[1]

Standard #1: Foundations	
CC1K1	Models, theories, and philosophies that form the basis for special education practice.
CC1K2	Laws, policies, and ethical principles regarding behavior management planning and implementation.
CC1K3	Relationship of special education to the organization and function of educational agencies.
CC1K4	Rights and responsibilities of students, parents, teachers and other professionals, and schools related to exceptional learning needs.
CC1K5	Issues in definition and identification of individuals with exceptional learning needs, including those from culturally and linguistically diverse backgrounds.
CC1K6	Issues, assurances, and due process rights related to assessment, eligibility, and placement within a continuum of services.
CC1K7	Family systems and the role of families in the educational process.
CC1K8	Historical points of view and contribution of culturally diverse groups.
CC1K9	Impact of the dominant culture on shaping schools and the individuals who study and work in them.
CC1K10	Potential impact of differences in values, languages, and customs that can exist between the home and school.
PH1K1	Issues and educational definitions of individuals with physical and health disabilities.
PH1K2	Historical foundations related to knowledge and practices in physical and health disabilities.
PH1K3	Laws and policies related to the provision of specialized health care in the educational setting.
CC1S1	Articulate personal philosophy of special education.
PH1S1	Articulate the service delivery for individuals with physical and health disabilities.
Standard #2: Development and Characteristics of Learners	
CC2K1	Typical and atypical human growth and development.
CC2K2	Educational implications of characteristics of various exceptionalities.
CC2K3	Characteristics and effects of the cultural and environmental milieu of the individual with exceptional learning needs and the family.
CC2K4	Family systems and the role of families in supporting development.
CC2K5	Similarities and differences of individuals with and without exceptional learning needs.
CC2K6	Similarities and differences among individuals with exceptional learning needs.
CC2K7	Effects of various medications on individuals with exceptional learning needs.
PH2K1	Medical terminology related to physical and health disabilities.
PH2K2	Etiology and characteristics of physical and health disabilities across the life span.
PH2K3	Secondary health care issues that accompany specific physical and health disabilities.
PH2K4	Types and transmission routes of infectious and communicable diseases.
Standard #3: Individual Learning Differences	
CC3K1	Effects an exceptional condition(s) can have on an individual's life.
CC3K2	Impact of learners' academic and social abilities, attitudes, interests, and values on instruction and career development.
CC3K3	Variations in beliefs, traditions, and values across and within cultures and their effects on relationships among individuals with exceptional learning needs, family, and schooling.
CC3K4	Cultural perspectives influencing the relationships among families, schools, and communities as related to instruction.

[1]*Note On Coding:* CC in the number code indicates a Common Core item; EC indicates an Early Childhood Special Education item; K indicates a Knowledge item; S indicates a Skill item.

CC3K5	Differing ways of learning of individuals with exceptional learning needs including those from culturally diverse backgrounds and strategies for addressing these differences.
PH3K1	Impact of physical and health disabilities on individuals, families, society.

Standard #4: Instructional Strategies

PH4K1	Instructional practices, strategies, and adaptations necessary to accommodate the physical and communication characteristics of individuals with physical and health disabilities.
PH4K2	Sources of specialized materials, equipment, and assistive technology for individuals with physical and health disabilities.
CC4S1	Use strategies to facilitate integration into various settings.
CC4S2	Teach individuals to use self-assessment, problem-solving, and other cognitive strategies to meet their needs.
CC4S3	Select, adapt, and use instructional strategies and materials according to characteristics of the individual with exceptional learning needs.
CC4S4	Use strategies to facilitate maintenance and generalization of skills across learning environments.
CC4S5	Use procedures to increase the individual's self-awareness, self-management, self-control, self-reliance, and self-esteem.
CC4S6	Use strategies that promote successful transitions for individuals with exceptional learning needs.
PH4S1	Use adaptations and assistive technology to provide individuals with physical and health disabilities full participation and access to the general curriculum.

Standard #5: Learning Environments and Social Interactions

CC5K1	Demands of learning environments.
CC5K2	Basic classroom management theories and strategies for individuals with exceptional learning needs.
CC5K3	Effective management of teaching and learning.
CC5K4	Teacher attitudes and behaviors that influence behavior of individuals with exceptional learning needs.
CC5K5	Social skills needed for educational and other environments.
CC5K6	Strategies for crisis prevention and intervention.
CC5K7	Strategies for preparing individuals to live harmoniously and productively in a culturally diverse world.
CC5K8	Ways to create learning environments that allow individuals to retain and appreciate their own and each others' respective language and cultural heritage.
CC5K9	Ways specific cultures are negatively stereotyped.
CC5K10	Strategies used by diverse populations to cope with a legacy of former and continuing racism.
PH5K1	Adaptations of educational environments necessary to accommodate individuals with physical and health disabilities.
PH5K2	Specialized health care interventions for individuals with physical and health disabilities in educational settings.
PH5K3	Barriers to accessibility and acceptance of individuals with physical and health disabilities.
CC5S1	Create a safe, equitable, positive, and supportive learning environment in which diversities are valued.
CC5S2	Identify realistic expectations for personal and social behavior in various settings.
CC5S3	Identify supports needed for integration into various program placements.
CC5S4	Design learning environments that encourage active participation in individual and group activities.
CC5S5	Modify the learning environment to manage behaviors.
CC5S6	Use performance data and information from all stakeholders to make or suggest modifications in learning environments.
CC5S7	Establish and maintain rapport with individuals with and without exceptional learning needs.
CC5S8	Teach self-advocacy.
CC5S9	Create an environment that encourages self-advocacy and increased independence.

CC5S10	Use effective and varied behavior management strategies.
CC5S11	Use the least intensive behavior management strategy consistent with the needs of the individual with exceptional learning needs.
CC5S12	Design and manage daily routines.
CC5S13	Organize, develop, and sustain learning environments that support positive intracultural and intercultural experiences.
CC5S14	Mediate controversial intercultural issues among students within the learning environment in ways that enhance any culture, group, or person.
CC5S15	Structure, direct, and support the activities of paraeducators, volunteers, and tutors.
CC5S16	Use universal precautions.
PH5S1	Use techniques of physical positioning and management of individuals with physical and health disabilities to ensure participation in academic and social environments.
PH5S2	Demonstrate appropriate body mechanics to ensure student and teacher safety in transfer, lifting, positioning, and seating.
PH5S3	Use positioning techniques that decrease inappropriate tone and facilitate appropriate postural reactions to enhance participation.
PH5S4	Assist individuals to develop sensitivity toward those who have communicable diseases.

Standard #6: Language

CC6K1	Effects of cultural and linguistic differences on growth and development.
CC6K2	Characteristics of one's own culture and use of language and the ways in which these can differ from other cultures and uses of languages.
CC6K3	Ways of behaving and communicating among cultures that can lead to misinterpretation and misunderstanding.
CC6K4	Augmentative and assistive communication strategies.
PH6K1	Communication and social interaction alternatives for individuals who are nonspeaking.
CC6S1	Use strategies to support and enhance communication skills of individuals with exceptional learning needs.
CC6S2	Use communication strategies and resources to facilitate understanding of subject matter for students whose primary language is not the dominant language.

Standard #7: Instructional Planning

CC7K1	Theories and research that form the basis of curriculum development and instructional practice.
CC7K2	Scope and sequences of general and special curricula.
CC7K3	National, state or provincial, and local curricula standards.
CC7K4	Technology for planning and managing the teaching and learning environment.
CC7K5	Roles and responsibilities of the paraeducator related to instruction, intervention, and direct service.
CC7S1	Identify and prioritize areas of the general curriculum and accommodations for individuals with exceptional learning needs.
CC7S2	Develop and implement comprehensive, longitudinal individualized programs in collaboration with team members.
CC7S3	Involve the individual and family in setting instructional goals and monitoring progress.
CC7S4	Use functional assessments to develop intervention plans.
CC7S5	Use task analysis.
CC7S6	Sequence, implement, and evaluate individualized learning objectives.
CC7S7	Integrate affective, social, and life skills with academic curricula.
CC7S8	Develop and select instructional content, resources, and strategies that respond to cultural, linguistic, and gender differences.
CC7S9	Incorporate and implement instructional and assistive technology into the educational program.
CC7S10	Prepare lesson plans.
CC7S11	Prepare and organize materials to implement daily lesson plans.

CC7S12	Use instructional time effectively.
CC7S13	Make responsive adjustments to instruction based on continual observations.
CC7S14	Prepare individuals to exhibit self-enhancing behavior in response to societal attitudes and actions.
PH7S1	Develop and use technology plan based on assistive technology assessment.
PH7S2	Interpret sensory and physical information to create or adapt appropriate learning plans for individuals with physical and health disabilities.
PH7S3	Design and implement instructional programs that address independent living and career education for individuals with physical and health disabilities.
PH7S4	Design and implement curriculum and instructional strategies for medical self-management procedures.
PH7S5	Integrate an individual's health care plan into daily programming.

Standard #8: Assessment

CC8K1	Basic terminology used in assessment.
CC8K2	Legal provisions and ethical principles regarding assessment of individuals.
CC8K3	Screening, prereferral, referral, and classification procedures.
CC8K4	Use and limitations of assessment instruments.
CC8K5	National, state or provincial, and local accommodations and modifications.
PH8K1	Specialized terminology used in assessing individuals with physical and health disabilities.
PH8K2	Specialized policies on referral and placement procedures for students with physical and health disabilities.
CC8S1	Gather relevant background information.
CC8S2	Administer nonbiased formal and informal assessments.
CC8S3	Use technology to conduct assessments.
CC8S4	Develop or modify individualized assessment strategies.
CC8S5	Interpret information from formal and informal assessments.
CC8S6	Use assessment information in making eligibility, program, and placement decisions for individuals with exceptional learning needs, including those from culturally and/or linguistically diverse backgrounds.
CC8S7	Report assessment results to all stakeholders using effective communication skills.
CC8S8	Evaluate instruction and monitor progress of individuals with exceptional learning needs.
CC8S9	Develop or modify individualized assessment strategies.
CC8S10	Create and maintain records.
PH8S1	Modify and adapt assessment procedures for use with individuals with physical and health disabilities.
PH8S2	Assess reliable method(s) of response of individuals with physical and health disabilities.
PH8S3	Use results of specialized evaluations to make instructional decisions for individuals with physical and health disabilities.
PH8S4	Monitor the effects of medication on individual performance.

Standard #9: Professional and Ethical Practice

CC9K1	Personal cultural biases and differences that affect one's teaching.
CC9K2	Importance of the teacher serving as a model for individuals with exceptional learning needs.
CC9K3	Continuum of lifelong professional development.
CC9K4	Methods to remain current regarding research-validated practice.
PH9K1	Organizations and publications relevant to the field of physical and health disabilities.
CC9S1	Practice within the CEC Code of Ethics and other standards of the profession.
CC9S2	Uphold high standards of competence and integrity and exercise sound judgment in the practice of the profession.
CC9S3	Act ethically in advocating for appropriate services.

CC9S4	Conduct professional activities in compliance with applicable laws and policies.
CC9S5	Demonstrate commitment to developing the highest education and quality-of-life potential of individuals with exceptional learning needs.
CC9S6	Demonstrate sensitivity for the culture, language, religion, gender, disability, socioeconomic status, and sexual orientation of individuals.
CC9S7	Practice within one's skills limit and obtain assistance as needed.
CC9S8	Use verbal, nonverbal, and written language effectively.
CC9S9	Conduct self-evaluation of instruction.
CC9S10	Access information on exceptionalities.
CC9S11	Reflect on one's practice to improve instruction and guide professional growth.
CC9S12	Engage in professional activities that benefit individuals with exceptional learning needs, their families, and one's colleagues.
PH9S1	Seek information about protocols and procedures to assist individuals with physical and health disabilities to participate in school and community activities.
PH9S2	Participate in the activities of professional organizations in the field of physical and health disabilities.
Standard #10: Collaboration	
CC10K1	Models and strategies of consultation and collaboration.
CC10K2	Roles of individuals with exceptional learning needs, families, and school and community personnel in planning of an individualized program.
CC10K3	Concerns of families of individuals with exceptional learning needs and strategies to help address these concerns.
CC10K4	Culturally responsive factors that promote effective communication and collaboration with individuals with exceptional learning needs, families, school personnel, and community members.
CC10S1	Maintain confidential communication about individuals with exceptional learning needs.
CC10S2	Collaborate with families and others in assessment of individuals with exceptional learning needs.
CC10S3	Foster respectful and beneficial relationships between families and professionals.
CC10S4	Assist individuals with exceptional learning needs and their families in becoming active participants in the educational team.
CC10S5	Plan and conduct collaborative conferences with individuals with exceptional learning needs and their families.
CC10S6	Collaborate with school personnel and community members in integrating individuals with exceptional learning needs into various settings.
CC10S7	Use group problem-solving skills to develop, implement, and evaluate collaborative activities.
CC10S8	Model techniques and coach others in the use of instructional methods and accommodations.
CC10S9	Communicate with school personnel about the characteristics and needs of individuals with exceptional learning needs.
CC10S10	Communicate effectively with families of individuals with exceptional learning needs from diverse backgrounds.
CC10S11	Observe, evaluate, and provide feedback to paraeducators.
PH10K1	Organizations and publications relevant to the field of physical and health disabilities.
PH10K2	Services, networks, and organizations for individuals with physical and health disabilities.
PH10K3	Roles and responsibilities of school and community-based medical and related services personnel.
PH10S1	Participate in the selection and implementation of augmentative or alternative communication systems.
PH10S2	Use local, community, and state or provincial resources to assist the programming for individuals with physical and health disabilities.
PH10S3	Coordinate activities of related service personnel to maximize direct instruction time for individuals with physical and health disabilities.

PH10S4	Collaborate with service providers to facilitate access and full participation for individuals with physical and health disabilities.
PH10S5	Collaborate with families of and service providers to individuals who are chronically or terminally ill.
PH10S6	Participate in transdisciplinary teams to provide integrated care and transition services.
PH10S7	Participate in the activities of professional organizations in the field of physical and health disabilities.

Notes:

"Individual with exceptional learning needs" is used throughout to include individuals with disabilities and individuals with exceptional gifts and talents.

"Exceptional condition" is used throughout to include both single and co-existing conditions. These may be two or more disabling conditions or exceptional gifts or talents co-existing with one or more disabling conditions.

"Special curricula" is used throughout to denote curricular areas not routinely emphasized or addressed in general curricula; e.g., social, communication, motor, independence, self-advocacy.

CEC Knowledge and Skill Base for All Entry-Level Special Education Teachers of Students with Visual Impairment[1]

Standard #1: Foundations	
CC1K1	Models, theories, and philosophies that form the basis for special education practice.
CC1K2	Laws, policies, and ethical principles regarding behavior management planning and implementation.
CC1K3	Relationship of special education to the organization and function of educational agencies.
CC1K4	Rights and responsibilities of students, parents, teachers, and other professionals, and schools related to exceptional learning needs.
CC1K5	Issues in definition and identification of individuals with exceptional learning needs, including those from culturally and linguistically diverse backgrounds.
CC1K6	Issues, assurances, and due process rights related to assessment, eligibility, and placement within a continuum of services.
CC1K7	Family systems and the role of families in the educational process.
CC1K8	Historical points of view and contribution of culturally diverse groups.
CC1K9	Impact of the dominant culture on shaping schools and the individuals who study and work in them.
CC1K10	Potential impact of differences in values, languages, and customs that can exist between the home and school.
VI1K1	Federal entitlements that provide specialized equipment and materials for individuals with visual impairments.
VI1K2	Historical foundations of education of individuals with visual impairments.
VI1K3	Educational definitions, identification criteria, labeling issues, and incidence and prevalence figures for individuals with visual impairments.
VI1K4	Basic terminology related to the structure and function of the human visual system.
VI1K5	Basic terminology related to diseases and disorders of the human visual system.
VI1K6	Issues and trends in special education and the field of visual impairment.
CC1S1	Articulate personal philosophy of special education.

Standard #2: Development and Characteristics of Learners	
CC2K1	Typical and atypical human growth and development.
CC2K2	Educational implications of characteristics of various exceptionalities.
CC2K3	Characteristics and effects of the cultural and environmental milieu of the individual with exceptional learning needs and the family.
CC2K4	Family systems and the role of families in supporting development.
CC2K5	Similarities and differences of individuals with and without exceptional learning needs.
CC2K6	Similarities and differences among individuals with exceptional learning needs.
CC2K7	Effects of various medications on individuals with exceptional learning needs.
VI2K1	Development of the human visual system.
VI2K2	Development of secondary senses when vision is impaired.
VI2K3	Effects of visual impairment on development.
VI2K4	Impact of visual impairment on learning and experience.
VI2K5	Psychosocial aspects of visual impairment.
VI2K6	Effects of medications on the visual system.

Standard #3: Individual Learning Differences	
CC3K1	Effects an exceptional condition(s) can have on an individual's life.

[1]*Note On Coding:* CC in the number code indicates a Common Core item; EC indicates an Early Childhood Special Education item; K indicates a Knowledge item; S indicates a Skill item.

CC3K2	Impact of learners' academic and social abilities, attitudes, interests, and values on instruction and career development.
CC3K3	Variations in beliefs, traditions, and values across and within cultures and their effects on relationships among individuals with exceptional learning needs, family, and schooling.
CC3K4	Cultural perspectives influencing the relationships among families, schools, and communities as related to instruction.
CC3K5	Differing ways of learning of individuals with exceptional learning needs including those from culturally diverse backgrounds and strategies for addressing these differences.
VI3K1	Effects of visual impairment on the family and the reciprocal impact on the individual's self-esteem.
VI3K2	Impact of additional exceptionalities on individuals with visual impairments.
VI3K3	Attitudes and actions of teachers that affect the behaviors of individuals with visual impairments.

Standard #4: Instructional Strategies

VI4K1	Strategies for teaching Braille reading and writing.
VI4K2	Strategies for teaching handwriting to individuals with low vision.
VI4K3	Strategies for teaching signature writing to individuals who are blind.
VI4K4	Strategies for teaching listening and compensatory auditory skills.
VI4K5	Strategies for teaching typing and keyboarding skills.
VI4K6	Strategies for teaching technology skills to individuals with visual impairments.
VI4K7	Strategies for teaching use of the abacus, talking calculator, tactile graphics, and adapted science equipment.
VI4K8	Strategies for teaching basic concepts to individuals with visual impairments.
VI4K9	Strategies for teaching visual efficiency skills and use of print adaptations, optical devices, and nonoptical devices.
VI4K10	Strategies for teaching organization and study skills to individuals with visual impairments.
VI4K11	Strategies to prepare individuals for structured pre-cane orientation and mobility assessment and instruction.
VI4K12	Strategies for teaching tactual perceptual skills to individuals with visual impairments.
VI4K13	Strategies for teaching human sexuality to individuals with visual impairments.
VI4K14	Strategies for teaching adapted physical and recreational skills to individuals with visual impairments.
VI4K15	Strategies for teaching social, daily living, and functional life skills to individuals with visual impairments.
VI4K16	Strategies for teaching career-vocational skills and providing vocational counseling for individuals with visual impairments.
VI4K17	Strategies for promoting self-advocacy in individuals with visual impairments.
VI4K18	Techniques for modifying instructional methods and materials for individuals with visual impairments.
VI4K19	Strategies to prepare students with progressive eye conditions to achieve a positive transition to alternative skills.
CC4S1	Use strategies to facilitate integration into various settings.
CC4S2	Teach individuals to use self-assessment, problem-solving, and other cognitive strategies to meet their needs.
CC4S3	Select, adapt, and use instructional strategies and materials according to characteristics of the individual with exceptional learning needs.
CC4S4	Use strategies to facilitate maintenance and generalization of skills across learning environments.
CC4S5	Use procedures to increase the individual's self-awareness, self-management, self-control, self-reliance, and self-esteem.
CC4S6	Use strategies that promote successful transitions for individuals with exceptional learning needs.
VI4S1	Teach individuals with visual impairments to use thinking, problem-solving, and other cognitive strategies.

VI4S2	Prepare adapted or modified materials in Braille, accessible print, and other formats.
VI4S3	Transcribe, proofread, and interline materials in contracted literary and Nemeth Braille codes.
VI4S4	Use Braillewriter, slate and stylus, and computer technology to produce Braille materials.
VI4S5	Prepare individuals with visual impairments to access information and services from the community.

Standard #5: Learning Environments and Social Interactions

CC5K1	Demands of learning environments.
CC5K2	Basic classroom management theories and strategies for individuals with exceptional learning needs.
CC5K3	Effective management of teaching and learning.
CC5K4	Teacher attitudes and behaviors that influence behavior of individuals with exceptional learning needs.
CC5K5	Social skills needed for educational and other environments.
CC5K6	Strategies for crisis prevention and intervention.
CC5K7	Strategies for preparing individuals to live harmoniously and productively in a culturally diverse world.
CC5K8	Ways to create learning environments that allow individuals to retain and appreciate their own and each others' respective language and cultural heritage.
CC5K9	Ways specific cultures are negatively stereotyped.
CC5K10	Strategies used by diverse populations to cope with a legacy of former and continuing racism.
VI5K1	Roles of paraeducators who work directly with individuals with visual impairments
VI5K2	Role models with visual impairments and their importance.
CC5S1	Create a safe, equitable, positive, and supportive learning environment in which diversities are valued.
CC5S2	Identify realistic expectations for personal and social behavior in various settings.
CC5S3	Identify supports needed for integration into various program placements.
CC5S4	Design learning environments that encourage active participation in individual and group activities.
CC5S5	Modify the learning environment to manage behaviors.
CC5S6	Use performance data and information from all stakeholders to make or suggest modifications in learning environments.
CC5S7	Establish and maintain rapport with individuals with and without exceptional learning needs.
CC5S8	Teach self-advocacy.
CC5S9	Create an environment that encourages self-advocacy and increased independence.
CC5S10	Use effective and varied behavior management strategies.
CC5S11	Use the least intensive behavior management strategy consistent with the needs of the individual with exceptional learning needs.
CC5S12	Design and manage daily routines.
CC5S13	Organize, develop, and sustain learning environments that support positive intracultural and intercultural experiences.
CC5S14	Mediate controversial intercultural issues among students within the learning environment in ways that enhance any culture, group, or person.
CC5S15	Structure, direct, and support the activities of paraeducators, volunteers, and tutors.
CC5S16	Use universal precautions.
VI5S1	Enhance instruction for individuals with visual impairments through modification of the environment.
VI5S2	Design multisensory learning environments that encourage active participation by individuals with visual impairments in group and individual activities.
VI5S3	Create learning environments that encourage self-advocacy and independence for individuals with visual impairments.

Standard #6: Language

CC6K1	Effects of cultural and linguistic differences on growth and development.
CC6K2	Characteristics of one's own culture and use of language and the ways in which these can differ from other cultures and uses of languages.
CC6K3	Ways of behaving and communicating among cultures that can lead to misinterpretation and misunderstanding.
CC6K4	Augmentative and assistive communication strategies.
VI6K1	Strategies for teaching alternatives to nonverbal communication.
CC6S1	Use strategies to support and enhance communication skills of individuals with exceptional learning needs.
CC6S2	Use communication strategies and resources to facilitate understanding of subject matter for students whose primary language is not the dominant language.
VI6S1	Prepare individuals with visual impairments to respond constructively to societal attitudes and actions.

Standard #7: Instructional Planning

CC7K1	Theories and research that form the basis of curriculum development and instructional practice.
CC7K2	Scope and sequences of general and special curricula.
CC7K3	National, state or provincial, and local curricula standards.
CC7K4	Technology for planning and managing the teaching and learning environment.
CC7K5	Roles and responsibilities of the paraeducator related to instruction, intervention, and direct service.
VI7K1	Relationships among assessment, individualized education program development, and placement as they affect vision-related services.
VI7K2	Model programs for individuals with visual impairments.
CC7S1	Identify and prioritize areas of the general curriculum and accommodations for individuals with exceptional learning needs.
CC7S2	Develop and implement comprehensive, longitudinal individualized programs in collaboration with team members.
CC7S3	Involve the individual and family in setting instructional goals and monitoring progress.
CC7S4	Use functional assessments to develop intervention plans.
CC7S5	Use task analysis.
CC7S6	Sequence, implement, and evaluate individualized learning objectives.
CC7S7	Integrate affective, social, and life skills with academic curricula.
CC7S8	Develop and select instructional content, resources, and strategies that respond to cultural, linguistic, and gender differences.
CC7S9	Incorporate and implement instructional and assistive technology into the educational program.
CC7S10	Prepare lesson plans.
CC7S11	Prepare and organize materials to implement daily lesson plans.
CC7S12	Use instructional time effectively.
CC7S13	Make responsive adjustments to instruction based on continual observations.
CC7S14	Prepare individuals to exhibit self-enhancing behavior in response to societal attitudes and actions.
VI7S1	Select and use technologies to accomplish instructional objectives for individuals with visual impairments.
VI7S2	Sequence, implement, and evaluate learning objectives based on the expanded core curriculum for individuals with visual impairments.
VI7S3	Obtain and organize special materials to implement instructional goals for individuals with visual impairments.

Standard #8: Assessment

CC8K1	Basic terminology used in assessment.

CC8K2	Legal provisions and ethical principles regarding assessment of individuals.
CC8K3	Screening, prereferral, referral, and classification procedures.
CC8K4	Use and limitations of assessment instruments.
CC8K5	National, state or provincial, and local accommodations and modifications.
VI8K1	Specialized terminology used in assessing individuals with visual impairments.
VI8K2	Ethical considerations, laws, and policies for assessment of individuals with visual impairments
VI8K3	Specialized policies on referral and placement procedures for individuals with visual impairments.
VI8K4	Specialized procedures for screening, prereferral, referral, and identification of individuals with visual impairments.
VI8K5	Alternative assessment techniques for individuals with visual impairments.
VI8K6	Interpretation and application of scores from assessments of individuals with visual impairments.
CC8S1	Gather relevant background information.
CC8S2	Administer nonbiased formal and informal assessments.
CC8S3	Use technology to conduct assessments.
CC8S4	Develop or modify individualized assessment strategies.
CC8S5	Interpret information from formal and informal assessments.
CC8S6	Use assessment information in making eligibility, program, and placement decisions for individuals with exceptional learning needs, including those from culturally and/or linguistically diverse backgrounds.
CC8S7	Report assessment results to all stakeholders using effective communication skills.
CC8S8	Evaluate instruction and monitor progress of individuals with exceptional learning needs.
CC8S9	Develop or modify individualized assessment strategies.
CC8S10	Create and maintain records.
VI8S1	Interpret eye reports and other vision-related diagnostic information.
VI8S2	Use disability-specific assessment instruments.
VI8S3	Adapt and use assessment procedures when evaluating individuals with visual impairments.
VI8S4	Maintain disability-related records for individuals with visual impairments.
VI8S5	Gather background information and family history related to the individual's visual status.
VI8S6	Interpret and use assessment data for instructional planning with individuals with visual impairments.

Standard #9: Professional and Ethical Practice

CC9K1	Personal cultural biases and differences that affect one's teaching.
CC9K2	Importance of the teacher serving as a model for individuals with exceptional learning needs.
CC9K3	Continuum of lifelong professional development.
CC9K4	Methods to remain current regarding research-validated practice.
VI9K1	Organizations and publications relevant to the field of visual impairment.
CC9S1	Practice within the CEC Code of Ethics and other standards of the profession.
CC9S2	Uphold high standards of competence and integrity and exercise sound judgment in the practice of the profession.
CC9S3	Act ethically in advocating for appropriate services.
CC9S4	Conduct professional activities in compliance with applicable laws and policies.
CC9S5	Demonstrate commitment to developing the highest education and quality-of-life potential of individuals with exceptional learning needs.
CC9S6	Demonstrate sensitivity for the culture, language, religion, gender, disability, socioeconomic status, and sexual orientation of individuals.
CC9S7	Practice within one's skills limit and obtain assistance as needed.
CC9S8	Use verbal, nonverbal, and written language effectively.

CC9S9	Conduct self-evaluation of instruction.
CC9S10	Access information on exceptionalities.
CC9S11	Reflect on one's practice to improve instruction and guide professional growth.
CC9S12	Engage in professional activities that benefit individuals with exceptional learning needs, their families, and one's colleagues.
VI9S2	Participate in the activities of professional organizations in the field of visual impairment.

Standard #10: Collaboration

CC10K1	Models and strategies of consultation and collaboration.
CC10K2	Roles of individuals with exceptional learning needs, families, and school and community personnel in planning of an individualized program.
CC10K3	Concerns of families of individuals with exceptional learning needs and strategies to help address these concerns.
CC10K4	Culturally responsive factors that promote effective communication and collaboration with individuals with exceptional learning needs, families, school personnel, and community members.
VI10K1	Strategies for assisting families and other team members in planning appropriate transitions for individuals with visual impairments.
VI10K2	Services, networks, publications, and organizations for individuals with visual impairments.
CC10S1	Maintain confidential communication about individuals with exceptional learning needs.
CC10S2	Collaborate with families and others in assessment of individuals with exceptional learning needs.
CC10S3	Foster respectful and beneficial relationships between families and professionals.
CC10S4	Assist individuals with exceptional learning needs and their families in becoming active participants in the educational team.
CC10S5	Plan and conduct collaborative conferences with individuals with exceptional learning needs and their families.
CC10S6	Collaborate with school personnel and community members in integrating individuals with exceptional learning needs into various settings.
CC10S7	Use group problem-solving skills to develop, implement, and evaluate collaborative activities.
CC10S8	Model techniques and coach others in the use of instructional methods and accommodations.
CC10S9	Communicate with school personnel about the characteristics and needs of individuals with exceptional learning needs.
CC10S10	Communicate effectively with families of individuals with exceptional learning needs from diverse backgrounds.
CC10S11	Observe, evaluate, and provide feedback to paraeducators.
VI10S1	Help families and other team members understand the impact of a visual impairment on learning and experience.
VI10S2	Structure and supervise the activities of paraeducators and tutors who work with individuals with visual impairments.

Notes:

"Individual with exceptional learning needs" is used throughout to include individuals with disabilities and individuals with exceptional gifts and talents.

"Exceptional condition" is used throughout to include both single and co-existing conditions. These may be two or more disabling conditions or exceptional gifts or talents co-existing with one or more disabling conditions.

"Special curricula" is used throughout to denote curricular areas not routinely emphasized or addressed in general curricula; e.g., social, communication, motor, independence, self-advocacy.

CEC Knowledge and Skill Base for
Special Education Diagnosticians[1, 2]

Standard #1: Foundations	
ED1K1	Philosophies of assessment.
ED1K2	Laws and policies related to assessing individuals with exceptional learning needs.

Standard #2: Development and Characteristics of Learners	
ED2K1	Range of individual abilities within categories of exceptionalities.
ED2K2	Factors that influence the overrepresentation and stigmatization of individuals with cultural and linguistic diversity.

Standard #3: Individual Learning Differences	
ED3K1	Influences of diversity on assessment results.

Standard #4: Instructional Strategies	
None specified for this set of advanced standards.	

Standard #5: Learning Environments and Social Interactions	
None specified for this set of advanced standards.	

Standard #6: Language	
None specified for this set of advanced standards.	

Standard #7: Instructional Planning	
None specified for this set of advanced standards.	

Standard #8: Assessment	
ED8K1	Qualifications necessary to administer and interpret tests.
ED8K2	Standards for test reliability.
ED8K3	Standards for test validity.
ED8K4	Procedures used in standardizing assessment instruments.
ED8K5	Use of standard error of measure in the field of measurement.
ED8K6	Possible sources of test error.
ED8K7	Uses and limitations of assessment information.
ED8K8	Vocational and career assessment.
ED8K9	Motor skills assessment.
ED8S1	Select and utilize assessment materials based on technical quality.
ED8S2	Collect thorough assessment data.
ED8S3	Score assessment instruments accurately.
ED8S4	Select or modify appropriate assessment procedures and instruments to ensure nonbiased results.
ED8S5	Use observation techniques.
ED8S6	Assess basic academic skills.
ED8S7	Assess language skills.
ED8S8	Assess adaptive behavior.
ED8S9	Assess behavior.
ED8S10	Assess perceptual skills.

[1]*Note On Coding:* CC in the number code indicates a Common Core item; EC indicates an Early Childhood Special Education item; K indicates a Knowledge item; S indicates a Skill item.

[2]These standards were developed with the assumption that candidates would have had previous training in special education.

ED8S11	Make individualized recommendations for eligibility, instruction, and transition, based on assessment results.
ED8S12	Prepare assessment reports.
ED8S13	Teach informal and observational techniques of data collection.
ED8S14	Keep accurate and detailed records of assessment and related proceedings.

Standard #9: Professional and Ethical Practice

ED9K1	Scope and role of an educational diagnostician.
ED9K2	Organizations and publications relevant to the field of educational diagnosis.
ED9S1	Participate in the activities of professional organizations in the field of educational diagnosis.

Standard #10: Collaboration

ED10S1	Communicate assessment purposes, methods, results, and implications to team members.

Notes:

"Individual with exceptional learning needs" is used throughout to include individuals with disabilities and individuals with exceptional gifts and talents.

"Exceptional condition" is used throughout to include both single and co-existing conditions. These may be two or more disabling conditions or exceptional gifts or talents co-existing with one or more disabling conditions.

"Special curricula" is used throughout to denote curricular areas not routinely emphasized or addressed in general curricula; e.g., social, communication, motor, independence, self-advocacy.

CEC Knowledge and Skill Base for
Special Education Administrators[1,2]

Standard #1: Foundations	
SA1K1	Laws and policies for general and special education.
SA1K2	Evolution of laws and policies that impact the lives of individuals with exceptionalities and their families from birth through adulthood.
SA1K3	Political and economic issues that affect policy development.
SA1K4	Models, theories, and philosophies that provide the basis for educational systems.
SA1K5	Development and implementation of policies and regulations for individuals with exceptional learning needs and their families.
SA1K6	Laws and policies regarding assessment, program evaluation, and accountability related to individuals with exceptional learning needs.
SA1K7	General curriculum theories and implications for individuals with exceptional learning needs.
SA1K8	Research related to educational change.
SA1K9	Education, social, and health agency fiscal policies.
SA1K10	Human resources management, recruitment, personnel assistance and development, and evaluation.
SA1K11	Sources of funding.
SA1K12	Laws and policies governing the discipline of all students and implications for individuals with exceptional learning needs.
SA1K13	Legal and ethical issues of behavior management of individuals with exceptional learning needs.
SA1K14	Family systems and the role of families in supporting development and educational progress of the individual with exceptional learning needs.
SA1S1	Interpret laws and policies pertaining to individuals with exceptional learning needs.
Standard #2: Development and Characteristics of Learners	
SA2K1	Human development, principles of learning, and the relationships to individuals with exceptional learning needs.
SA2K2	Characteristics of individuals with exceptional learning needs and implications for the development of programs and services.
Standard #3: Individual Learning Differences	
SA3K1	Impact of diversity on educational expectations and programming.
Standard #4: Instructional Strategies	
None specified for this set of advanced standards.	
Standard #5: Learning Environments and Social Interactions	
None specified for this set of advanced standards.	
Standard #6: Language	
None specified for this set of advanced standards.	
Standard #7: Instructional Planning	
SA7K1	General curriculum, instruction, and how special education services support access to the general curriculum.
SA7S1	Develop and implement a continuum of services that responds to individual educational needs and family characteristics.
SA7S2	Incorporate postschool outcomes for individuals with exceptional learning needs in the general curriculum standards.

[1]*Note On Coding:* CC in the number code indicates a Common Core item; EC indicates an Early Childhood Special Education item; K indicates a Knowledge item; S indicates a Skill item.

[2]These standards were developed with the assumption that candidates would have had previous training in special education.

SA7S3	Design and implement professional development and constructive evaluation procedures that are designed to improve instructional content and practices.
SA7S4	Develop and implement a plan to provide instructional and assistive technologies.
SA7S5	Develop collaborative programs that ensure that individuals with exceptional learning needs have access to and participate in the general curriculum.
SA7S6	Develop and implement flexible service delivery that addresses the range of needs of individuals with exceptional learning needs.
SA7S7	Develop and implement prevention strategies and programs.
SA7S8	Develop budgets to ensure the efficient and effective allocation of resources.
SA7S9	Use a variety of technologies to enhance management of resources and programs.
SA7S10	Develop and implement discipline policy and procedures for individuals with exceptional learning needs.
SA7S11	Implement a range of strategies that promote positive behavior, crisis intervention, and family involvement and support.

Standard #8: Assessment

SA8S1	Advocate for the participation of individuals with exceptional learning needs in accountability systems.
SA8S2	Implement procedures within the assessment accountability system to ensure the participation of individuals with exceptional learning needs.
SA8S3	Develop and implement ongoing evaluations of special education programs and practices.

Standard #9: Professional and Ethical Practice

SA9K1	Organizations and publications relevant to the field of special education administration.
SA9S1	Communicate a personal inclusive vision for meeting the needs of individuals with exceptional learning needs.
SA9S2	Advocate for individuals with exceptional learning needs and their families.
SA9S3	Respect and support individuals with exceptional learning needs in self-advocacy.
SA9S4	Communicate and demonstrate a high standard of ethical practice.
SA9S5	Make decisions concerning individuals with exceptional learning needs based on open communication, trust, mutual respect, and dignity.
SA9S6	Participate in the activities of the professional organization relevant to the field of Special Education Administration.

Standard #10: Collaboration

SA10K1	Approaches for involving parents, family, and community members in educational planning, implementation, and evaluation.
SA10K2	Role of parent and advocacy organizations as they support individuals with exceptionalities and their families.
SA10S1	Develop and implement intra- and interagency agreements that create programs with shared responsibility for individuals with exceptional learning needs.
SA10S2	Promote seamless transitions of individuals with exceptional learning needs across educational and other programs from birth through adulthood.
SA10S3	Implement administrative procedures to ensure clear communication among administrators, instructional staff, and related service personnel.
SA10S4	Develop family education and other support programs.
SA10S5	Engage in shared decision making to support programs for individuals with exceptional learning needs.
SA10S6	Provide ongoing communication with families of individuals with exceptional learning needs.
SS10S7	Consult and collaborate in administrative and instructional settings.

Notes:

"Individual with exceptional learning needs" is used throughout to include individuals with disabilities and individuals with exceptional gifts and talents.

"Exceptional condition" is used throughout to include both single and co-existing conditions. These may be two or more disabling conditions or exceptional gifts or talents co-existing with one or more disabling conditions.

"Special curricula" is used throughout to denote curricular areas not routinely emphasized or addressed in general curricula; e.g., social, communication, motor, independence, self-advocacy.

CEC Knowledge and Skill Base for
Special Education Technology Specialists[1,2]

Standard #1: Foundations	
TE1K1	Concepts and issues related to the use of technology in education and other aspects of our society.
TE1S1	Articulate a personal philosophy and goals for using technology in special education.
TE1S2	Use technology-related terminology in written and oral communication.
TE1S3	Describe legislative mandates and governmental regulations and their implications for technology in special education.
Standard #2: Development and Characteristics of Learners	
TE2K1	Impact of technology at all stages of development on individuals with exceptional learning needs.
Standard #3: Individual Learning Differences	
TE3K1	Issues in diversity and in the use of technology.
Standard #4: Instructional Strategies	
TE4S1	Identify and operate instructional and assistive hardware, software, and peripherals.
TE4S2	Provide technology support to individuals with exceptional learning needs who are receiving instruction in general education settings.
TE4S3	Arrange for demonstrations and trial periods with potential assistive or instructional technologies prior to making purchase decisions.
Standard #5: Learning Environments and Social Interactions	
TE5K1	Procedures for the organization, management, and security of technology.
TE5K2	Ergonomic principles to facilitate the use of technology.
TE5S1	Evaluate features of technology systems.
TE5S2	Use technology to foster social acceptance in inclusive settings.
TE5S3	Identify the demands of technology on the individual with exceptional learning needs.
Standard #6: Language	
TE6S1	Use communication technologies to access information and resources electronically.
Standard #7: Instructional Planning	
TE7K1	Procedures for evaluation of computer software and other technology materials for their potential application in special education.
TE7K2	Funding sources and processes of acquisition of assistive technology devices and services.
TE7K3	National, state, or provincial PreK–12 technology standards.
TE7S1	Assist the individual with exceptional learning needs in clarifying and prioritizing functional intervention goals regarding technology-based evaluation results.
TE7S2	Identify elements of the curriculum for which technology applications are appropriate and ways they can be implemented.
TE7S3	Identify and operate software that meets educational objectives for individuals with exceptional learning needs in a variety of educational environments.
TE7S4	Design, fabricate, and install assistive technology materials and devices to meet the needs of individuals with exceptional learning needs.
TE7S5	Provide consistent, structured training to individuals with exceptional learning needs to operate instructional and adaptive equipment and software until they have achieved mastery.
TE7S6	Verify proper implementation of mechanical and electrical safety practices in the assembly and integration of the technology to meet the needs of individuals with exceptional learning needs.

[1]*Note On Coding:* CC in the number code indicates a Common Core item; EC indicates an Early Childhood Special Education item; K indicates a Knowledge item; S indicates a Skill item.

[2]These standards were developed with the assumption that candidates would have had previous training in special education.

TE7S7	Develop and implement contingency plans in the event that assistive or instructional technology devices fail.
TE7S8	Develop specifications and/or drawings necessary for technology acquisitions.
TE7S9	Write proposals to obtain technology funds.

Standard #8: Assessment

TE8K1	Use of technology in the assessment, diagnosis, and evaluation of individuals with exceptional learning needs.
TE8S1	Match characteristics of individuals with exceptional learning needs with technology product or software features.
TE8S2	Use technology to collect, analyze, summarize, and report student performance data to aid instructional decision making.
TE8S3	Identify functional needs, screen for functional limitations, and identify if the need for a comprehensive assistive or instructional technology evaluation exists.
TE8S4	Monitor outcomes of technology-based interventions and reevaluate and adjust the system as needed.
TE8S5	Assist the individual with exceptional learning needs in clarifying and prioritizing functional intervention goals regarding technology-based evaluation results.
TE8S6	Work with team members to identify assistive and instructional technologies that can help individuals meet the demands placed upon them in their environments.
TE8S7	Identify placement of devices and positioning of the individual to optimize the use of assistive or instructional technology.
TE8S8	Examine alternative solutions prior to making assistive or instructional technology decisions.
TE8S9	Make technology decisions based on a continuum of options ranging from no technology to high technology.

Standard #9: Professional and Ethical Practice

TE9K1	Equity, ethical, legal, and human issues related to technology use in special education.
TE9K2	Organizations and publications relevant to the field of technology.
TE9S1	Maintain ongoing professional development to acquire knowledge and skills about new developments in technology.
TE9S2	Adhere to copyright laws about duplication and distribution of software and other copyrighted technology materials.
TE9S3	Advocate for assistive or instructional technology on individual and system change levels.
TE9S4	Participate in activities of professional organizations relevant to the field of technology.

Standard #10: Collaboration

TE10K1	Roles that related services personnel fulfill in providing technology services.
TE10K2	Guidelines for referring individuals with exceptional learning needs to another professional.
TE10S1	Conduct inservice training in applications of technology in special education.
TE10S2	Refer team members and families to assistive and instructional technology resources.
TE10S3	Collaborate with other team members in planning and implementing the use of assistive and adaptive devices.
TE10S4	Instruct others in the operation of technology, maintenance, warranties, and trouble-shooting techniques.

Notes:

"Individual with exceptional learning needs" is used throughout to include individuals with disabilities and individuals with exceptional gifts and talents.

"Exceptional condition" is used throughout to include both single and co-existing conditions. These may be two or more disabling conditions or exceptional gifts or talents co-existing with one or more disabling conditions.

"Special curricula" is used throughout to denote curricular areas not routinely emphasized or addressed in general curricula; e.g., social, communication, motor, independence, self-advocacy.

CEC Knowledge and Skill Base for
Special Education Transition Specialists[1, 2]

Standard #1: Foundations	
TS1K1	Theoretical and applied models of transition.
TS1K2	Transition-related laws and policies.
TS1K3	History of national transition initiatives.
TS1K4	Research on relationships between individual outcomes and transition practices.
TS1K5	Procedures and requirements for referring individuals to community service agencies.
Standard #2: Development and Characteristics of Learners	
TS2K1	Implications of individual characteristics with respect to postschool outcomes and support needs.
Standard #3: Individual Learning Differences	
None specified for this set of advanced standards.	
Standard #4: Instructional Strategies	
TS4K1	Methods for providing community-based education for individuals with exceptional learning needs.
TS4K2	Methods for linking academic content to transition goals.
TS4K3	Strategies for involving families and individuals with exceptional learning needs in transition planning and evaluation.
TS4S1	Arrange and evaluate instructional activities in relation to postschool goals.
Standard #5: Learning Environments and Social Interactions	
TS5K1	School and postschool services available to specific populations of individuals with exceptional learning needs.
TS5S1	Identify and facilitate modifications within work and community environments.
TS5S2	Use support systems to facilitate self-advocacy in transition planning.
Standard #6: Language	
None specified for this set of advanced standards.	
Standard #7: Instructional Planning	
TS7K1	Job seeking and job retention skills identified by employers as essential for successful employment.
TS7K2	Vocational education methods, models, and curricula.
TS7K3	Range of postschool options within specific outcome areas.
TS7S1	Identify outcomes and instructional options specific to the community and the individual.
TS7S2	Arrange and evaluate instructional activities in relation to postschool goals.
TS7S3	Ensure the inclusion of transition-related goals in the educational program plan.
TS7S4	Develop postschool goals and objectives, using interests and preferences of the individual.
Standard #8: Assessment	
TS8K1	Formal and informal approaches for identifying students' interests and preferences related to educational experiences and postschool goals.
TS8S1	Match skills and interests of the individuals to skills and demands required by vocational and postschool settings.
TS8S2	Interpret results of career and vocational assessment for individuals, families, and professionals.
TS8S3	Use a variety of formal and informal career, transition, and vocational assessment procedures.
TS8S4	Evaluate and modify transition goals on an ongoing basis.

[1]*Note On Coding:* CC in the number code indicates a Common Core item; EC indicates an Early Childhood Special Education item; K indicates a Knowledge item; S indicates a Skill item.

[2]These standards were developed with the assumption that candidates would have had previous training in special education.

| TS8S5 | Assess and develop natural support systems to facilitate transition to postschool environments. |

Standard #9: Professional and Ethical Practice

TS9K1	Scope and role of transition specialist.
TS9K2	Scope and role of agency personnel related to transition services.
TS9K3	Organizations and publications relevant to the field of transition.
TS9S1	Show positive regard for the capacity and operating constraints of community organizations involved in transition services.
TS9S2	Participate in activities of professional organizations in the field of transition.

Standard #10: Collaboration

TS10K1	Methods to increase transition service delivery through interagency agreements and collaborative funding.
TS10K2	Transition planning strategies that facilitate input from team members.
TS10S1	Design and use procedures to evaluate and improve transition education and services in collaboration with team members.
TS10S2	Provide information to families about transition education, services, support networks, and postschool options.
TS10S3	Involve team members in establishing transition policy.
TS10S4	Provide transition-focused technical assistance and professional development in collaboration with team members.
TS10S5	Collaborate with transition-focused agencies.
TS10S6	Develop interagency strategies to collect, share, and use student assessment data.
TS10S7	Use strategies for resolving differences in collaborative relationships and interagency agreements.
TS10S8	Assist teachers to identify educational program planning team members.
TS10S9	Assure individual, family, and agency participation in transition planning and implementation.

Notes:

"Individual with exceptional learning needs" is used throughout to include individuals with disabilities and individuals with exceptional gifts and talents.

"Exceptional condition" is used throughout to include both single and co-existing conditions. These may be two or more disabling conditions or exceptional gifts or talents co-existing with one or more disabling conditions.

"Special curricula" is used throughout to denote curricular areas not routinely emphasized or addressed in general curricula; e.g., social, communication, motor, independence, self-advocacy.

B. CEC Standards for the Accreditation of Teacher Preparation Programs

The CEC standards for the preparation of special educators are divided into three parts: Field Experiences and Clinical Practice Standards, Assessment System Standards, and 10 Special Education Content Standards.

The CEC Special Education Content Standards are made up of 10 narrative standards, which are the same for all programs. However, it is expected that faculty will use the Knowledge and Skills Standards (Learning Disabilities, Early Childhood, General Curriculum Reference, etc.) to inform their curriculum development to ensure that the Content Standards are met. Programs are *not* expected to include a specific response to each of the knowledge and skills, but must respond to the 10 Special Education Content Standards. The program's assessment system should comprehensively address each of the 10 Content Standards as informed by its area of specialization.

State licensure frameworks for special education are the most diverse of any education discipline. Some states license by disability category. Many states group categories together in various multicategorical licenses, but these groupings vary from state to state. Since preparation programs are required to meet state standards, preparation programs typically follow state licensure frameworks. Consequently, there is extraordinary diversity in how special education teachers are prepared. While CEC does not advocate for this level of licensing diversity, CEC continues to provide options to preparation programs through its Knowledge and Skill Bases. As stated above, the 10 CEC Content Standards are identical for all programs. CEC has Knowledge and Skill Bases that are disability specific (e.g., Learning Disabilities, Emotionally and Behavioral Disorders, Visually Impaired), multicategorical (Individualized General Curriculum and Individualized Independence Curriculum), and age-specific (Early Childhood). These options provide programs the flexibility to select the Knowledge and Skill Bases that most closely align with their program.

If a program is unsure how to address the CEC standards, please contact the CEC Professional Services Unit (cecprof@cec.sped.org).

FIELD EXPERIENCES AND CLINICAL PRACTICE STANDARDS

Special education candidates progress through a series of developmentally sequenced field experiences for the full range of ages, types and levels of abilities, and collaborative opportunities that are appropriate to the license or roles for which they are preparing. These field and clinical experiences are supervised by qualified professionals.

ASSESSMENT SYSTEM STANDARDS

The CEC Assessment System Standards have been developed using the NCATE Specialty Area Studies Board (SASB) "Principles for Performance-Based Assessment Systems in Professional Education Programs." Each component in the "Principles" has been included in the following CEC standards:

1. Assessments address components of each content standard.
2. Assessments are relevant and consistent with each content standard.
3. Assessments are planned, refined, and implemented by key stakeholders (i.e., professional and local community).
4. Multiple measures (both internal and external) are used and are systematic and ongoing across components of the program (e.g., content, course work, field experiences).
5. The assessment system is clearly delineated and communicated to candidates.
6. Assessments are credible and rigorous.
7. The assessment system includes critical decision points.
8. The assessment data are regularly and systematically compiled, analyzed, and summarized.
9. Assessment data are used for program improvement.

CEC Content Standards[1]

Special Education Content Standard #1: Foundations

Special educators understand the field as an evolving and changing discipline based on philosophies, evidence-based **principles and theories,** relevant **laws and policies,** diverse and **historical** points of view, and **human issues** that have historically influenced and continue to influence the field of special education and the education and treatment of individuals with exceptional needs both in school and society. Special educators understand how these **influence professional practice,** including assessment, instructional planning, implementation, and program evaluation. Special educators understand how **issues of human diversity** can impact families, cultures, and schools, and how these complex human issues can interact with issues in the delivery of special education services. They understand the **relationships of organizations of special education** to the organizations and functions of schools, school systems, and other agencies. Special educators use this knowledge as a ground upon which to construct their own personal understandings and philosophies of special education.

Beginning special educators demonstrate their mastery of this standard through the mastery of the CEC Common Core Knowledge and Skills, as well as through the appropriate CEC Specialty Area(s) Knowledge and Skills for which the program is preparing candidates.

Special Education Content Standard #2: Development and Characteristics of Learners

Special educators know and **demonstrate respect** for their students first as unique human beings. Special educators understand the **similarities and differences in human development** and the characteristics between and among individuals with and without exceptional learning needs (ELN). Moreover, special educators understand how **exceptional conditions** can interact with the domains of human development and they **use this knowledge to respond to the varying abilities and behaviors of individuals with ELN.** Special educators understand how the experiences of individuals with ELN can impact families, as well as the individual's ability to learn, interact socially, and live as fulfilled contributing members of the community.

Beginning special educators demonstrate their mastery of this standard through the mastery of the CEC Common Core Knowledge and Skills, as well as through the appropriate CEC Specialty Area(s) Knowledge and Skills for which the preparation program is preparing candidates.

Special Education Content Standard #3: Individual Learning Differences

Special educators understand the **effects that an exceptional condition** can have **on an individual's learning** in school and throughout life. Special educators understand that the beliefs, traditions, and values across and within cultures can affect relationships among and between students, their families, and the school community. Moreover, special educators are **active and resourceful in seeking to understand how primary language, culture, and familial backgrounds interact with the individual's exceptional condition** to impact the individual's academic and social abilities, attitudes, values, interests, and career options. The understanding of these learning differences and their possible interactions **provides the foundation** upon which **special educators individualize instruction** to provide meaningful and challenging learning for individuals with ELN.

Beginning special educators demonstrate their mastery of this standard through the mastery of the CEC Common Core Knowledge and Skills, as well as through the appropriate CEC Specialty Area(s) Knowledge and Skills for which the program is preparing candidates.

[1]*Note:* **Bold** = primary.

Special Education Content Standard #4: Instructional Strategies

Special educators possess a repertoire of evidence-based **instructional strategies to individualize instruction** for individuals with ELN. Special educators select, adapt, and use these instructional strategies to promote **positive learning results in general and special curricula** and to appropriately **modify learning environments** for individuals with ELN. They enhance the **learning of critical thinking, problem-solving, and performance skills** of individuals with ELN, and increase their self-awareness, self-management, self-control, self-reliance, and self-esteem. Moreover, special educators emphasize the **development, maintenance, and generalization** of knowledge and skills across environments, settings, and the lifespan.

Beginning special educators demonstrate their mastery of this standard through the mastery of the CEC Common Core Knowledge and Skills, as well as through the appropriate CEC Specialty Area(s) Knowledge and Skills for which the program is preparing candidates.

Special Education Content Standard #5: Learning Environments and Social Interactions

Special educators actively **create learning environments** for individuals with ELN that foster cultural understanding, safety and emotional well-being, positive social interactions, and **active engagement** of individuals with ELN. In addition, special educators **foster environments in which diversity is valued** and individuals are taught to live harmoniously and productively in a culturally diverse world. Special educators shape **environments to encourage the independence,** self-motivation, self-direction, personal empowerment, and self-advocacy of individuals with ELN. Special educators **help their general education colleagues integrate individuals** with ELN in regular environments and engage them in meaningful learning activities and interactions. Special educators use **direct motivational and instructional interventions** with individuals with ELN to teach them to respond effectively to current expectations. When necessary, special educators can safely **intervene with individuals with ELN in crisis.** Special educators coordinate all these efforts and provide **guidance and direction to paraeducators and others,** such as classroom volunteers and tutors.

Beginning special educators demonstrate their mastery of this standard through the mastery of the CEC Common Core Knowledge and Skills, as well as through the appropriate CEC Specialty Area(s) Knowledge and Skills for which the preparation program is preparing candidates.

Special Education Content Standard #6: Language

Special educators understand **typical and atypical language development** and the ways in which exceptional conditions can interact with an individual's experience with and use of language. Special educators use individualized strategies to **enhance language development and teach communication skills** to individuals with ELN. Special educators are familiar with **augmentative, alternative, and assistive technologies** to support and enhance communication of individuals with exceptional needs. Special educators match their communication methods to an individual's language proficiency and cultural and linguistic differences. Special educators provide **effective language models** and they use communication strategies and resources to **facilitate understanding of subject matter for individuals with ELN whose primary language is not English.**

Beginning special educators demonstrate their mastery of language for and with individuals with ELN through the mastery of the CEC Common Core Knowledge and Skills, as well as through the appropriate CEC Specialty Area(s) Knowledge and Skills for which the preparation program is preparing candidates.

Special Education Content Standard #7: Instructional Planning

Individualized decision making and instruction is at the center of special education practice. Special educators develop **long-range individualized instructional plans** anchored in both general and special curricula. In addition, special educators systematically translate these individualized plans into carefully selected **shorter-range goals and objectives** taking into consideration an individual's abilities and needs, the learning environment, and a myriad of cultural and linguistic factors. Individualized instructional plans emphasize **explicit modeling** and **efficient guided practice** to assure acquisition and fluency through maintenance and generalization. Understanding of these factors as well as the implications of an individual's exceptional condition, guides the special educator's selection, adaptation, and creation of materials, and the use of powerful instructional variables. Instructional plans are **modified based on ongoing analysis of the individual's learning progress.** Moreover, special educators facilitate this instructional planning in a **collaborative context** including the individuals with exceptionalities, families, professional colleagues, and personnel from other agencies as appropriate. Special educators also develop a variety of **individualized transition plans,** such as transitions from preschool to elementary school and from secondary settings to a variety of postsecondary work and learning contexts. Special educators are comfortable using **appropriate technologies** to support instructional planning and individualized instruction.

Beginning special educators demonstrate their mastery of this standard through the mastery of the CEC Common Core Knowledge and Skills, as well as through the appropriate CEC Specialty Area(s) Knowledge and Skills for which the program is preparing candidates.

Special Education Content Standard #8: Assessment

Assessment is integral to the decision making and teaching of special educators and special educators use **multiple types of assessment information** for a variety of educational decisions. Special educators use the results of assessments to help identify exceptional learning needs and to develop and implement individualized instructional programs, as well as to adjust instruction in response to ongoing learning progress. Special educators understand the **legal policies and ethical principles of measurement and assessment** related to referral, eligibility, program planning, instruction, and placement for individuals with ELN, including those from culturally and linguistically diverse backgrounds. Special educators understand **measurement theory and practices** for addressing issues of validity, reliability, norms, bias, and interpretation of assessment results. In addition, special educators understand the appropriate **use and limitations** of various types of assessments. Special educators collaborate with families and other colleagues to assure **nonbiased, meaningful assessments and decision making.** Special educators conduct **formal and informal assessments** of behavior, learning, achievement, and environments to design learning experiences that support the growth and development of individuals with ELN. Special educators use assessment information to **identify supports and adaptations** required for individuals with ELN to access the general curriculum and to participate in school, system, and statewide assessment programs. Special educators **regularly monitor the progress** of individuals with ELN in general and special curricula. Special educators **use appropriate technologies** to support their assessments.

Beginning special educators demonstrate their mastery of this standard through the mastery of the CEC Common Core Knowledge and Skills, as well as through the appropriate CEC Specialty Area(s) Knowledge and Skills for which the preparation program is preparing candidates.

Special Education Content Standard #9: Professional and Ethical Practice

Special educators are guided by the profession's ethical and professional practice standards. Special educators practice in multiple roles and complex situations across wide age and developmental ranges. Their practice requires ongoing attention to **legal matters** along with serious professional and **ethical considerations.** Special educators engage in **professional activities** and participate in learning communities that benefit individuals with ELN, their families, colleagues, and their own professional growth. Special educators view themselves as **lifelong learners** and regularly reflect on and adjust their practice. Special educators are aware of how their own and others' attitudes, behaviors, and ways of communicating can influence their practice. Special educators understand that culture and language can interact with exceptionalities, and are **sensitive to the many aspects of diversity** of individuals with ELN and their families. Special educators actively plan and engage in activities that foster their professional growth and keep them **current with evidence-based best practices.** Special educators know their own limits of practice and practice within them.

Beginning special educators demonstrate their mastery of this standard through the mastery of the CEC Common Core Knowledge and Skills, as well as through the appropriate CEC Specialty Area(s) Knowledge and Skills for which the preparation program is preparing candidates.

Special Education Content Standard #10: Collaboration

Special educators routinely and effectively **collaborate with families, other educators, related service providers, and personnel from community agencies in culturally responsive ways.** This collaboration assures that the needs of individuals with ELN are addressed throughout schooling. Moreover, special educators embrace their special role as advocate for individuals with ELN. Special educators promote and advocate the learning and well-being of individuals with ELN across a wide range of settings and a range of different learning experiences. Special educators are viewed as specialists by a myriad of people who actively seek their collaboration to effectively include and teach individuals with ELN. Special educators are a **resource to their colleagues** in understanding the laws and policies relevant to individuals with ELN. Special educators use collaboration to **facilitate the successful transitions** of individuals with ELN across settings and services.

Beginning special educators demonstrate their mastery of this standard through the mastery of the CEC Common Core Knowledge and Skills, as well as through the appropriate CEC Specialty Area(s) Knowledge and Skills for which the preparation program is preparing candidates.

NOTES

"Individual with exceptional learning needs" is used throughout to include individuals with disabilities and individuals with exceptional gifts and talents.

"Exceptional condition" is used throughout to include both single and co-existing conditions. These may be two or more disabling conditions or exceptional gifts or talents co-existing with one or more disabling conditions.

"Special curricula" is used throughout to denote curricular areas not routinely emphasized or addressed in general curricula; e.g., social, communication, motor, independence, self-advocacy.

C. CEC Standards for Initial Licensure

In this newest set of CEC standards, CEC has rearranged its Knowledge and Skill Sets so that each explicitly aligns with the Interstate New Teacher and Assessment and Support Consortium's (INTASC) Model Standards for Teacher licensure. Each set has been reorganized into 10 domain areas that parallel the domain areas of each of the 10 INTASC Core Principles. This alignment is demonstrated in Table 4.1. [see p. 13 for a complete description of this reorganization].

One of the primary purposes of this change was to support states, especially those states that use the INTASC standards as a key component of their licensure frameworks, to use the CEC Standards as they develop state standards for licensure of special education teachers.

CEC's Standards for Preparation and Licensure are written in two tiers. The foundational standards are the Knowledge and Skill Sets. These sets have been developed to meet the variety of state licensure frameworks.

There are standards for both categorical, multi-categorical licensure frameworks. CEC also developed a set of 10 Content Standards, based on the Knowledge and Skill Standards, one for each of the domain areas listed in Table 4.1. (See Appendix 2 for a complete description of their development.) The Content Standards are written at a general level and are a single set—that is, they do not delineate the differences between the competencies needed by early childhood special education teachers, teachers of students with mild to moderate disabilities, teachers of students who are deaf and hard of hearing, etc. This level of specificity is found in the Knowledge and Skill Sets of Standards.

In Section 3 of this publication, CEC has provided two tools states can use to align their state standards with either the CEC Content Standards or the CEC Knowledge and Skill Standards. All of the CEC Standards, along with the electronic version of these forms, can be found on the CEC Web site at www.cec. sped. org.

TABLE 4.1
Alignment of INTASC Core Principles and CEC Standard Domain Areas

INTASC Core Principles	CEC Standard Domain Areas
1. Content Knowledge	1. Foundations
2. Learner Development	2. Characteristics of Learners
3. Learner Diversity	3. Individual Differences
4. Instructional Strategies	4. Instructional Strategies
5. Learning Environment	5. Learning Environments and Social Interactions
6. Communication	6. Language
7. Planning for Instruction	7. Instructional Strategies
8. Assessment	8. Assessment
9. Reflective Practice and Professional Development	9. Ethics and Professional Practice
10. Community	10. Collaboration

D. CEC Mentoring and Continuing Education Standards

MENTORSHIP

The CEC Standard for Mentoring:

In addition, each new professional in special education should receive a minimum of a 1-year mentorship during the first year of professional special education practice. The mentor should be an experienced professional in the same or a similar role as the mentee who can provide expertise and support on a continuing basis.

Even with quality preparation, the beginning special educator faces new challenges in applying and generalizing new skills and knowledge. Like other professionals, special educators who have the support of more senior colleagues become proficient more quickly, and are more likely to remain in the profession. The goals of the mentorship program should include

- Facilitating the application of knowledge and skills learned.
- Conveying advanced knowledge and skills.
- Acculturating into the school's learning community.
- Reducing job stress and enhancing job satisfaction.
- Supporting professional induction.

When special educators begin practice in a new area of licensure, they should have the opportunity to work with mentors who are experienced professionals in similar roles. The purpose of mentors is to provide expertise and support to the teachers on a continuing basis for at least the first year of practice in that area of certification. The mentorship is part of continuing education; thus, it is a requirement for maintaining licensure, not a requirement for initial licensure.

The mentorship is a professional relationship between the new teacher and an experienced teacher that aids the new teacher in further developing knowledge and skills in the area of certification and provides the support required to sustain the new teacher in practice.

The mentorship is collegial, not supervisory. It is essential that a mentor have knowledge, skills, and experience relevant to the new teacher's position in order to provide the expertise and support the new teacher requires to practice effectively. Thus, it is essential that new teachers practice in environments where mentors are available. Members of the special education profession are expected to serve as mentors as part of their professional responsibilities, and they should receive the resources and support necessary to carry out this responsibility effectively.

The CEC Standards provide that special education teachers should receive mentorships when they begin practice in each area of licensure. Thus, for example, an experienced teacher of students with visual impairments who, after the necessary preparation, becomes licensed to teach students in early childhood should receive a mentorship during the first year of practice in early childhood in order to maintain the license in early childhood.

CONTINUING PRACTICE IN THE PROFESSION

The CEC Standard for Continuing Practice in the Profession:

Both state licensure and national certification of individuals for professional practice in the field of special education should be for a limited period of time with periodic renewal. Each professional in the field of educating individuals with exceptionalities shall participate in an average of 36 contact hours (or an average of 3.6 continuing education units) each year of planned, organized, and recognized professional development activities related to the professional's field of practice.

The day has passed when one can assume that they have mastered a job and no longer need new skills. Today the average worker will change careers at least three times in their work life. And even within the same career, essential skills are changing at a dramatic rate. Just 10 years ago, many teachers saw technology skills as peripheral to their jobs.

Just as teachers in general must be lifelong learners, so too must special educators pursue new knowledge and skills throughout their careers. Licensure or certification must be time limited, and renewal must be based on planned, organized, and recognized professional development activities related to the professional's field of practice.

CEC has approved the following guidelines to implement the continuing practice standard.

- Each professional shall have a Professional Development Plan (PDP) that meets the standard and guidelines.
- Activities used in the PDP to earn continuing education units (CEU) can be selected from the following categories: career related academic course work, conducting or supporting research, participating in inservice workshops, teaching courses, delivering presentations, publishing, participating in supervised collegial support, providing service to professional association(s), participating in approved educational travel, and other appropriate projects.
- The PDP is reviewed and amended at least annually.
- Activities in the PDP are above and beyond routine job functions of the professional, and no single activity or category makes up the plan.
- The PDP includes an average of 3.6 CEUs per year.
- CEUs are earned in at least 3 of the past 5 years.

Section 5

Standards for Paraprofessionals Serving Individuals with Exceptional Learning Needs

THE PARAPROFESSIONAL IN SPECIAL EDUCATION

For more than 50 years, paraprofessionals have helped special educators provide important services to students with exceptional learning conditions. Historically, they provided services ranging from clerical tasks to assisting with individualized functional living tasks. Today they have become an essential part of the special education team in delivering individualized services and playing an increasingly prominent role in the instruction of individuals with exceptional learning needs at all ages. According to the Study of Personnel Needs in Special Education (SPENSE, n.d.), today paraprofessionals in the United States spend at least 10% of their time on the following activities:

- Providing instructional support in small groups.
- Providing one-to-one instruction.
- Modifying materials.
- Implementing behavior plans.
- Monitoring hallways, study halls, etc.
- Meeting with teachers.
- Collecting data on students.
- Providing personal care assistance.

The qualified special education paraprofessional is an employee who performs tasks as prescribed and is supervised by a fully licensed special education professional. Qualified paraprofessionals deliver individualized services to individuals with exceptional learning needs in a wide variety of settings, including general education classes, community-based functional learning sites, and just about everywhere that a special education professional can be found.

Paraprofessionals bring a wide variety of backgrounds and experience to their jobs (SPENSE, n.d.). In the United States, 29% have high school diplomas, 38% have completed some college, and 32% hold an associate's degree or higher. Paraprofessionals with college experience have increased confidence in collaborating and communicating with teachers. The majority of paraprofessionals are supervised by special education teachers and overwhelmingly they feel supported by their special education supervisors.

To ensure that paraprofessionals have the required skills for their expanded roles, CEC, in collaboration with the National Resource Center for Paraeducators, developed and validated the following preparation standards for paraprofessionals who serve individuals with exceptional learning needs. CEC expects that agencies will ensure that all paraprofessionals working with students with exceptional learning needs have, at a minimum, mastered these standards.

In addition, paraprofessionals should have available ongoing, effective, continuing training with professional educators and training that is specifically targeted for paraprofessionals.

SPECIAL EDUCATION PARAEDUCATOR EVALUATION FORMS

The following charts are tools paraeducators and paraeducator training programs can use to ensure that they are meeting the CEC Standards for Special Education Paraeducators.

Form 1 is a tool paraeducator training programs can use to evaluate whether or not their program sufficiently addresses the CEC Standards for the Preparation of Special Education

Paraeducators. Preparation programs can use the chart in several ways. If developing a new program, faculty can use the chart to ensure that the essential knowledge and skills are included in the course curriculum. This can be done by cross-referencing each of the standards to the course content, field experiences, etc. Programs can also use these standards to ensure that their assessments adequately evaluate the paraeducator's knowledge and skills. This can be done by cross-referencing required assessments to each of the standards.

Form 2 is a self-evaluation instrument designed to be used by students in paraeducator training programs to evaluate their progress in learning and applying the paraeducator knowledge and skills. Students can use this as a self-assessment tool as they move through the program, checking off each knowledge and skill as it is mastered. This could also be used as a summative assessment at the end of the training program.

REFERENCES

Study of Personnel Needs in Special Education, Table 2.91. (n.d.). Retrieved October 24, 2003, from http://ferdig. coe.ufl.edu/spense/scripts/tables/htdocs/TABLE2_91. htm

CEC Knowledge and Skill Base for All
Entry-Level Special Education Paraeducators

Standard #1: Foundations	
Knowledge:	
PE1K1	Purposes of programs for individuals with exceptional learning needs.
PE1K2	Basic educational terminology regarding students, programs, roles, and instructional activities.
Skills:	

Standard #2: Development and Characteristics of Learners	
Knowledge:	
PE2K1	Effects an exceptional condition(s) can have on an individual's life.
Skills:	

Standard #3: Individual Learning Differences	
Knowledge:	
PE3K1	Rights and responsibilities of families and children as they relate to individual learning needs.
PE3K2	Indicators of abuse and neglect.
Skills:	
PE3S1	Demonstrate sensitivity to the diversity of individuals and families.

Standard #4: Instructional Strategies	
Knowledge:	
PE4K1	Basic instructional and remedial strategies and materials.
PE4K2	Basic technologies appropriate to individuals with exceptional learning needs.
Skills:	
PE4S1	Use strategies, equipment, materials, and technologies, as directed, to accomplish instructional objectives.
PE4S2	Assist in adapting instructional strategies and materials as directed.
PE4S3	Use strategies as directed to facilitate effective integration into various settings.
PE4S4	Use strategies that promote the learner's independence as directed.
PE4S5	Use strategies as directed to increase the individual's independence and confidence.

Standard #5: Learning Environments and Social Interactions	
Knowledge:	
PE5K1	Demands of various learning environments.
PE5K2	Rules and procedural safeguards regarding the management of behaviors of individuals with exceptional learning needs.
Skills:	
PE5S1	Establish and maintain rapport with learners.
PE5S2	Use universal precautions and assist in maintaining a safe, healthy learning environment.
PE5S3	Use strategies for managing behavior as directed.
PE5S4	Use strategies as directed, in a variety of settings, to assist in the development of social skills.

Standard #6: Language	
Knowledge:	
PE6K1	Characteristics of appropriate communication with stakeholders.

Skills:	

Standard #7: Instructional Planning

Knowledge:	

Skills:	
PE7S1	Follow written plans, seeking clarification as needed.
PE7S2	Prepare and organize materials to support teaching and learning as directed.

Standard #8: Assessment

Knowledge:	
PE8K1	Rationale for assessment.

Skills:	
PE8S1	Demonstrate basic collection techniques as directed.
PE8S2	Make and document objective observations as directed.

Standard #9: Professional and Ethical Practice

Knowledge:	
PE9K1	Ethical practices for confidential communication about individuals with exceptional learning needs.
PE9K2	Personal cultural biases and differences that affect one's ability to work with others.

Skills:	
PE9S1	Perform responsibilities as directed in a manner consistent with laws and policies.
PE9S2	Follow instructions of the professional.
PE9S3	Demonstrate problem solving, flexible thinking, conflict management techniques, and analysis of personal strengths and preferences.
PE9S4	Act as a role model for individuals with exceptional learning needs.
PE9S5	Demonstrate commitment to assisting learners in achieving their highest potential.
PE9S6	Demonstrate the ability to separate personal issues from one's responsibilities as a paraeducator.
PE9S7	Maintain a high level of competence and integrity.
PE9S8	Exercise objective and prudent judgment.
PE9S9	Demonstrate proficiency in academic skills, including oral and written communication.
PE9S10	Engage in activities to increase one's own knowledge and skills.
PE9S11	Engage in self-assessment.
PE9S12	Accept and use constructive feedback.
PE9S13	Demonstrate ethical practices as guided by the CEC Code of Ethics and other standards and policies.

Standard #10: Collaboration

Knowledge:	
PE10K1	Common concerns of families of individuals with exceptional learning needs.
PE10K2	Roles of stakeholders in planning an individualized program.

Skills:	
PE10S1	Assist in collecting and providing objective, accurate information to professionals.
PE10S2	Collaborate with stakeholders as directed.
PE10S3	Foster respectful and beneficial relationships.
PE10S4	Participate as directed in conferences as members of the educational team.
PE10S5	Function in a manner that demonstrates a positive regard for the distinctions between roles and responsibilities of paraeducators and those of professionals.

Special Education Paraeducator Training Program Evaluation:
Are the Standards Addressed and Assessed?

Standard	What opportunities do candidates have to master this standard?	How does the program assess that candidates have mastered this standard?
Standard 1: Foundations		
Knowledge:		
PE1K1 Purposes of programs for individuals with exceptional learning needs.		
PE1K2 Basic educational terminology regarding students, programs, roles, and instructional activities.		
Standard 2: Development and Characteristics of Learners		
Knowledge:		
PE2K1 Effects an exceptional condition(s) can have on an individual's life.		
Standard 3: Individual Learning Differences		
Knowledge:		
PE3K1 Rights and responsibilities of families and children as they relate to individual learning needs.		
PE3K2 Indicators of abuse and neglect.		
Skills:		
PE3S1 Demonstrate sensitivity to the diversity of individuals and families.		
Standard 4: Instructional Strategies		
Knowledge:		
PE4K1 Basic instructional and remedial strategies and materials.		
PE4K2 Basic technologies appropriate to individuals with exceptional learning needs.		
Skills:		
PE4S1 Use strategies, equipment, materials, and technologies, as directed, to accomplish instructional objectives.		
PE4S2 Assist in adapting instructional strategies and materials as directed.		
PE4S3 Use strategies as directed to facilitate effective integration into various settings.		
PE4S4 Use strategies that promote the learner's independence as directed.		
PE4S5 Use strategies as directed to increase the individual's independence and confidence.		

continued

Standard	What opportunities do candidates have to master this standard?	How does the program assess that candidates have mastered this standard?
Standard 5: Learning Environments and Social Interactions		
Knowledge:		
PE5K1 Demands of various learning environments.		
PE5K2 Rules and procedural safeguards regarding the management of behaviors of individuals with exceptional learning needs.		
Skills:		
PE5S1 Establish and maintain rapport with learners.		
PE5S2 Use universal precautions and assist in maintaining a safe, healthy learning environment.		
PE5S3 Use strategies for managing behavior as directed.		
PE5S4 Use strategies as directed, in a variety of settings, to assist in the development of social skills.		
Standard 6: Language		
Knowledge:		
PE6K1 Characteristics of appropriate communication with stakeholders.		
Standard 7: Instructional Planning		
Skills:		
PE7S1 Follow written plans, seeking clarification as needed.		
PE7S2 Prepare and organize materials to support teaching and learning as directed.		
Standard 8: Assessment		
Knowledge:		
PE8K1 Rationale for assessment.		
Skills:		
PE8S1 Demonstrate basic collection techniques as directed.		
PE8S2 Make and document objective observations as directed.		
Standard 9: Professional and Ethical Practice		
Knowledge:		
PE9K1 Ethical practices for confidential communication about individuals with exceptional learning needs.		
PE9K2 Personal cultural biases and differences that affect one's ability to work with others.		

continued

Standard		What opportunities do candidates have to master this standard?	How does the program assess that candidates have mastered this standard?
Skills:			
PE9S1	Perform responsibilities as directed in a manner consistent with laws and policies.		
PE9S2	Follow instructions of the professional.		
PE9S3	Demonstrate problem-solving, flexible thinking, conflict management techniques, and analysis of personal strengths and preferences.		
PE9S4	Act as a role model for individuals with exceptional learning needs.		
PE9S5	Demonstrate commitment to assisting learners in achieving their highest potential.		
PE9S6	Demonstrate the ability to separate personal issues from one's responsibilities as a paraeducator.		
PE9S7	Maintain a high level of competence and integrity.		
PE9S8	Exercise objective and prudent judgment.		
PE9S9	Demonstrate proficiency in academic skills, including oral and written communication.		
PE9S10	Engage in activities to increase one's own knowledge and skills.		
PE9S11	Engage in self-assessment.		
PE9S12	Accept and use constructive feedback.		
PE9S13	Demonstrate ethical practices as guided by the CEC Code of Ethics and other standards and policies.		
Standard 10: Collaboration			
Knowledge:			
PE10K1	Common concerns of families of individuals with exceptional learning needs.		
PE10K2	Roles of stakeholders in planning an individualized program.		
Skills:			
PE10S1	Assist in collecting and providing objective, accurate information to professionals.		
PE10S2	Collaborate with stakeholders as directed.		
PE10S3	Foster respectful and beneficial relationships.		
PE10S4	Participate as directed in conferences as members of the educational team.		
PE10S5	Function in a manner that demonstrates a positive regard for the distinctions between roles and responsibilities of paraeducators and those of professionals.		

FORM 2
Special Education Paraeducator Self-Evaluation:
Have I Mastered the Standards?

Standard	What is my level of mastery of this standard?	
	Novice	Proficient
Standard 1: Foundations		
Knowledge:		
PE1K1 — Purposes of programs for individuals with exceptional learning needs.		
PE1K2 — Basic educational terminology regarding students, programs, roles, and instructional activities.		
Standard 2: Development and Characteristics of Learners		
Knowledge:		
PE2K1 — Effects an exceptional condition(s) can have on an individual's life.		
Standard 3: Individual Learning Differences		
Knowledge:		
PE3K1 — Rights and responsibilities of families and children as they relate to individual learning needs.		
PE3K2 — Indicators of abuse and neglect.		
Skills:		
PE3S1 — Demonstrate sensitivity to the diversity of individuals and families.		
Standard 4: Instructional Strategies		
Knowledge:		
PE4K1 — Basic instructional and remedial strategies and materials.		
PE4K2 — Basic technologies appropriate to individuals with exceptional learning needs.		
Skills:		
PE4S1 — Use strategies, equipment, materials, and technologies, as directed, to accomplish instructional objectives.		
PE4S2 — Assist in adapting instructional strategies and materials as directed.		
PE4S3 — Use strategies as directed to facilitate effective integration into various settings.		
PE4S4 — Use strategies that promote the learner's independence as directed.		
PE4S5 — Use strategies as directed to increase the individual's independence and confidence.		
Standard 5: Learning Environments and Social Interactions		
Knowledge:		
PE5K1 — Demands of various learning environments.		

continued

Standard		What is my level of mastery of this standard?	
		Novice	Proficient
PE5K2	Rules and procedural safeguards regarding the management of behaviors of individuals with exceptional learning needs.		
Skills:			
PE5S1	Establish and maintain rapport with learners.		
PE5S2	Use universal precautions and assist in maintaining a safe, healthy learning environment.		
PE5S3	Use strategies for managing behavior as directed.		
PE5S4	Use strategies as directed, in a variety of settings, to assist in the development of social skills.		
Standard 6: Language			
Knowledge:			
PE6K1	Characteristics of appropriate communication with stakeholders.		
Standard 7: Instructional Planning			
Skills:			
PE7S1	Follow written plans, seeking clarification as needed.		
PE7S2	Prepare and organize materials to support teaching and learning as directed.		
Standard 8: Assessment			
Knowledge:			
PE8K1	Rationale for assessment.		
Skills:			
PE8S1	Demonstrate basic collection techniques as directed.		
PE8S2	Make and document objective observations as directed.		
Standard 9: Professional and Ethical Practice			
Knowledge:			
PE9K1	Ethical practices for confidential communication about individuals with exceptional learning needs.		
PE9K2	Personal cultural biases and differences that affect one's ability to work with others.		
Skills:			
PE9S1	Perform responsibilities as directed in a manner consistent with laws and policies.		
PE9S2	Follow instructions of the professional.		
PE9S3	Demonstrate problem-solving, flexible thinking, conflict management techniques, and analysis of personal strengths and preferences.		

continued

Standard		What is my level of mastery of this standard?	
		Novice	*Proficient*
PE9S4	Act as a role model for individuals with exceptional learning needs.		
PE9S5	Demonstrate commitment to assisting learners in achieving their highest potential.		
PE9S6	Demonstrate the ability to separate personal issues from one's responsibilities as a paraeducator.		
PE9S7	Maintain a high level of competence and integrity.		
PE9S8	Exercise objective and prudent judgment.		
PE9S9	Demonstrate proficiency in academic skills, including oral and written communication.		
PE9S10	Engage in activities to increase one's own knowledge and skills.		
PE9S11	Engage in self-assessment.		
PE9S12	Accept and use constructive feedback.		
PE9S13	Demonstrate ethical practices as guided by the CEC Code of Ethics and other standards and policies.		
Standard 10: Collaboration			
Knowledge:			
PE10K1	Common concerns of families of individuals with exceptional learning needs.		
PE10K2	Roles of stakeholders in planning an individualized program.		
Skills:			
PE10S1	Assist in collecting and providing objective, accurate information to professionals.		
PE10S2	Collaborate with stakeholders as directed.		
PE10S3	Foster respectful and beneficial relationships.		
PE10S4	Participate as directed in conferences as members of the educational team.		
PE10S5	Function in a manner that demonstrates a positive regard for the distinctions between roles and responsibilities of paraeducators and those of professionals.		

APPENDICES

Appendix 1

A Brief Timeline of CEC
Professional Standards Events

1922	The establishment of professional standards for the field of special education is declared as one of the fundamental aims of CEC.
1962	Professional Standards is the theme of the national convention.
1963	CEC purpose statement includes standards for professional personnel.
1965	CEC Conference on Professional Standards.
1966	*Professional Standards for Personnel in the Education of Exceptional Children* is published.
1976	*Guidelines for Personnel in the Education of Exceptional Children* is published. CEC and the National Council for Accreditation of Teacher Education (NCATE) form a partnership for approving training programs.
1980	CEC standards adopted by NCATE.
1981	CEC Delegate Assembly charges CEC to develop, promote, and implement preparation and certification standards, and a code of ethics.
1982	CEC called to establish and promote appropriate professional standards in the organization's mission statement.
1983	CEC adopts Code of Ethics, Standards for Professional Practice, Standards for the Preparation of Special Education Personnel, and Standards for Entry Into Professional Practice. The Professional Standard Committee is charged with their implementation.
1984	NCATE adopts CEC's revised standards. NCATE adopts their "Redesign" where colleges and universities submit their folios to the respective professional organizations.
1985	NCATE adopts Guidelines for Program Approval of both basic and advanced special education preparation programs.
1986	CEC begins reviewing folios of programs seeking national accreditation. Guidelines for folio preparation adopted by CEC.
1987	*Standards and Guidelines for Curriculum Excellence in Personnel Preparation Programs in Special Education* is published.
1989	CEC Delegate Assembly adopts policy framework for CEC Standards for Entry into Professional Practice.
1990	NCATE adopts CEC's revised Guidelines for Program Approval of both basic and advanced special education preparation programs.
1992	CEC adopts the Common Core of Knowledge and Skills Essential for All Beginning Special Education Teachers. CEC adopts non-NCATE Guidelines for Program Approval for intitutions of higher education (IHE) including institutional, faculty, and program resources.
1993	CEC Standards for Entry Into Professional Practice are revised. CEC revises non-NCATE Guidelines for Program Approval for IHEs including institutional, faculty, and program resources.

1995	CEC adopts initial areas of specialization knowledge and skill standards.
	New standards published and submitted for NCATE adoption.
	What Every Special Educator Must Know: The International Standards for the Preparation and Certification of Special Education Teachers is published.
1996	*What Every Special Educator Must Know: The International Standards for the Preparation and Certification of Special Education Teachers* (2nd edition) is published.
1997	CEC initiates the Professionally Recognized Special Educator, a national special education certification program with certificates for special education teachers, administrators, and diagnosticians.
	NCATE initiates the NCATE 2000 project that shifts the focus of program accreditation to candidate performance.
1998	Knowledge and Skill Standards for Transition Specialists, Special Education Administrators, Educational Diagnosticians, and Special Education Paraeducators are approved.
	The Standards for Entry Into Professional Practice are revised.
	Guidelines for continuing education are approved.
	Revisions to the Common Core of Knowledge and Skills Essential for All Beginning Special Education Teachers are approved.
	The Curriculum Referenced Licensing and Program Accreditation Framework is approved.
	What Every Special Educator Must Know: The International Standards for the Preparation and Certification of Special Educators (3rd edition) is published.
2000	The Knowledge and Skill Standards are edited to improve clarity and reduce redundancy.
	Multicultural standards added to the CEC Common Core.
	What Every Special Educator Must Know: The Standards for the Preparation and Certification of Special Educators (4th edition) is published.
	All Knowledge and Skill Standard sets are rearranged into 10 domain areas that parallel the domain areas of the Interstate New Teacher and Assessment and Support Consortium's (INTASC) Core Principles.
	CEC Accreditation Standards, to be used by programs developing performance assessment systems, are written.
2001	NCATE approves CEC performance standards and review procedures.
2003	CEC revises procedures for the validation of Knowledge and Skill Standards.

Appendix 2

Development of and Procedures for Validation of the Knowledge and Skills Standards

CEC carries out the development of professional standards through the Professional Standards and Practice Standing Committee (PSPSC) and its relevant subcommittees. One of the major responsibilities of the PSPSC has been the development, validation, and updating of the knowledge and skills bases in the various areas of special education.

DEVELOPMENT OF THE STANDARDS

In 1989, the PSPSC established the first Knowledge and Skills Subcommittee (KSS), co-chaired by Barbara Sirvis, of New York, and Bill Swan, of Georgia, and composed of CEC division representatives and past CEC Teachers of the Year. It set out to accomplish the following two major tasks:

- Identify a common core of knowledge and skills for all beginning special education teachers.
- Create specialty sets of knowledge and skills that are necessary to teach in a particular area of exceptionality or age group.

The KSS gathered materials from literature; state, provincial, and local governments; institutions of higher education; and elsewhere. The KSS then identified and organized thousands of competencies into major categories, culled them down to 195 statements, and determined the importance of each by surveying a 1,000-person sample of CEC's membership. Based on the response (54%), the KSS reduced the number of statements to 107.

CEC adopted these validated statements, which became "The CEC Common Core of Knowledge and Skills Essential for All Beginning Special Education Teachers," published in the fall 1992 issue of *TEACHING Exceptional Children.*

Alan Koenig, of Texas, assumed the chairmanship of the 1993 KSS and began developing specialty sets of knowledge and skills to supplement the Common Core. The exceptionality and age-specific CEC divisions took the lead, developing sets of knowledge and skills necessary to teach in their areas of specialization. The KSS worked with the divisions to ensure that the specialty sets were formatted properly and that the statements supplemented the Common Core.

The KSS also developed a survey, which was sent to a random sample of the division's membership to validate the specialty sets. Each survey was sent to a sample of CEC members, half of whom were teachers and other direct service providers. Modifications were made in consultation with the division. Generally, there was a high level of concurrence with the work the division produced.

In 1996, after initial publication of *What Every Special Educator Must Know,* comments were received from the field regarding the knowledge and skills statements. After review of all of the comments, CEC approved in the spring of 1996 a number of technical and clarifying changes. These were included in the second edition of this publication.

In 1996, the KSS began to develop a procedure for developing a set of standards that would be curriculum-referenced rather than disability-category-specific. In 1998, the KSS, now chaired by Rachelle Bruno of Kentucky, completed the development of this Curriculum Referenced Licensing and Program Accreditation Framework. This new framework was approved by the PSPSC in April 1998. The KSS also approved Knowledge and Skill sets for educational diagnosticians and special education administrators.

The special education paraeducator knowledge and skills were approved in 1998 with the close collaboration of the National Resource Center for Paraeducators, the National Education Association, and the American Federation of Teachers.

In 2000, the KSS, now chaired by Kathlene Shank of Illinois, successfully completed a revision of the Common Core and a Knowledge and Skill set for Technology Specialist and Transition Specialists. The KSS also began a major effort to refine and update the standards. In order to provide assistance to the more than 30 states that use the 10 Interstate New Teacher and Assessment and Support Consortium (INTASC) principles, the KSS reorganized all of the CEC Knowledge and Skill standards from the 8 domain areas of the current standards (Characteristics of Learners, Assessment, etc.) to the 10 domain areas of the INTASC principles. They then edited all of the Knowledge and Skill sets to eliminate redundancy and to increase the precision of the language. In addition, several new items were validated and added to the Common Core in the areas of multicultural competence, access to the general education curriculum, technology, and collaboration.

KSS then wrote the CEC Content Standards that will now be used by teacher preparation programs as the benchmark for a candidate performance assessment system. Instead of lists of knowledge and skill standards, the 2001 Content Standards consist of 10 narrative standards. These standards were written to reflect the content of the validated knowledge and skills in each of the 10 domain areas of the Knowledge and Skill Standards. The Knowledge and Skill Standards inform the Content Standards. The Content Standards are the same for all programs.

PROCEDURES FOR THE VALIDATION OF THE KNOWLEDGE AND SKILLS STANDARDS

The following process was approved in 2003 for the development, validation, and revalidation of the Knowledge and Skill Standards. The process was amended to ensure that there was an explicit documentation of the research and literature base for the standards. Please note that any member or recognized unit within CEC may recommend additions or amendments to the Knowledge and Skill Standards by submitting the request to the Assistant Executive Director for Professional Standards at CEC Headquarters.

1. The PSPSC determines Knowledge and Skill sets to be developed and/or revalidated. The PSPSC identifies a set group facilitator (SF) to guide the process.

2. The KSS Chair and SF establish a small focused work group.

3. The work group identifies possible items for validation, documents the professional literature that supports each proposed knowledge and skill statement, summarizes the literature base, formats the items, and submits this information to the KSS.

4. The KSS reviews the work of the group to ensure readiness of the standards for survey.

5. The PSPU conducts the survey of CEC members using a targeted stratified random sample and Knowledge and Skill statements and submits its results to the KSS Chair and the SF.

6. A select group of experts, selected by the PSPSC Chair in consultation with the SF, reviews the standards and the survey data.

7. The KSS reviews and approves the revalidated or validated set of Knowledge and Skills.

8. The PSPSC oversees the process, makes a determination regarding the KSS recommendations, and submits its decision to the CEC Board of Directors.

Appendix 3

Knowledge and Skills from the CEC Common Core That Address Specific Domain Areas

CEC often gets questions regarding the knowledge and skills in several domains of interest. For the readers' convenience, the following two sets have been excerpted from the CEC Common Core: Appendix 3A: Multicultural Competence and Appendix 3B: Self-Determination.

Two other areas of current interest are supervision of paraeducators and practitioners' use of evidence-based research. The CEC Common Core Standards include the following three standards that deal with supervising paraeducators:

CEC COMMON CORE STANDARDS THAT ADDRESS SUPERVISION OF PARAEDUCATORS

CC5S15 Structure, direct, and support the activities of paraeducators, volunteers, and tutors.

CC7K5 Roles and responsibilities of the paraeducators related to instruction, intervention, and direct service.

CC10S11 Observe, evaluate, and provide feedback to paraeducators.

CEC COMMON CORE STANDARDS THAT ADDRESS TEACHERS' USE OF RESEARCH

A foundation assumption of the CEC standards is that all special education professionals will use evidence-based research in their decision-making. This is indicated in the standards by the numerous times the standards call for teachers to use "effective" strategies. There are also two Common Core Standards that deal specifically with this issue.

CC7K1 Theories and research that form the basis of curriculum development and instructional practice.

CC9K4 Methods to remain current regarding research-validated practice.

Appendix 3A
The Knowledge and Skills for All Entry-Level Special Educators (excerpted from the CEC Common Core) That Address Multicultural Competence

Standard Number	Standard
CC1K5	Issues in definition and identification of individuals with exceptional learning needs, including those from culturally and linguistically diverse backgrounds.
CC1K8	Historical points of view and contribution of culturally diverse groups.
CC1K9	Impact of the dominant culture on shaping schools and the individuals who study and work in them.
CC1K10	Potential impact of differences in values, languages, and customs that can exist between the home and school.
CC2K3	Characteristics and effects of the cultural and environmental milieu of the individual with exceptional learning needs and the family.
CC3K2	Impact of learners' academic and social abilities, attitudes, interests, and values on instruction and career development.
CC3K3	Variations in beliefs, traditions, and values across and within cultures and their effects on relationships among individuals with exceptional learning needs, family, and schooling.
CC3K4	Cultural perspectives influencing the relationships among families, schools, and communities as related to instruction.
CC3K5	Differing ways of learning of individuals with exceptional learning needs including those from culturally diverse backgrounds and strategies for addressing these differences.
CC5K4	Teacher attitudes and behaviors that influence behavior of individuals with exceptional learning needs.
CC5K7	Strategies for preparing individuals to live harmoniously and productively in a culturally diverse world.
CC5K8	Ways to create learning environments that allow individuals to retain and appreciate their own and each other's respective language and cultural heritage.
CC5K9	Ways specific cultures are negatively stereotyped.
CC5K10	Strategies used by diverse populations to cope with a legacy of former and continuing racism.
CC5S1	Create a safe, equitable, positive, and supportive learning environment in which diversities are valued.
CC5S13	Organize, develop, and sustain learning environments that support positive intracultural and intercultural experiences.
CC5S14	Mediate controversial intercultural issues among students within the learning environment in ways that enhance any culture, group, or person.
CC6K1	Effects of cultural and linguistic differences on growth and development.
CC6K2	Characteristics of one's own culture and use of language and the ways in which these can differ from other cultures and uses of languages.
CC6K3	Ways of behaving and communicating among cultures that can lead to misinterpretation and misunderstanding.

CC6S2	Use communication strategies and resources to facilitate understanding of subject matter for students whose primary language is not the dominant language.
CC7S8	Develop and select instructional content, resources, and strategies that respond to cultural, linguistic, and gender differences.
CC7S14	Prepare individuals to exhibit self-enhancing behavior in response to societal attitudes and actions.
CC8S2	Administer nonbiased formal and informal assessments.
CC8S6	Use assessment information in making eligibility, program, and placement decisions for individuals with exceptional learning needs, including those from culturally and/or linguistically diverse backgrounds.
CC9K1	Personal cultural biases and differences that affect one's teaching.
CC9S6	Demonstrate sensitivity for the culture, language, religion, gender, disability, socio-economic status, and sexual orientation of individuals.
CC10K4	Culturally responsive factors that promote effective communication and collaboration with individuals with exceptional learning needs, families, school personnel, and community members.
CC10S10	Communicate effectively with families of individuals with exceptional learning needs from diverse backgrounds.

Appendix 3B

The Knowledge and Skills for All Entry-Level Special Educators (excerpted from the CEC Common Core) That Address Student Self-Determination

Standard Code	Standard
CC4S2	Teach individuals to use self-assessment, problem solving, and other cognitive strategies to meet their needs.
CC4S5	Use procedures to increase the individual's self-awareness, self-management, self-control, self-reliance, and self-esteem.
CC5S8	Teach self-advocacy.
CC5S9	Create an environment that encourages self-advocacy and increased independence.
CC7S3	Involve the individual and family in setting instructional goals and monitoring progress.
CC7S14	Prepare individuals to exhibit self-enhancing behavior in response to societal attitudes and actions.
CC8S7	Report assessment results to all stakeholders using effective communication skills.
CC10S4	Assist individuals with exceptional learning needs and their families in becoming active participants in the educational team.
CC10S5	Plan and conduct collaborative conferences with individuals with exceptional learning needs and their families.
CC10S7	Use group problem-solving skills to develop, implement, and evaluate collaborative activities.

Appendix 4

CEC Professional Policies*

SECTION THREE - PART 1

BASIC COMMITMENTS AND RESPONSIBILITIES TO EXCEPTIONAL CHILDREN

*Taken from CEC Policy Manual.

CHAPTER 01
RESPONSIBILITIES OF THE COUNCIL FOR EXCEPTIONAL CHILDREN

Para. 1 - Purpose

The Council for Exceptional Children is an association of professional and other persons whose principal purpose is to obtain optimal educational opportunity for all children and youth with exceptionalities. These children's needs differ sufficiently from other children's so that they require special educational and related services in addition to those presently available through regular education programs and other human service delivery systems. While the legal criteria that define children and youth with exceptionalities vary greatly from one governmental jurisdiction to another, The Council for Exceptional Children is primarily concerned about children and youth having sensory deficits, physical handicaps, mental retardation, behavioral disorders, communication disorders, special learning disabilities, multiple handicaps, gifts and talents, and children who are developmentally delayed or abused and neglected. Children and youth with exceptionalities are found in all communities regardless of socioeconomic or cultural factors.

Para. 2 - Governmental Relations

Public policy legislation, litigation, appropriation, regulation, and negotiated agreements are the means by which children and youth with exceptionalities have been guaranteed the educational opportunities of our society. The Council is deeply committed to the effective implementation of existing public policy in the interest of children and youth with exceptionalities. In addition, The Council seeks extension and creation of public policy in a manner which will encourage and augment quality service programs at all governmental levels. To provide the scope and kind of services needed, The Council endorses public policies that strengthen and enhance instructional programs for all children and youth. While such general provisions should benefit the exceptional child, The Council believes that specific policy provisions are necessary to offer those children and youth with exceptional needs the opportunity to develop to their fullest potential. In carrying out its governmental activities, The Council will be guided by the policies adopted by its members and by the directives of its governance.

Para. 3 - Advocacy by Members

The Council believes that all persons concerned about the education of children and youth with exceptionalities must initiate and maintain efforts to ensure that appropriate public policy is adopted, fully implemented, and enforced.

The Council recognizes that the provision of public services to children and youth with exceptionalities is a function of the governmental process. For this reason, The Council urges and supports the active involvement of its members in activities which will build greater awareness on the part of parents, communities, and governmental officials regarding the needs of children and youth with exceptionalities and will extend appropriate information to such bodies in their efforts to carry out the objectives of this policy statement.

The Council believes that it is the responsibility of all persons concerned about the needs of children and youth with exceptionalities to continually seek to improve government provisions for their education. In this regard, The Council pledges its assistance in providing needed information and in helping to develop the necessary strategies to attain improvement of educational services for children and youth with exceptionalities.

In our democratic societies, we have created systems of law to protect the individual from the abuses of society, particularly from abuses of the agencies established by society to serve its needs. In the attempt to provide what appear to be needed services, the rights of the individual may be overlooked. For this reason, The Council urges constant vigilance on the part of all persons engaged in the education of children and youth with exceptionalities to assure that the rights of these individuals and their families are understood and observed. The Council further suggests that all public programs and private programs utilizing public funds be open to review and that flexibility be provided to allow for judicial consideration of such matters.

Para. 4 - Accessibility

The Council for Exceptional Children provides a physical and emotional environment which is sensitive to the needs, feelings, and opinions of persons with varying mobility and communication needs. CEC makes special efforts to encourage the participation of members with exceptionalities in its activities and the utilization of its services. The Council for Exceptional Children:

a. Identifies CEC members and other professionals with exceptionalities who would make use of communication, accessibility, and mobility resources.

b. Facilitates communication between professionals with exceptionalities and CEC Headquarters staff.

c. Orients CEC members and headquarters staff to the needs of professionals with exceptionalities.

d. Informs professionals with exceptionalities about the resources available through CEC to enable their equitable participation in all CEC activities.

e. Guarantees that all CEC sponsored activities are conducted in accessible and usable facilities and communication modes to ensure full and equitable participation of professionals with exceptionalities.

CHAPTER 02
EDUCATIONAL RIGHTS AND RESPONSIBILITIES

Para. 1 - Education is the Right of All Children

The principle of education for all is based on democracy's philosophical premise that every person is valuable in his or her own right and should be afforded equal opportunities to develop his or her full potential. Thus, no democratic society should deny educational opportunities to any child, regardless of the child's potential for making a contribution to society. Since the passage of the first public school laws in the mid-nineteenth century, this principle has received general endorsement and qualified execution. While lip service has been paid to the intent of the principle, various interpretations of the terms "education" and "all children" have deprived many children of their rights.

The ordinary educational opportunities provided by the schools have tended to neglect or exclude children with unusual learning needs: the gifted and talented; those having sensory deficits, physical handicaps, mental retardation, behavioral disorders, communication disorders, specific learning disabilities, or multiple handicaps; and children who are developmentally delayed or abused and neglected. These children need special education and, in order to be able to benefit fully from this education, they need the opportunity to view themselves as acceptable to society. They need stable and supportive home lives, wholesome community interactions, and the opportunity to view themselves and others in a healthy manner.

Because of their exceptionality, many children need to begin their school experiences at an earlier age than is customary; many need formal educational services well into adulthood; and many require health and social services that are closely coordinated with school programs. Meeting these needs is essential to the total development of children with exceptionalities as individuals and as members of society.

For some decades now, educators and schools have been responding to the challenges of educating children with exceptionalities. Still, not all children are being provided for fully; the intellectually gifted child, for example, and many other children who need highly specialized services, are not receiving them. The community should extend its demand that school personnel learn to understand and serve the individual needs of these children as well as those more easily accommodated in the educational system. The surge of interest among educators in individualizing instruction hopefully will mean more sensitivity to the educational needs of all children, and particularly those with special needs.

Programs for children and youth with exceptionalities should be varied in nature and conducted in a variety of settings, depending on the individual needs of the child, the child's family, and the community. It is The Council's belief that society should have the legal responsibility to extend the opportunity for every individual to be educated to the full extent of his or her capacities, whatever they may be or however they may be attenuated by special circumstances. There is no dividing line which excludes some children and includes others in educational programs. Clearly, every exceptional child has the right to a free appropriate public education which may not in any instance be compromised because of inadequacies in the educational system or existing public policies.

Para. 2 - Government Responsibilities for Special Education in Intermediate and Local School Districts

Intermediate and local school districts carry major responsibility for the quality of educational services to children and youth with exceptionalities and for leadership and coordination with other agencies to achieve comprehensive child centered services. Intermediate and local school districts should provide continuing leadership for all educational services in the community, including participation in the financing of every education program in the district and of any program outside the district which serves children and youth with exceptionalities at the district's request.

The Council believes that school districts should be responsible for an annual review of children and youth with exceptionalities who are legal residents of the district to assure that their education is proceeding adequately, even though they may be receiving their educational services outside their district of residence.

Para. 3 - State or Provincial Governments

The basic responsibility for guaranteeing an education to all children rests with state or provincial governments through their state or provincial education agencies; however, the fulfillment of this responsibility is effected in cooperation with federal and local education authorities. The Council believes that it is the responsibility of the state/province to guarantee each child comprehensive educational opportunities without cost to the child or the child's family. Special financial support should be offered to the intermediate and local districts or combinations of these units so that no excess local cost is involved in providing specialized quality programs, services, and facilities. While the cost of services for children and youth with exceptionalities varies greatly, such considerations should not affect the goal of optimal programming for every child. The Council believes that no financial incentive should be provided to encourage the adoption of a less than optimal education program. A particular responsibility of state/province governments is to provide progressive leadership and direction to coordinated state/provincial programs of special education and to provide coordination among the several departments of government other than education which may be called upon to serve children and youth with exceptionalities and their families.

Para. 4 - Federal Governments of the United States and Canada

The Council believes the federal government should give major attention to guaranteeing educational opportunities to children and youth whose education has been neglected. The federal government has a responsibility for assuring that the rights of children with exceptionalities are not violated. Because education of children and youth with exceptionalities has, in general, been a neglected area, special categories of support should be directed to meeting their needs. Federal financial aid should be directed to state or provincial governments for the education of children with exceptionalities.

The federal government should provide for support of professional leadership in the field of special education with emphasis on assessment of needs, planning of needed programs, preparation of personnel, and research.

The federal government should provide financial support to colleges, universities, and other appropriate agencies to assist in operating programs to prepare all needed personnel to conduct comprehensive special education programs and services.

The federal government should provide financial support to school districts and combinations of school districts that wish to provide innovative or exemplary programs for children and youth with exceptionalities or that, for any reason, enroll an unusually high proportion of children and youth with special needs.

The federal government should provide major support to programs in the field of special education that serve regional or national needs such as the education of migrant children.

In instances where the federal government assumes primary responsibility for the education of a group of children (i.e., American Indian and Alaska Native children in Bureau of Indian Affairs operated and contracted schools and the education of dependents in Department of Defense schools and programs), it must also provide appropriate special education to these groups. As one means of accomplishing this goal, the Department of Interior, Bureau of Indian Affairs, should maintain a specific budget line item for special education and related services for children with exceptionalities.

Para. 5 - Intergovernmental Planning

The success of the functions of federal, state/provincial, and local government requires close cooperative planning of a short- and long-term nature. Such planning requires excellence in communicative skills and facilities. Such plans for the education of children and youth with exceptionalities should form the basis for new and improved legislative and government policies at all levels of government.

Para. 6 - Compulsory Services and Attendance

The provision for universal education of children in a democratic society has been translated as a commitment to providing educational opportunities for every child, whatever may be his or her socioeconomic status; cultural or racial origins; physical, intellectual, or emotional status; potential contribution to society; and educational needs. This commitment to every child thus includes a commitment to children with unusual learning needs and to those with outstanding abilities and talents. Although providing education for these children may require a variety of specialized services and instructional programs, some costly and some requiring radical innovations in traditional educational structures, there is no basis for including some children and excluding others where the principle of universal education is concerned.

Some of the specialized services that may be essential if children with exceptionalities are to attend school include the provision of specialized transportation, functional architectural environments, personalized equipment and aids, individualized instructional programs, and special education and support personnel. Certainly the fiscal requirements for such programs may be great; if they are not instituted and maintained, however, the cost of neglect is infinitely greater and must be borne mainly by the children as well as by their families, communities, and society as a whole.

The commitment to education for all encompasses the responsibility for providing special forms of education to children and youth with exceptional characteristics and needs. This responsibility extends to all types of exceptionalities, regardless of the degree to which a child may eventually be able to contribute to society. To this end, The Council supports efforts to eliminate exclusionary clauses in compulsory school attendance laws and other such laws and administrative practices which deny children and youth with exceptionalities the educational opportunity they require.

Para. 7 -Maintenance of Educational Opportunity

The requirement to provide a free, appropriate, public education is constitutionally-based and cannot be abrogated for any child or group of children, regardless of any characteristics, disabilities, or traits of such children. Many children, including children with exceptionalities have been excluded from schools on the unacceptable grounds that they are disruptive, are perceived to be uneducable, or have undesirable characteristics.

Schools today face a growing challenge in educating students who are dangerously violent or destructive. In order for educational environments to be acceptably conducive to learning, behavior which impedes the ability of children to learn and teachers to teach must be minimized or eliminated. Schools have the responsibility to immediately consider changing the educational setting for any students who behave in a dangerously violent or destructive manner. If such an alternative educational placement is determined to be appropriate, such students must be placed in educational settings designed to meet their learning, safety, and behavioral management needs.

Few students receiving appropriate special education services become a danger to self and/or others. Rather, students with disabilities are more likely to be victimized than their nondisabled peers and would benefit directly from safer schools.

Policy: The exemption, exclusion, or expulsion of any child from receiving a free, appropriate, public education creates a greater problem for society and therefore should not be permitted. At the same time violent and destructive behavior is unacceptable in our schools. Acknowledging that such behavior occurs, CEC believes that schools have the responsibility to quickly and unilaterally move students who exhibit dangerously violent or destructive behavior to an alternative educational setting in which ongoing safety/behavioral goals and educational goals are addressed by appropriately trained or qualified personnel. This setting must meet the school's dual responsibilities of providing an appropriate, public education and a safe learning/working environment in an age- and culturally-appropriate manner.

Alternative placements and programs should meet standards of quality that promote learning environments that benefit students in positive and productive ways. Less than desirable alternative placements that serve to merely contain students without meaningful learner benefits should not be used. If the student has a disability, this setting must be selected by the student's individualized education program committee. If the student does not have a disability, another appropriate education committee should make this decision. If the alternative setting is contested, the current alternative setting will continue until the resolution of applicable due process procedures for a student with or without disabilities.

During the time a student is in an alternative educational setting, the local education agency must conduct a committee meeting (in the case of a student with a disability, an individualized education program committee meeting) as soon as possible. During this meeting, the following must be considered:

a. Whether the student's violent behavior was an isolated incident and is not likely to happen again;

b. Whether the environment in which the violent behavior occurred was appropriate given the student's age, cultural background, disability, related needs, and characteristics;

c. Whether or not there are new characteristics within the student or environment necessitating further evaluation or, in the case of a student with a disability, a revision of the individualized education program;

d. Whether the student's return to the previous educational setting with appropriate supports and related services would provide safety for self and others; and

e. Whether the placement was the least restrictive environment for the student.

In determining an appropriate temporary placement for a student or when developing a new program if one is necessary, educators, parents, and other appropriate professionals should consider a variety of possibilities, such as:

a. Maintaining the current placement with additional support services.

b. Providing educational alternatives to suspension that afford students quality learning experiences.

c. Utilizing documented effective behavioral interventions, curricular modifications, and accommodation strategies appropriate to the student's culture and designed to assist the student in controlling behavior.

Schools should ensure that all general and special educators involved in implementing the student's education program have opportunities for staff development to acquire the knowledge and skills necessary for effective implementation of the student's program. Providing systematic education about appropriate behavior to all students in the educational environment is also necessary. CEC also stresses the importance of the involvement and commitment of families and communities. CEC recommends that school districts, in collaboration with state/provincial agencies, community agencies, and juvenile justice systems, create appropriate alternative settings. The creation and maintenance of appropriate educational settings provide positive opportunities for all to work and learn and thus reduce the likelihood of future inappropriate behavior.

Para. 8 - Responsibility of the Schools for Early Childhood Education

Schools have traditionally assumed educational responsibility for children beginning at about age 5 or 6 and ending with late adolescence. Increasingly, it is apparent that formal educational experiences at earlier ages would pay rich dividends in the full development of the capabilities of many children with exceptionalities. Special educators have useful knowledge and many techniques for working with very young children with exceptionalities. What is needed is the identification of children who could benefit from early education and the actual implementation of programs.

Communities should make their schools responsible for conducting search and census operations through which children who may need specialized education at very early ages can be identified. The voluntary enrollment of such children by their parents is inadequate because many parents may not be aware of the child's special needs or of available forms of assistance. Procedures for child study that encourage adaptations to the particular needs of very young children with exceptionalities are an important part of early education programs.

Schools should provide educational services for individuals according to their needs and regardless of age.

Schools should actively seek out children who may have specialized educational needs in the first years of their lives. A particular commitment should be made to initiate home care training programs for parents of infants with special needs, to establish specialized early childhood and kindergarten programs, and to utilize specialized components of regular early education programs to serve children with exceptionalities.

Para. 9 - Services to Children with Exceptionalities Ages Birth Through Five

The provision of services to children with exceptionalities from birth through 5 years of age must be made a priority. It is the premise of The Council that lack of such services currently represents the most serious impediment to the development of children with exceptionalities. There is mounting evidence of the effectiveness of programs for very young children with exceptionalities and their families.

Services to young children with exceptionalities are presently provided by a variety of systems at national, state, provincial, and local levels. There is little systematic coordination between agencies, and major service gaps remain unfilled. A national initiative is needed to establish plans for systematic coordination among the social, educational, and health agencies currently serving children with exceptionalities from birth through 5 years so as to ensure maximum benefits for these children and their families, and to plan for the future provision of additional programs to fill major gaps in service to this population.

Wide variations in service arrangements are necessary to meet the individual needs of children. The Council strongly supports the principle that services for young children with exceptionalities, whenever appropriate, be provided in a context which includes children without exceptionalities. Effective integrated experiences can further the development of children with exceptionalities and also can form the roots of respect for diversity in all children. Since the success of integrated programs relies heavily on the provision of specialized teacher training and supportive resources, the importance of such supports should be reflected in legislative and funding directives.

In expanding services for children with exceptionalities from birth through 5 years, it is essential that the central role of the parent in the young child's development be recognized. Programs must be designed to incorporate parental participation and to provide support for families in their role as the child's primary care provider. The training of teachers of young children with exceptionalities should be expanded to include skills in working with parents in mutually helpful ways so that parental and agency efforts in helping the child are strengthened.

Para. 10 - Responsibilities for Providing Continuing Education Services to Exceptional Youth

The Council believes that education is a lifelong process and that, instead of age, competency and maximal development should be the terminating factor with regard to formal schooling. It also believes that individuals with learning problems, particularly exceptional youth, frequently need education and periodic reeducation beyond the traditional school attendance ages to encourage their continuing development. These options might include postsecondary education, vocational education, job training, employment counseling, community living skills, and placement services in order to maximize their ability to contribute to society.

Para. 11 - Migrant Exceptional Students

Exceptional students who are mobile, due to their parents' migrant employment, experience reduced opportunities for an appropriate education and a reduced likelihood of completing their education. Child-find and identification policies and practices, designed for a stationary population, are inadequate for children who move frequently. Incomplete, delayed, or inadequate transfer of records seriously impedes educational continuity. Interstate/provincial differences in special education eligibility requirements, programs and resources, minimum competency testing, and graduation requirements result in repetition of processing formalities, gaps in instruction, delays in the resumption of services, an inability to accumulate credits for graduation, and other serious inequities. In addition to the disruption of learning, mobility disrupts health care, training, teacher-student rapport, and personal relationships.

The Council believes that educational policies and practices should be developed at federal, state/provincial, and local levels to improve access to education for migrant children and youth with exceptionalities. These policies should include:

a. A national system for the maintenance and transferal of special education records for migrant students with exceptionalities.

b. Intrastate/provincial and interstate/provincial cooperation in the transfer of records and of credits.

c. Flexibility in high school credit accumulation for migrant students with exceptionalities.

d. Joint planning, coordination, and shared responsibility among special education, migrant education, bilingual education, and related programs.

e. Funding patterns that adjust for variations in enrollment.

f. Flexible scheduling and other programming options that adjust for student mobility.

g. Routine monitoring of activities undertaken to identify the migrant exceptional student and to ensure educational continuity.

h. Ongoing research efforts to promote, improve, support, and evaluate the education of migrant students with exceptionalities.

i. Personnel training.

j. Parent and family information programs to facilitate record transfer.

Para. 12 - Children with Exceptionalities in Charter Schools

CEC vigorously supports educational reforms within the public schools which promote rigorous learning standards, strong educational outcomes, shared decision making, diverse educational offerings, and the removal of unnecessary administrative requirements. Charter schools, a form of public schools, are one approach many believe can be effective in achieving these objectives. However, such schools must reflect this country's commitment to free and universal public education, with equality of educational opportunity for all -- including students with disabilities.

Regardless of who takes responsibility for the delivery of educational services for children with disabilities who attend a charter school, the chartering agency—and, ultimately, state or provincial authorities—must ensure that the rights of children with exceptionalities are upheld. It is the position of CEC that the following criteria with respect to children with disabilities be adhered to when parents, professionals, and school district authorities consider the development of charter school policy, the content of contracts or agreements establishing individual charter schools, and the actual operation of charter schools.

- **Student Access.** Charter schools must be required to abide by the same federal or provincial nondiscrimination and equal education opportunity laws that apply to other public schools. Charter schools must not discriminate in their admissions policies, nor should they charge tuition or other mandatory fees. Disability status cannot be used as a criterion for excluding a child with a disability from attending a charter school, and policies governing admissions and students' participation in the school program should not inadvertently exclude children with disabilities.

- **Provision of Free, Appropriate Public Education.** As public schools, charter schools must be required to provide a free, appropriate, public education to students with disabilities, and to ensure all of the other basic fundamental procedural rights in accordance with applicable federal and provincial laws, such as the Individuals with Disabilities Education Act and Section 504 of the Rehabilitation Act in the United States, including children's physical access to the education program offered. Enrollment in a charter school cannot be used to deny to a student with disabilities the free, appropriate education to which they have a right.

- **Financing the Education of Children with Disabilities.** Educational and other services required by children with disabilities, including special education and related services, can be provided directly by the charter school, or through alternative arrangements with other public schools, with local school districts, or with state or provincial education agencies. State, provincial and local policies for charter schools and, when appropriate, charter agreements themselves should explicitly identify responsibility for providing and paying for any special services associated with educating children with disabilities in charter schools, including the cost of building renovations and the provision of education and related services.

- **Accountability.** Charter schools must be held accountable by state or provincial education agencies and, when appropriate local school districts, for providing special education and related services to children with disabilities, consistent with applicable federal, provincial and state laws, just as other public schools are. The standards that apply to educating children with disabilities in charter schools must be the same as those that apply to other public schools, and enforcement of these standards must be conducted in a manner that is consistent with enforcement activities and penalties that apply in determining compliance of other public schools.

CHAPTER 03
SPECIAL EDUCATION WITHIN THE SCHOOLS

Para. 1 - The Relationship Between Special and Regular School Programs

Special education is an integral part of the total educational enterprise, not a separate order. In any school system, special education is a means of enlarging the capacity of the system to serve the educational needs of all children.

The particular function of special education within the schools (and the education departments of other institutions) is to identify children with unusual needs and to aid in the effective fulfillment of those needs. Both regular and special school programs play a role in meeting the educational needs of children with exceptionalities. A primary goal of educators should be to help build accommodative learning opportunities for children with exceptionalities in regular educational programs. In the implementation of this goal, special education can serve as a support system, and special educators can assist regular school personnel in managing the education of children with exceptionalities.

When the special placement of a child is required, the aim of the placement should be to maximize the development and freedom of the child rather than to accommodate the regular classroom.

Special education should function within and as a part of the regular, public school framework. Within this framework, the function of special education should be to participate in the creation and maintenance of a total educational environment suitable for all children.

From their base in the regular school system, special educators can foster the development of specialized resources by coordinating their specialized contributions with the contributions of the regular school system. One of the primary goals of special educators should be the enhancement of regular school programs as a resource for all children.

Para. 2 - Administrative Organization

The system of organization and administration developed for special education should be linked with regular education (a) to increase the capability of the total system to make more flexible responses to changes in the behavior of individual pupils and to changing conditions in schools and society, and (b) to permit all elements of the system to influence the policies and programs of the others.

Special education must provide an administrative organization to facilitate achievement for children with exceptionalities of the same educational goals as those pursued by other children. This purpose can be achieved through structures that are sufficiently compatible with those employed by regular education to ensure easy, unbroken passage of children across regular-special education administrative lines for whatever periods of time may be necessary, as well as by structures that are sufficiently flexible to adjust quickly to changing task demands and child growth needs.

The major purpose of the special education administrative organization is to provide and maintain those environmental conditions in schools that are most conducive to the growth and learning of children with special needs.

Under suitable conditions, education within the regular school environment can provide the optimal opportunity for most children with exceptionalities. Consequently, the system for the delivery of special education must enable the incorporation of special help and opportunities in regular educational settings.

Children should spend only as much time outside regular class settings as is necessary to control learning variables that are critical to the achievement of specified learning goals.

Para. 3 - Scope of Program

Education for children and youth with exceptionalities requires the well planned and purposeful coordination of many disciplines. Special education is a cross-disciplinary, problem-oriented field of services which is directed toward mobilizing and improving a variety of resources to meet the educational needs of children and youth with exceptionalities.

Para. 4 - The Goal and Commitment of Special Education

The fundamental purposes of special education are the same as those of regular education: the optimal development of the student as a skillful, free, and purposeful person, able to plan and manage his or her own life and to reach his or her highest potential as an individual and as a member of society. Indeed, special education developed as a highly specialized area of education in order to provide children with exceptionalities with the same opportunities as other children for a meaningful, purposeful, and fulfilling life.

Perhaps the most important concept that has been developed in special education as the result of experiences with children with exceptionalities is that of the fundamental individualism of every child. The aspiration of special educators is to see every child as a unique composite of potentials, abilities, and learning needs for whom an educational program must be designed to meet his or her particular needs. From its beginnings, special education had championed the cause of children with learning problems. It is as the advocates of such children and of the concept of individualization that special education can come to play a major creative role in the mainstream of education.

The special competencies of special educators are more than a collection of techniques and skills. They comprise a body of knowledge, methods, and philosophical tenets that are the hallmark of the profession. As professionals, special educators are dedicated to the optimal education of children with exceptionalities and they reject the misconception of schooling that is nothing but custodial care.

The focus of all education should be the unique learning needs of the individual child as a total functioning organism. All educators should recognize and accept that special and regular education share the same fundamental goals.

Special education expands the capacity of schools to respond to the educational needs of all students.

As advocates of the right of all children to an appropriate education, special educators affirm their professionalism.

Para. 5 - Educational Environments for Exceptional Students

Special education takes many forms and can be rovided with a broad spectrum of administrative arrangements. Children with special educational needs should be served in regular classes and neighborhood schools insofar as these arrangements are conducive to good educational progress. The Council believes that the goal of educating children with exceptionalities together with children without exceptionalities is desirable if the individual program is such that it will enhance the child's (with exceptionalities) educational, social, emotional, and vocational development.

It is sometimes necessary, however, to provide special supplementary services for children with exceptionalities or to remove them from parts or all of the regular educational program. It may even be necessary to remove some children from their homes and communities in order for them to receive education and related services in residential schools, hospitals, or training centers. The Council believes that careful study and compelling reasons are necessary to justify such removal.

The Council charges each public agency to ensure that a continuum of alternative placements, ranging from regular class programs to residential settings, is available to meet the needs of children with exceptionalities.

Children with exceptionalities enrolled in special school programs should be given every appropriate opportunity to participate in educational, nonacademic, and extracurricular programs and services with children who are not disabled or whose disabilities are less severe.

While special schools for children with exceptionalities and other separate educational facilities may function as part of an effective special educational delivery system, it is indefensible to confine groups of exceptional pupils inappropriately in such settings as a result of the failure to develop a full continuum of less restrictive programs. The Council condemns as educationally and morally indefensible the practice of categorical isolation by exceptionality without full consideration of the unique needs of each student, and the rejection of children who are difficult to teach from regular school situations. When insufficient program options exist and when decisions are poorly made, children with exceptionalities are denied their fundamental rights to free public education. In so acting, education authorities violate the basic tenets of our democratic societies.

Like all children, children with exceptionalities need environmental stability, emotional nurturance, and social acceptance. Decisions about the delivery of special education to children with exceptionalities should be made after careful consideration of their home, school, and community relationships, their personal preferences, and effects on self-concept, in addition to other sound educational considerations.

Para. 6 - Inclusive Schools and Community Settings

The Council for Exceptional Children believes all children, youth, and young adults with disabilities are entitled to a free and appropriate education and/or services that lead to an adult life characterized by satisfying relations with others, independent living, productive engagement in the community, and participation in society at large. To achieve such outcomes, there must exist for all children, youth, and young adults a rich variety of early intervention, educational, and vocational program options and experiences. Access to these programs and experiences should be based on individual educational need and desired outcomes. Furthermore, students and their families or guardians, as members of the planning team, may recommend the placement, curriculum option, and the exit document to be pursued.

CEC believes that a continuum of services must be available for all children, youth, and young adults. CEC also believes that the concept of inclusion is a meaningful goal to be pursued in our schools and communities. In addition, CEC believes children, youth, and young adults with disabilities should be served whenever possible in general education classrooms in inclusive neighborhood schools and community settings. Such settings should be strengthened and supported by an infusion of specially trained personnel and other appropriate supportive practices according to the individual needs of the child.

Policy Implications

Schools. In inclusive schools, the building administrator and staff with assistance from the special education administration should be primarily responsible for the education of children, youth, and young adults with disabilities. The administrator(s) and other school personnel must have available to them appropriate support and technical assistance to enable them to fulfill their responsibilities. Leaders in state/provincial and local governments must redefine rules and regulations as necessary, and grant school personnel greater authority to make decisions regarding curriculum, materials, instructional practice, and staffing patterns. In return for greater autonomy, the school administrator and staff should establish high standards for each child, youth, and young adult, and should be held accountable for his or her progress toward outcomes.

Communities. Inclusive schools must be located in inclusive communities; therefore, CEC invites all educators, other professionals, and family members to work together to create early intervention, educational, and vocational programs and experiences that are collegial, inclusive, and responsive to the diversity of children, youth, and young adults. Policy makers at the highest levels of state/provincial and local government, as well as school administration, also must support inclusion in the educational reforms they espouse. Further, the policy makers should fund programs in nutrition, early intervention, health care, parent education, and other social support programs that prepare all children, youth, and young adults to do well in school. There can be no meaningful school reform, nor inclusive schools, without funding of these key prerequisites. As important, there must be interagency agreements and collaboration with local governments and business to help prepare students to assume a constructive role in an inclusive community.

Professional Development. And finally, state/provincial departments of education, local educational districts, and colleges and universities must provide high-quality preservice and continuing professional development experiences that prepare all general educators to work effectively with children, youth, and young adults representing a wide range of abilities and disabilities, experiences, cultural and linguistic backgrounds, attitudes, and expectations. Moreover, special educators should be trained with an emphasis on their roles in inclusive schools and community settings. They also must learn the importance of establishing ambitious goals for their students and of using appropriate means of monitoring the progress of children, youth, and young adults.

Para. 7 - Staff Preparation for Placement

Essential to the appropriate placement of the child with an exceptionality is the preparation of the environment for that child through preservice and/or inservice training of staff and any other necessary accommodations.

Teacher training institutions are challenged to instruct all teacher candidates about current trends in the education of exceptional children.

State and provincial departments of education are charged with the responsibility to promote inservice activities that will update all professional educators and provide ongoing, meaningful staff development programs.

Administrators can have a significant positive influence upon the professional lives of teaching staff and, therefore, upon the educational lives of children. Administrative personnel of school districts are, therefore, charged with the responsibility to promote inservice education and interprofessional exchanges which openly confront contemporary issues in the education of all children.

Para. 8 - Individualized Education Programs

The creation and operation of a series of alternative settings for exceptional persons to live their lives and to develop to the greatest degree possible requires that service providers continuously strive to deliver the highest quality services possible. The Council believes that the central element for the delivery of all the services required by a person with an exceptionality must be an individually designed program. Such a program must contain the objectives to be attained, resources to be allocated, evaluation procedures and time schedule to be employed, and a termination date for ending the program and procedure for developing a new one. The process for developing an individualized program must adhere to all the procedural safeguards of due process of law and must involve the individual person and his or her family, surrogate, advocate, or legal representative.

Para. 9 - Due Process Protections (Procedural Safeguards)

As a final component of quality control, The Council believes that no decisions can be made on behalf of any individual without strict adherence to due process of law. Most significant is our position that all individuals are entitled to adequate representation when such decisions are being made. We support the increasing efforts on the part of governments to officially require the assignment of a surrogate when a family member is not available for purposes of adequately representing the interests of the person with an exceptionality. Ultimately, however, whenever possible, a member of the individual's family provides the most desirable representation. It is also our position that the individual consumer must be given every opportunity to make his or her own decisions, that this is a right provided to all citizens, and that any abridgement of that individual right can only occur upon the proper exercise of law.

Para. 10 - Confidentiality

The Council for Exceptional Children urges members to adhere to ethical principles and act in compliance with laws and regulations which protect children and their family's right to privacy and which control the use of confidential information regarding children.

Para. 11 - Program Evaluation

Programs designed for the purpose of providing educational opportunities for children and youth with exceptionalities must not be viewed as static, for the end product must always be the exceptional child and his or her personal improvement. For this reason, all programs should contain plans to evaluate their effectiveness, and the results of such evaluations should be presented for public review.

The Council believes that all legislation to fund existing programs or create new programs should contain mechanisms for effective evaluation and that governmental advisory bodies should review the findings of evaluations on a regular basis. External as well as internal systems of evaluation should be developed to aid in the evaluation of programs for children and youth with exceptionalities.

Para. 12 - Labeling and Categorizing of Children

The field of special education is concerned with children who have unique needs and with school programs that employ specialized techniques. As the result of early attitudes and programs that stressed assistance for children with severe disabilities, the field developed a vocabulary and practices based on the labeling and categorizing of children. In recent decades, labeling and categorizing were extended to children with milder degrees of exceptionality. Unfortunately, the continued use of labels tends to rigidify the thinking of all educators concerning the significance and purpose of special education and thus to be dysfunctional and even harmful for children.

Words such as "defective," "disabled," "retarded," "impaired," "disturbed," and "disordered," when attached to children with special needs, are stigmatic labels that produce unfortunate results in both the children and in the community's attitudes toward the children. These problems are magnified when the field organizes and regulates its programs on the basis of classification systems that define categories of children according to such terms. Many of these classifications are oriented to etiology, prognosis, or necessary medical treatment rather than to educational classifications. They are thus of little value to the schools. Simple psychometric thresholds, which have sometimes been allowed to become pivotal considerations in educational decision making, present another set of labeling problems.

Special education's most valuable contribution to education is its specialized knowledge, competencies, values, and procedures for individualizing educational programs for individual children, whatever their special needs. Indeed, special educators at their most creative are the advocates of children who are not well served by schools except through special arrangements. To further the understanding of and programming for such children, special educators as well as other educational personnel should eliminate the use of simplistic categorizing.

No one can deny the importance of some of the variables of traditional significance in special education such as intelligence, hearing, and vision. However, these variables in all their complex forms and degrees must be assessed in terms of educational relevance for a particular child. Turning them into typologies that may contribute to excesses in labeling and categorizing children is indefensible and should be eliminated.

In the past, many legislative and regulatory systems have specified criteria for including children in an approved category as the starting point for specialized programming and funding. This practice places high incentives on the labeling of children and undoubtedly results in the erroneous placement of many children.

It is desirable that financial aids be tied to educational programs rather than to children and that systems for allocating children to specialized programs be much more open than in the past.

Special educators should enhance the accommodative capacity of schools and other educational agencies to serve children with special needs more effectively. In identifying such children, special educators should be concerned with the identification of their educational needs, not with generalized labeling or categorizing of children.

Decisions about the education of children should be made in terms of carefully individualized procedures that are explicitly oriented to children's developmental needs.

To further discourage the labeling and categorizing of children, programs should be created on the basis of educational functions served rather than on the basis of categories of children served.

Regulatory systems that enforce the rigid categorization of pupils as a way of allocating them to specialized programs are indefensible. Financial aid for special education should be tied to specialized programs rather than to finding and placing children in those categories and programs.

Para. 13 - Group Intelligence Testing

a. Psychological tests of many kinds saturate our society and their use can result in the irreversible deprivation of opportunity to many children, especially those already burdened by poverty and prejudice.

b. Most group intelligence tests are multileveled and standardized on grade samples, thus necessitating the use of interpolated and extrapolated norms and scores.

c. Most group intelligence tests, standardized on LEAs rather than individual students, are not standardized on representative populations.

d. In spite of the use of nonrepresentative group standardization procedures, the norms are expressed in individual scores.

e. Most group intelligence tests, standardized on districts which volunteer, may have a bias in the standardization.

f. Many of the more severely handicapped and those expelled or suspended have no opportunity to influence the norms.

g. Group intelligence tests are heavily weighted with language and will often yield spurious estimates of the intelligence of non-English speaking or language different children.

h. A group intelligence test score, although spurious, may still be a good predictor of school performance for some children.

i. School achievement predicts future school performance as well as group intelligence tests, thus leaving little justification for relying on group intelligence tests.

j. One of the most frequent abuses of group intelligence tests is the use of such tests with populations for which they are inappropriate.

The Council goes on record in full support of the recommendations of the "Classification Project" (Hobbs, *The Futures of Children*, 1975, pp. 237-239) pertaining to group intelligence testing as follows:

a. "... That there be established a National Bureau of standards for Psychological Tests and Testing."

b. That there be established "minimum guidelines with respect to the utilization of psychological tests for the classification of children."

c. "That organizations that make extensive use of educational and psychological tests...should establish review boards to monitor their testing programs."

Until these three recommendations are accomplished, The Council encourages a moratorium on the use of group intelligence tests by individual school districts for the purpose of identifying children with exceptionalities.

Para. 14 - Performance Assessment

While most students with exceptional needs have been assured their right to public education along with their peers, they have not been similarly assured of the opportunity to complete their education, graduate, and receive a diploma signifying their achievement. There exist considerable variations and inconsistencies within and among the states and provinces regarding graduation requirements, student standards, and performance assessment for students with exceptional needs and the procedures for their receiving, or not receiving, a diploma.

Within the school reform movement, emerging issues which compound these variations and inconsistencies in graduation requirements, student standards, and performance assessment include the increased emphasis on accountability and the growing use of district and state-wide student assessment results not only for the granting of diplomas and the determination of grade placement, but also in high stakes assessments in which teacher salaries and other incentives are tied to student performance. Educational policies need to be formulated to resolve these inconsistencies, eliminate potentially discriminatory practices, and assure that graduation and grade placement requirements are equitably applied to all students. Unless this happens, many of the educational gains made by students with exceptional needs could be threatened or delayed.

The Council believes that educational guidelines for performance assessment and graduation and/or grade placement requirements for students with exceptional needs should be developed at the national, state, provincial, and local levels. These guidelines should incorporate the following principles:

a. Every student with exceptional needs should have available the opportunity to demonstrate performance using valid and reliable assessment.

b. Assessment processes and instruments should be used that have been developed and validated on student samples that have included students who have exceptionalities and that validly demonstrate their performances.

c. Assessment accommodations and alternative performance assessments should be available when needed for students with exceptionalities to assure that relevant performance, rather than the cultural diversity, linguistic diversity, or exceptionality, is being assessed.

d. The use of common or differential standards, the purpose and benefits of the assessment, and the procedures for assessing students, including the range of accommodations and modifications used in such assessments, should be addressed annually in each student's individual education program.

e. If performance assessments are not currently being used for students with exceptionalities, as is the case with all assessments, adequate time should be provided to develop or field test assessments, and to validate such assessments, accommodations, or alternative assessments with students who have exceptionalities.

f. Performance assessments that are designed to measure learning outcomes should not be given if students have not had an opportunity to learn the knowledge or skills being assessed. They should also have adequate time and appropriate programs to address areas in which performance is not sufficiently demonstrated.

g. It may not be appropriate to use the results of performance assessments given for purposes of school or system accountability to make individual student educational decisions.

h. A diploma should be granted to all students who complete high school, and it should be accompanied by grade transcripts, course-of-study description, and/or descriptions of student learning and accomplishments..

i. Systems should be in place to allow credits toward graduation for approved study outside of school such as work, service, and project-based learning in the community and vocational/technical, community college, and university/college coursework.

j. The successful implementation of a performance assessment program, including its application to students with exceptional needs, requires the cooperative efforts of general/regular educators, special educators, parents, and students in its planning, application, and evaluation.

Para. 15 - Surgical and Chemical Interventions to Control the Behavior of Human Beings

The Council condemns the inappropriate use of surgical and chemical interventions to control the behavior of human beings. Although these procedures often simplify care and maintenance, the integrity of the individual must transcend any institution's desire for administrative convenience. The Council recognizes that in certain circumstances such interventions may be appropriate; however, they should never be used without the approval of the individual to be treated, or the individual's parents or guardians, or, in circumstances where the individual is a ward of the state, the approval of an appropriate review body before which the individual or his or her representatives are guaranteed all legal due-process rights.

Para. 16 - Physical Intervention

The Council recognizes the right to the most effective educational strategies to be the basic educational right of each special education child. Furthermore, The Council believes that the least restrictive positive educational strategies should be used, as it relates to physical intervention, to respect the child's dignity and personal privacy. Additionally, The Council believes that such interventions shall assure the child's physical freedom, social interaction and individual choice. The intervention must not include procedures which cause pain or trauma. Intervention techniques must focus not only on eliminating a certain undesirable behavior, but also upon a determination of the purpose of that behavior, and the provision/instruction of a more appropriate behavior. Lastly, behavior intervention plans must be specifically described in the child's written educational plan with agreement from the education staff, the parents and, when appropriate, the child.

The Council recommends that physical intervention be used only if all the following requirements are met:

a. The child's behavior is dangerous to herself/himself or others, or the behavior is extremely detrimental to or interferes with the education or development of the child.

b. Various positive reinforcement techniques have been implemented appropriately and the child has repeatedly failed to respond as documented in the child's records.

c. It is evident that withholding physical intervention would significantly impede the child's educational progress as explicitly defined in his/her written educational plan.

d. The physical intervention plan specifically will describe the intervention to be implemented, the staff to be responsible for the implementation, the process for documentation, the required training of staff and supervision of staff as it relates to the intervention and when the intervention will be replaced.

e. The physical intervention plan will become a part of the written educational plan.

f. The physical intervention plan shall encompass the following provisions:

  1. A comprehensive analysis of the child's environment including variables contributing to the inappropriate behavior.

  2. The plan to be developed by a team including professionals and parents/guardians, as designated by state/provisional and federal law.

  3. The personnel implementing the plan shall receive specific training congruent with the contents of the plan and receive ongoing supervision from individuals who ware trained and skilled in the techniques identified in the plan.

  4. The health and medical records of the child must be reviewed to ensure that there are no physical conditions present that would contraindicate the use of the physical intervention proposed.

  5. The impact of the plan on the child's behavior must be consistently evaluated, the results documented, and the plan modified when indicated.

The Council supports the following prohibitions:

a. Any intervention that is designed to, or likely to, cause physical pain.

b. Releasing noxious, toxic or otherwise unpleasant sprays, mists, or substances in proximity to the child's face.

c. Any intervention which denies adequate sleep, food, water, shelter, bedding, physical comfort, or access to bathroom facilities.

d. Any intervention which is designed to subject, used to subject, or likely to subject the individual to verbal abuse, ridicule or humiliation, or which can be expected to cause excessive emotional trauma.

e. Restrictive interventions which employ a device or material or objects that simultaneously immobilize all four extremities, including the procedure known as prone containment, except that prone containment may be used by trained personnel as a limited emergency intervention.

f. Locked seclusion, unless under constant surveillance and observation.

g. Any intervention that precludes adequate supervision of the child.

h. Any intervention which deprives the individual of one or more of his or her senses.

The Council recognizes that emergency physical intervention may be implemented if the child's behavior poses an imminent and significant threat to his/her physical well-being or to the safety of others. The intervention must be documented and parents/guardians must be notified of the incident.

However, emergency physical intervention shall not be used as a substitute for systematic behavioral intervention plans that are designed to change, replace, modify, or eliminate a targeted behavior.

Furthermore, The Council expects school districts and other educational agencies to establish policies and comply with state/provincial and federal law and regulations to ensure the protection of the rights of the child, the parent/guardian, the education staff, and the school and local educational agency when physical intervention is applied.

Para. 17 - Corporal Punishment

The Council for Exceptional Children supports the prohibition of the use of corporal punishment in special education. Corporal punishment is here defined as a situation in which all of the following elements are present: an authority accuses a child of violating a rule and seeks from the child an explanation, whereupon a judgment of guilt is made, followed by physical contact and pain inflicted on the child. The Council finds no conditions under which corporal punishment so defined would be the treatment of choice in special education.

Para. 18 - Child Abuse and Neglect

The Council recognizes abused and neglected children as children with exceptionalities. As professionals concerned with the physical, emotional, and mental well-being of children, educators must take an active role in the protection of children from abuse and neglect. The Council reminds its members and citizens in general, of the availability of assault and battery statutes and calls upon its members to utilize such statutes when applicable in cases of child abuse. When child abuse occurs, swift action must be taken to report the incident and protect the child. Delays caused by not knowing what to do or failure to take action, contribute to the child's injury. Educators and related personnel are urged to learn how to recognize and report child abuse and neglect and to know the community resources for treating suspected cases.

Para. 19 - Managing Communicable and Contagious Diseases

Controlling the spread of communicable and contagious diseases within the schools has always been a problem faced by educators, the medical profession, and the public. Effective policies and procedures for managing such diseases in the schools have historically been developed by health agencies and implemented by the schools. These policies and procedures were primarily designed to manage acute, temporary conditions rather than chronic conditions which require continuous monitoring and remove children from interaction with other children while the condition is contagious or communicable.

Recent public awareness of chronic infectious diseases such as those with hepatitis B-virus, cytomegalovirus, herpes simplex virus, and HIV have raised concerns necessitating the reassessment or at least clarification of school policies and procedures. The Council believes that having a chronic infection does not in itself result in a need for special education. Further, The Council believes that schools and public health agencies should assure that any such infectious and communicable disease policies and procedures:

a. Do not exclude the affected child from the receipt of an appropriate education even when circumstances require the temporary removal of the child from contact with other children.

b. Provide that determination of a nontemporary alteration of a child's educational placement should be done on an individual basis, utilizing an interdisciplinary/interagency approach including the child's physician, public health personnel, the child's parents, and appropriate educational personnel.

c. Provide that decisions involving exceptional children's nontemporary alterations of educational placements or services constitute a change in the child's Individualized Education Program and should thus follow the procedures and protections required.

d. Recognize that children vary in the degree and manner in which they come into contact with other children and school staff.

e. Provide education staff with the necessary information, training, and hygienic resources to provide for a safe environment for students and educational staff.

f. Provide students with appropriate education about infectious diseases and hygienic measures to prevent the spread of such diseases.

g. Provide, where appropriate, infected children with education about the additional control measures that they can practice to prevent the transmission of the disease agent.

h. Enable educational personnel who are medically at high risk to work in environments which minimize such risk.

i. Provide educational personnel with adequate protections for such personnel and their families if they are exposed to such diseases through their employment.

The Council believes that special education personnel preparation programs should:

a. Educate students about infectious diseases and appropriate methods for their management.

b. Counsel students as to how to determine their level of medical risk in relation to certain diseases and the implications of such risk to career choice.

The Council believes that the manner in which policies for managing infectious diseases are developed and disseminated is important to their effective implementation. Therefore the following must be considered integral to any such process:

a. That they be developed through the collaborative efforts of health and education agencies at both the state, provincial and local levels, reflecting state, provincial and local educational, health and legal requirements.

b. That provision is made for frequent review and revision to reflect the ever-increasing knowledge being produced through research, case reports, and experience.

c. That policies developed be based on reliable identified sources of information and scientific principles endorsed by the medical and educational professions.

d. That such policies be understandable to students, professionals, and the public.

e. That policy development and dissemination be a continual process and disassociated from pressures associated with precipitating events.

Para. 20 - Career Education

Career education is the totality of experience through which one learns to live a meaningful, satisfying work life. Within the career education framework, work is conceptualized as conscious effort aimed at producing benefits for oneself and/or others. Career education provides the opportunity for children to learn, in the least restrictive environment possible, the academic, daily living, personal-social and occupational knowledge, and specific vocational skills necessary for attaining their highest levels of economic, personal, and social fulfillment. The individual can obtain this fulfillment though work (both paid and unpaid) and in a variety of other social roles and personal lifestyles, including his or her pursuits as a student, citizen, volunteer, family member, and participant in meaningful leisure time activities.

Children with exceptionalities (i.e., those whose characteristics range from profoundly and severely disabled to those who are richly endowed with talents and/or intellectual giftedness) include individuals whose career potentials range from sheltered to competitive work and living arrangements. Children with exceptionalities require career education experiences which will develop to the fullest extent possible their wide range of abilities, needs, and interests.

It is the position of The Council that individualized appropriate education for children with exceptionalities must include the opportunity for every student to attain his or her highest level of career potential through career education experiences. Provision for these educational experiences must be reflected in an individualized education program for each exceptional child which must include the following:

a. Nondiscriminatory, ongoing assessment of career interests, needs, and potentials which assures recognition of the strengths of the individual which can lead to a meaningful, satisfying career in a work oriented society. Assessment materials and procedures must not be discriminatory on the basis of race, sex, national origin, or exceptionality.

b. Career awareness, exploration, preparation, and placement experiences in the least restrictive school, living, and community environments that focus on the needs of the exceptional individual from early childhood through adulthood.

c. Specification and utilization of community and other services related to the career development of exceptional individuals (e.g., rehabilitation, transportation, industrial and business, psychological).

d. Involvement of parents or guardians and the exceptional student in career education planning.

Career education must not be viewed separately from the total curriculum. Rather, career education permeates the entire school program and even extends beyond it. It should be an infusion throughout the curriculum by knowledgeable teachers who modify the curriculum to integrate career development goals with current subject matter, goals, and content. It should prepare individuals for the several life roles that make up an individual's career. These life roles may include an economic role, a community role, a home role, an avocational role, a religious or moral role, and an aesthetic role. Thus, career education is concerned with the total person and his or her adjustment for community working and living.

Para. 21 - Treatment of Exceptional Persons in Textbooks

The Council proposes the following points as guidelines for early childhood, elementary, secondary, and higher education instructional materials so they more accurately and adequately reflect persons with exceptionalities as full and contributing members of society.

a. In print and nonprint educational materials, 10% of the contents should include or represent children or adults with an exceptionality.

b. Representation of persons with exceptionalities should be included in materials at all levels (early childhood through adult) and in all areas of study.

c. The representation of persons with exceptionalities should be accurate and free from stereotypes.

d. Persons with exceptionalities should be shown in the least restrictive environment. They should be shown participating in activities in a manner that will include them as part of society.

e. In describing persons with exceptionalities, the language used should be nondiscriminatory and free from value judgments.

f. Persons with exceptionalities and persons without exceptionalities should be shown interacting in ways that are mutually beneficial

g. Materials should provide a variety of appropriate role models of persons with exceptionalities.

h. Emphasis should be on uniqueness and worth of all persons, rather than on the differences between persons with and without exceptionalities.

i. Tokenism should be avoided in the representation of persons with exceptionalities.

Para. 22 - Technology

The Council for Exceptional Children recognizes that the appropriate application and modification of present and future technologies can improve the education of exceptional persons. CEC believes in equal access to technology and supports equal educational opportunities for technology utilization by all individuals. Present technologies include electronic tools, devices, media, and techniques such as (a) computers and microprocessors; (b) radio, television, and videodisc systems; © information and communication systems;

(d) robotics; and (e) assistive and prosthetic equipment and techniques. The Council believes in exploring and stimulating the utilization of these technologies in school, at home, at work, and in the community.

CEC encourages the development of product standards and consumer education that will lead to the appropriate and efficient matching of technological applications to individual and local conditions. CEC recognizes the need to communicate market needs and market expectations to decision makers in business, industry, and government.

CEC supports the continuous education of professionals who serve exceptional individuals, through (a) collection and dissemination of state-of-the-art information, (b) professional development, and © professional preparation of personnel to perform educational and other services for the benefit of exceptional individuals.

Para. 23 - Students with Special Health Care Needs

The Council for Exceptional Children believes that having a medical diagnosis that qualifies a student as one with a special health care need does not in itself result in a need for special education. Students with specialized health care needs are those who require specialized technological health care procedures for life support and/or health support during the school day. The Council believes the policies and procedures developed by schools and health care agencies that serve students with special health care needs should: (1) not exclude a student from receipt of appropriate special education and related services; (2) not exclude a student from receipt of appropriate educational services in the least restrictive environment; (3) not require educational agencies to assume financial responsibility for noneducationally related medical services; (4) define clearly the type, nature, and extent of appropriate related services to be provided and the nature of the appropriate provider; (5) assure that placement and service decisions involve interdisciplinary teams of personnel knowledgeable about the student, the meaning of evaluation data, and placement options; (6) promote a safe learning environment, including reasonable standards for a clean environment in which health risks can be minimized for all involved; (7) provide assurance that health care services are delivered by appropriate and adequately trained personnel; (8) provide appropriate medical and legal information about the special health care needs of students for all staff; (9) provide appropriate support mechanisms for students, families, and personnel involved with students with special health care needs; and (10) provide appropriate and safe transportation.

The Council for Exceptional Children believes that special education personnel preparation and continuing education programs should provide knowledge and skills related to: (1) the nature and management of students with special health care needs; (2) exemplary approaches and models for the delivery of services to students with special health care needs; and (3) the importance and necessity for establishing support systems for students, parents/families, and personnel.

Recognizing that this population of students is unique and relatively small, The Council for Exceptional Children still believes that the manner in which policies are developed and disseminated related to students with special health care needs is critically important to effective implementation. In development of policy and procedure for this low-incidence population, the following must be considered integral to any such process: (1) that it be developed through collaborative efforts of health and education agencies at state, provincial, and local levels; (2) that it reflects federal, state, provincial, and local educational, health, and legal requirements; (3) that it provides for frequent review and revision of intervention techniques and programs as a result of new knowledge identified through research, program evaluation and monitoring, and other review mechanisms; (4) that policies are supported by data obtained from medical and educational professions; (5) that policy development is easily understandable by students, professionals, and the public at large; and (6) that policy development and dissemination should be a continual process and disassociated from pressures associated with precipitating events.

Para. 24 - Use of Interpreters or Transliterators for Individuals Who are Deaf/Hard of Hearing

CEC recognizes that an increasing number of students who are deaf/hard of hearing are being educated in the public schools. CEC impresses upon the education field the importance of using appropriately trained and qualified persons to interpret and transliterate for students who are deaf/hard of hearing. CEC opposes the practice of using non-related or non-certified individuals to interpret or transliterate in classrooms. Additionally, CEC opposes the notion that "one size fits all" when ommunication modes and languages are involved. Therefore, CEC supports the following statements.

1. The practice of spontaneously pulling non-professional persons from their regularly assigned duties to fulfill the role of interpreter/transliterator when appropriate training has not been provided should be avoided altogether.

2. School districts, agencies, private schools or other employers/users should exhaust all means of obtaining professional personnel who are competent in the mode of communication used by the students before seeking the assistance of interpreters/transliterators.

3. Individuals certified to assess the communication needs of students who are deaf/hard of hearing should be consulted to determine the appropriate mode or language needed by an individual child. Providing interpretation or transliteration in a mode or language not used by the child is equally as problematic as providing no interpretation/transliteration at all, and the average signer or oral interpreter is often not qualified to make this judgment.

4. Interpreters (from natural sign languages such as ASL or Auslan to the spoken form of the country in which that language is used and vice versa) and transliterators (from English-based sign system, Cued Speech, oral interpreters, and those who use any sign system designed to pattern the grammar of that country's spoken language) should be trained and credentialed in their mode and language of communication along with training in special education procedures and guidelines, normal child development, and the roles and responsibilities of educational interpreters. Professionals using interpreters and transliterators also should receive training in the appropriate use of these individuals to maximize effective communication among professionals, students, and parents.

5. Competencies of interpreters and transliterators must be determined before using their services. Evaluations should be conducted by certified individuals, agencies or organizations from the community familiar with the mode, language, and needs of children and youth. Competencies should include, but are not limited to, high proficiency levels in the spoken language of the country and the target language (eg, spoken English or Czech to ASL or CSL, spoken language such as Spanish to Cued Speech or oral transliteration), knowledge of the culture and linguistic nuances, including Deaf Culture and other cultures of other spoken languages; and knowledge of cross-cultural, gender, and generational differences and expectations.

6. Upon mastery of these competencies, a certification, approval, or rating system should be required to ensure that interpreters and transliterators possess the skills necessary for providing effective services.

CHAPTER 04
ADMINISTRATIVE AND FISCAL IDENTITY

Para. 1 - Responsibility Defined

Responsibility for administering special education programs should be clearly defined so that accountability for service effectiveness can be maintained.

In the administration of the special education system, it must be clarified (a) who is to be responsible for various functions and decisions and (b) what procedures can be developed to provide adequate protection of the individual child's rights. When services essential to the improvement of a child's condition are rendered under several administrative auspices, as is so often the case with children and youth with exceptionalities, which agent or agency is to be responsible for providing which aspects of treatment needs to be clearly defined at every level to produce the most effective outcomes for the child.

The major functions commonly assigned to administrators of special education programs include the following:

a. Establishing and maintaining effective ways of identifying children with special education needs.

b. Assessing the special needs of children to determine what kinds of special programs and services should be provided for them.

c. Planning and organizing an appropriate variety of interventions or program alternatives for children with exceptionalities.

d. Marshaling the resources needed to conduct a comprehensive program of special education.

e. Using direction, coordination, and consultation as required to guide the efforts of all those who are engaged in the special education enterprise.

f. Conducting evaluation and research activities to reflect new emphases and to incorporate new knowledge and constantly improve special instruction and the quality of special services.

g. Involving community representatives in planning programs to ensure their understanding and support.

h. Conducting programs for staff development, such as inservice or continuing education.

Para. 2 - Leadership

The Council urges state/provincial and local education agencies to develop administrative structures on a policy-making level and to staff such programs with professionally qualified personnel who can provide dynamic leadership. Creative leadership at all levels of government is imperative for the development and improvement of programs for children and youth with exceptionalities. For this reason, The Council supports efforts to improve the quality of leadership and administrative operations in all phases of educational endeavor.

Para. 3 - Administrative Hierarchy

Every school system should contain a visible central administrative unit for special education programs and services which is at the same administrative hierarchical level as other major instructional program units.

The parameters of regular and special education should be articulated so that children may be afforded equal educational opportunity through the resources of either or both instructional programs.

Such articulation should be achieved through sensitive negotiations between the responsible agents of both regular and special education who meet in full parity. To protect the rights of all children to equal educational opportunity, the policy-making bodies of school systems should include administrators of both regular and special education.

Programs to meet the needs of children with exceptionalities are no less important than those designed to meet the needs of other children. The importance of programs to meet human needs should not be judged on the basis of the number of clients the programs are expected to serve.

Para. 4 - Special Education and School Budgets

Success of all education programs is dependent on the provision of adequate funding. This is essentially true of programs for children and youth with exceptionalities. Often funding for such programs becomes buried in general budgeting procedures. In such cases, children and youth with exceptionalities do not have the opportunity to have their needs directly considered by the decision-making bodies of government. Therefore, The Council urges that efforts be undertaken to assure that budgetary provisions for children and youth with exceptionalities be clearly identified. The Council opposes general funding procedures that would circumvent direct aid to programs for children and youth with exceptionalities.

Since children with exceptionalities have the same rights to education as other children, the educational needs of children with exceptionalities cannot be delayed until the needs and service demands of the majority of children have been satisfied. Educational resources are always likely to be finite. The application of the principle of "the greatest good for the greatest number" to determine which children's needs shall be met first directly contradicts our democratic society's declared commitment to equal educational opportunity for all children. History confirms that the social injustices and ill effects that flow from the application of the majority-first principle to educational budgeting are too serious for this principle to be used in educational financing.

Children with exceptionalities constitute a minority of the school population. The programs serving them represent a comparatively high financial investment in relation to the numbers of children served. In some school systems, money allocated to special education is regarded as an alternative to the improvement of regular school programs. The climate of competitive interests thus produced can jeopardize the stability of special education services.

The interests of the community are ill served if competition for funds is conducted on the basis of special interests. What is needed, rather, is the cooperation of both regular and special educators to educate the public in the desirability of meeting the needs of all children without discrimination or favoritism.

There is every reason to believe that the public interest is best protected when the responsibility for the deployment of public resources is placed in the hands of persons who are qualified by training and experience to make the necessary judgments. Thus, special education should play an active role in determining how resources are to be allocated. However, the community has the ultimate responsibility to determine goals and to evaluate performance.

Resources should be allocated to special education on the basis of programs to be provided, not on the basis of traditional categorical incidence estimates.

The mandate to provide all children with equal educational opportunities requires that all educators, whether regular or special, be equally concerned with the funding of both regular and special education programs. No school system can fulfill the mandate if rivalries for dollars are permitted to supersede the needs of children.

CHAPTER 05
SPECIAL EDUCATION AND THE COMMUNITY OUTSIDE THE EDUCATION SYSTEM

Para. 1 - Liaison with Other Agencies and Organizations

Children and youth with exceptionalities and their families require the services of many agencies which deal with their various needs. In most cases, individual agency efforts can be made more effective through a cooperative interagency and interdisciplinary approach whereby special education has a primary function for liaison with other agencies and organizations. This approach will not only encourage a consistent effort on the part of all concerned with the child's education and development, but will provide for joint establishment of the priorities and respective responsibilities for meeting the child's needs. Public policy should be encouraged at the state, provincial, and federal levels for a coordinated approach to multifunded projects under one application procedure to ensure comprehensive services to the child. Such policies should support and facilitate intergovernmental cooperation as well as interagency linkage. The Council encourages policies which promote a coordinated approach to planning for the needs of children and youth with exceptionalities and which strengthen the relationships of special education to public and private agencies providing services. The Council at all levels should consistently support a coordinated effort.

Para. 2 - Public Participation

Administrative units at all levels of government responsible for providing leadership must have responsibility for developing policy regarding the education of children and youth with exceptionalities. However, such policy must reflect the thinking of all persons involved in the education of children and youth with exceptionalities. The Council believes that advisory committees can help government agencies assess problems, plan and set priorities, and develop and oversee policies regarding the education of children and youth with exceptionalities. The Council further believes that all policies involving education of children and youth with exceptionalities should be brought before recurring public and legislative scrutiny.

Para. 3 - The School and the Family

Parents must have access to all available necessary information in order to be able to make optimal decisions about the child's education and to fulfill the family's obligations to the child.

As a means of strengthening special education programs, the parents of children with exceptionalities and organized community groups should be given a responsible voice in educational policy formation and planning activities.

The primary consumers of educational services, the children, should not be ignored as a valuable resource in the evaluation of the organization and delivery of services.

As a means of strengthening the family in fulfilling its obligations to children with exceptional needs, the schools should provide educationally related counseling and family services. In cases of clear educational neglect, the schools, through qualified professional personnel, should make extraordinary arrangements for educational services.

Access includes making information available at convenient times and locations and providing information in the parent's native language or mode of communication whenever necessary.

Part. 4 - Private Sector

The private sector (nonprofit) has long played a significant role in the field of special education. The elements of the private sector (nonprofit) are varied and encompass the full gamut of levels of educational programs and services from preschool education through higher education, research, demonstration projects, personnel training, technology, and the development and production of media and materials. Increasingly, a working relationship has developed between the public and private sectors (nonprofit) regarding children and youth with exceptionalities.

The Council believes that private enterprise (nonprofit) can make major contributions to the development of adequate special education services. The Council urges cooperation between government and private enterprise (nonprofit) to meet the needs of children and youth with exceptionalities. The Council urges that legislation be flexible enough to allow administrative agencies to involve the private sector (nonprofit) in all aspects of program development.

The Council believes that the opportunity for all children to receive an education is a public responsibility, but that program operation of such services may be conducted in varied settings and through a variety of public and private (nonprofit) agencies. For this reason, The Council supports the development and provision of special services in both the public and private sectors (nonprofit) and the support for such services through public funds, under public control and supervision.

The Council believes that when children with exceptionalities receive their education in the private sector (nonprofit) as a matter of public policy, then the appropriate state public agency shall approve the education program and personnel in such facilities, certify that the program is appropriate to the child's educational needs and is provided at no expense to the child or his family, certify that the facility meets appropriate health and safety standards, and guarantee that all rights of children with exceptionalities and their families are maintained.

CHAPTER 06
COMMUNITY-BASED SERVICES

Para. 1 - Prerequisites

Significant nationwide trends, both to reduce the populations of institutions and to improve the services provided for those who are institutionalized, necessitate comprehensive public policies on community-based services. Numerous exceptional children and adults reside in institutions. The quantity and quality of educational and other service programs provided in these facilities vary greatly. Considerable evidence, however, has been collected demonstrating that many institutions for exceptional citizens have failed to meet the needs of their residents. Institutionalization, in many instances, has violated basic individual rights and fostered inhumane deprivation. Rights violated include the opportunity to live in a humane environment and be provided with individual programs of treatment designed to allow each person to develop to the greatest degree possible.

Despite public and professional awareness of deplorable institutional conditions, persons with exceptionalities who could not live in natural homes were routinely placed in institutions. Alternative service arrangements were usually not available and an implicit assumption was made that some persons with disabilities were incapable of growth. The lack of quality services and the stigma of negative attitudes must be changed.

The Council, recognizing the necessity for community-based services, maintains that the human services system must adhere to the principle of normalization to avoid destructive individual and societal consequences and adhere to the following prerequisites:

a. Central to a person's growth and dignity is a right to live within the community, with access to high quality and appropriate services.

b. A legal mandate with fixed responsibility must exist providing community services for all persons, including those now institutionalized.

c. The goal of community services is to assure the greatest developmental gains on the part of the individual through maximum flexibility in all services.

d. The ongoing process of normalizing the service system requires developing a continuum of community-based living environments and the selective use of the full range of services available to the entire community.

e. Multiple and diverse methods of safeguarding program quality are essential at every level of responsibility.

f. All programs provided to exceptional persons must include written standards governing service delivery.

g. When a state restricts an individual's fundamental liberty, it must adhere to the principle of least restrictive environment and, further, absolutely guarantee due process.

Para. 2 - Characteristics

A comprehensive community-based service system for exceptional persons should reflect the following characteristics:

a. Services must meet the needs of persons of all ages, must accommodate the problems of individuals possessing all degrees of disabilities, and be available when needed and where needed by the individual.

b. Services must be appropriately located in populous neighborhoods and should be compatible with the surrounding community.

c. Services must be based upon a systematic plan for continuity which interrelates with other established services.

d. Services must have a legally vested authority which enables the fixing of responsibility and accountability with implementation power.

e. Services must be designed to permit the placement of exceptional persons in high quality programs in the least restrictive environment.

f. Services must be economically sound in meeting human development needs.

Para. 3 - The Need for Flexibility and Development

Because of rapid changes and developments in the environmental factors that influence the characteristics of children and the conditions of their lives, special education should maintain a flexibility that permits it to adapt to changing requirements.

Some of the events and changes that have had major impact on special education in recent years are the following: a rubella epidemic, discovery of preventatives for retrolental fibroplasia, increasing numbers of premature births, increasing awareness of the deleterious effects of poverty and malnutrition, new techniques in surgical intervention, invention of individual electronic hearing aids, and adaptation of low-vision aids. Changes and developments in public health, medicine, technology, and social programs may have only a small total effect on school systems, but they frequently have major impacts on special education programs. Changes in one aspect of special education quickly are reflected in other aspects of the field as, for example, the rapid development of day school programs for children with exceptionalities which has been reflected in a more severely disabled population in residential schools.

Special educators must seek to be highly flexible in the provision of services and the use of technology and techniques to meet the changing needs of children with exceptionalities.

School administrators and special educators have particular responsibility for sustaining their professional awareness and development as a basis for changing programs to meet changing needs.

Para. 4 - Prevention of Handicapping Conditions

Increasing knowledge of the biological and social causes of many handicapping conditions now makes some conditions preventable. The Council believes that appropriate prenatal counseling and care and intervention services could prevent or reduce the severity of many handicapping conditions. Therefore, The Council believes that there should be substantial governmental attention and resources devoted to prevention and the amelioration of the impact of handicapping conditions including:

a. Research and development

b. Public awareness

c. Prenatal services

d. Child- and family-centered early intervention services

e. Family and parenting education and support programs for teenagers and other high-risk populations

f. Reduction of social and environmental factors that cause handicapping conditions.

CHAPTER 07
EDUCATION OF THE GIFTED AND TALENTED

Para. 1 - Gifted and Talented Children as Exceptional Children

Special education for the gifted is not a question of advantage to the individual versus advantage to society. It is a matter of advantage to both. Society has an urgent and accelerated need to develop the abilities and talents of those who promise high contribution. To ignore this obligation and this resource is not only shortsighted but does violence to the basic concept of full educational opportunity for all.

Special educators should vigorously support programs for the gifted and talented as consistent with their concept of the need for special assistance for all children with exceptionalities. Such programs should reflect both the cognitive and noncognitive needs of the gifted and talented.

Para. 2 - Identification

Gifted and talented children are those who are capable of high performance as identified by professionally qualified personnel. These children require different educational programs and/or services beyond those normally provided by the regular school program in order to realize their full potential in contribution to self and society.

Broad search and an early identification system for the identification of gifted and talented children within all sectors of the population should be the hallmark of an adequate educational system. Identification procedures should also reflect individual means of identifying children with general intellectual ability, specific academic abilities, leadership abilities, and abilities in the fine and performing arts.

Para. 3 - Delivery of Services

No single administrative plan or educational provision is totally appropriate for the gifted and talented. Certain administrative and instructional arrangements may provide settings in which the gifted and talented are likely to perform more adequately. In the final analysis, however, the task is one of accommodation to the needs of the individual.

New arrangements and new provisions must be utilized, including freedom to pursue interests which might not fit the prescribed curriculum, opportunities for open blocks of time, opportunities for consultation with persons and use of resources external to the classroom, and opportunities to bypass those portions of the curriculum which have been previously achieved by the individual. These kinds of arrangements must present options across all educational settings and procedures within all programs for the gifted and talented, whether in the regular classroom or in highly specialized situations.

Special education for the gifted and talented demands individualization within special programs in terms of student needs, as well as differentiation between programs for the gifted and talented and programs for other children and adults.

A program of special education for the gifted and talented should provide continuing and appropriate educational experiences from preschool into adult years.

Para. 4 - Preparation of School and Leadership Personnel

Special preparation is required for those educators who have either specific or general responsibilities for educating the gifted and talented. Teachers and other professional educators who work with the gifted and talented need special training in both program content and process skills. Such training should be recognized by appropriate certification in the case of teachers and should receive the general support of local, state, provincial, federal, and private interests.

Para. 5 - Demonstration Programs

The preparation of school personnel in the education of the gifted and talented should be carried out in settings which permit opportunities to examine relevant research and to observe innovative administrative provisions and exemplary instruction. This requires extensive library services, ongoing research or access to such research, and most importantly, centers in which teachers may observe and try out new styles of teaching appropriate to the education of the gifted and talented.

Special model or demonstration programs should be established to illustrate to educators and others the kind and range of innovative program efforts that are possible and effective in the education of gifted and talented students.

Para. 6 - Research and Development

Research and development resources should be focused on the needs of the gifted and talented in order to develop new methodologies and curricula and to allow educators and others to evaluate current and proposed methods.

Para. 7 - Parents and the Public

One responsibility of the special educator is to educate the parents of gifted and talented children concerning their children's needs and rights.

The educational needs of the gifted and talented also warrant planned programs of public information, particularly at the local community level. Special educators should accept these responsibilities as an important part of their professional involvement.

Para. 8 - Financial Support

Although programs for the gifted and talented can sometimes be initiated at relatively modest cost, it is important that funds for this purpose be earmarked at local, state or provincial, and national levels.

Principal expenditures should be directed toward the employment of leadership personnel, the development of methods and programs, and of particular importance at the local level, the preparation of persons for the support and implementation of such methods and programs in the schools.

The importance of optimal educational services for the gifted and talented merits the expenditure of funds in appropriate amounts toward this end by all levels of government as well as by other sources.

CHAPTER 08
ETHNIC AND MULTICULTURAL GROUPS

Para. 1 - Preamble

The Council believes that all policy statements previously adopted by CEC related to children with and without exceptionalities, as well as children with gifts and talents, are relevant and applicable to both minority and nonminority individuals. In order to highlight concerns of special interest to members of ethnic and multicultural groups, the following policy statements have been developed:

Para. 2 - Ethnicity and Exceptionality

The Council recognizes the special and unique needs of members of ethnic and multicultural groups and pledges its full support toward promoting all efforts which will help to bring them into full and equitable participation and membership in the total society.

Para. 3 - Identification, Testing, and Placement

The Council supports the following statements related to the identification, testing, and placement of children from ethnic and multicultural groups who are also exceptional.

a. Child-find procedures should identify children by ethnicity as well as type and severity of exceptionality or degree of giftedness.

b. Program service reporting procedures should identify children by ethnicity as well as exceptionality or degree of giftedness.

c. All testing and evaluation materials and methods used for the classification and placement of children from ethnic and multicultural groups should be selected and administered so as not to be racially or culturally discriminatory.

d. Children with exceptionalities who are members of ethnic and multicultural groups should be tested in their dominant language by examiners who are fluent in that language and familiar with the cultural heritage of the children being tested.

e. Communication of test results with parents of children from ethnic and multicultural groups should be done in the dominant language of those parents and conducted by persons involved in the testing or familiar with the particular exceptionality, fluent in that language, and familiar with the cultural heritage of those parents.

All levels of government should establish procedures to ensure that testing and evaluation materials and methods used for the purpose of classification and placement of children are selected and administered so as not to be linguistically, racially, or culturally discriminatory.

Para. 4 - Programming and Curriculum Adaptation

The Council supports the following statements related to programming and curriculum adaptation for children from ethnic and multicultural groups:

a. Long-term placement should be avoided unless students are reevaluated at prescribed intervals by individuals qualified in assessing such students with the most appropriate culture-free assessment instruments available.

b. All school districts should take necessary steps to ensure that both students and their parents fully comprehend the implications of and the reasons for proposed programming decisions, including the nature and length of placement. Parents should be fully involved in the decision-making process.

c. Culturally appropriate individualized education programs should be designed which include the child's present level of educational performance, annual goals, short-term objectives, and specific educational services to be provided.

d. It is of utmost importance to identify children's relative language proficiency so that language-appropriate special education programs may be provided (e.g., bilingual special education and special education programs incorporating English-as-a-Second-Language instruction).

e. Children with exceptionalities who are members of ethnic and multicultural groups should have access to special cultural and language programs provided to nonexceptional group members, with the necessary program adaptations to make the program beneficial to the exceptional child or youth.

f. Culturally appropriate educational materials should be readily available in ample quantity so that all students, including those from ethnic and multicultural groups, may benefit from their content.

g. Curriculum should be adapted or developed to meet the unique needs of children from all cultural groups. Curriculum should include a multicultural perspective which recognizes the value of diverse cultural traditions to society as well as the contributions of all cultural groups of American and Canadian society.

h. It is critical for teachers to recognize individual language and cultural differences as assets rather than deficits. Furthermore, those assets should be utilized to enhance education for all children, including those from ethnic and multicultural groups.

Para. 5 - Technical Assistance and Training

Special and unique concerns of Council members from ethnic and multicultural groups which are related to technical assistance, training, and services will receive the attention and support of the Special Assistant to the Executive Director for Ethnic and Multicultural Concerns.

Para. 6 - Special Projects

a. The Council will continue its interests in projects that meet the needs and concerns of all its membership. Furthermore, The Council will actively search for projects that include special concerns of members from ethnic and multicultural groups.

b. Projects that include special and unique concerns of members from ethnic and multicultural groups to be considered for development and implementation will receive the combined attention and support of various Council staff and the Special Assistant to the Executive Director for Ethnic and Multicultural Concerns.

c. All projects of The Council will include opportunities for perspective and participation by ethnic and multicultural groups in formulation, implementation, and evaluation phases.

Para. 7 - Cooperation with Organizations, Disciplines, and Individuals

a. The Council will support efforts to explore with other organizations mutual concerns and issues related to ethnic and multicultural children and their families. In the process, The Council will take care not to intervene in the internal affairs of any of the other organizations.

b. The Council will support efforts to work cooperatively with other organizations in activities and services related to children with exceptionalities from ethnic and multicultural groups and their families.

Para. 8 - Use of Interpreters/Translators for Culturally and Linguistically Diverse Individuals (Other than Hard of Hearing)

a. The practice of spontaneously pulling non-professional bilingual persons from their regularly assigned duties to fulfill the role of interpreter/translator when appropriate training has not been provided should be avoided altogether.

b. School districts, agencies, private schools or other employers/users should exhaust all means of obtaining professional personnel who are bilingual before seeking the assistance of interpreters/translators.

c. If the use of interpreters/translators is the only alternative, training should be provided in the briefing, interaction and debriefing processes on interpreting/translating, and in special education procedures and guidelines.

d. Professionals in organizations using interpreters/translators should also be trained in the appropriate use of these personnel to maximize effective communication among professionals, students and parents.

e. Competencies of interpreters/translators must be determined before using their services. Competencies should include, but are not limited to, high proficiency levels in English and the target language; knowledge of cultural and linguistic nuances; knowledge of cross-cultural, gender, and generational differences and expectations.

f. Upon mastery of the competencies, certification or rating through an approved system should be required to ensure that interpreters/translators possess the skills necessary for providing effective services.

CHAPTER 09
SPECIAL EDUCATION'S RESPONSIBILITIES TO ADULTS WITH DISABILITIES

Para. 1 - Preamble

The Council believes that most students can learn to become contributing citizens, family members, employees, learners, and active participants in meaningful vocational, recreational, and leisure pursuits. We believe, therefore, that it is an important purpose of education to assist students in the attainment of such outcomes. Further, we believe that education from early childhood through adult education should focus on assuring that students with exceptionalities attain such outcomes.

Para. 2 - Collaborative Responsibilities

In order to assist students with exceptionalities to become productive workers and independent adults, special education should work in collaboration with adult service agencies to influence the provision of needed services from such agencies. Collaboration should include:

a. Working with postsecondary vocational/technical institutions, adult education, rehabilitation, and independent living centers that assess, train, and place persons with exceptionalities in meaningful work situations.

b. Interaction and collaboration to provide relevant information to agencies and organizations that will assist them to conduct job site assessments, training follow-up, and continuing training or education for persons with exceptionalities.

c. Assisting appropriate special educators to become knowledgeable about their community's labor market needs and build close working relationships and partnerships with the business and industrial sector so that receptivity toward potential employees with exceptionalities is increased.

d. Promotion of adult and continuing education and literacy service opportunities for adults with exceptionalities.

e. Conducting systematic follow-up studies on former students so that curriculum and instruction can be appropriately modified to be responsive to employment and independent living needs.

f. Advocating the elimination of attitudinal and physical barriers which reduce the ability of these individuals to fully participate in society and increase vocational, recreational, and leisure opportunities.

g. Supporting the participation of special educators on advisory committees and in staff development and inservice training programs of agencies, organizations, and the business and industrial sector that address the needs of adults with exceptionalities and how they can be met.

h. Promoting an early close working relationship with adult service agency personnel, so secondary students can be provided more successful transition from school to adult life, and advocating for the provision of needed adult services by these agencies.

SECTION THREE - PART 2

PROFESSIONAL STANDARDS AND PRACTICE

CHAPTER 01
PREPARATION AND UTILIZATION OF PERSONNEL

Para. 1 - Right to Quality Instruction

The quality of educational services for children and youth with exceptionalities resides in the abilities, qualifications, and competencies of the personnel who provide the services. There is a serious deficit in the present availability of fully qualified personnel able to extend such services. This lack of competent personnel seriously hampers efforts to extend educational services to all children and youth with exceptionalities. There is a need to investigate new modes for evaluation of professional competence in the desire to accelerate the process of training effective professionals and paraprofessionals in significant numbers to meet the needs of the field. The Council affirms the principle that, through public policy, each student with an exceptionality is entitled to instruction and services by professionally trained and competent personnel. In addition, there is a need for new and appropriate training patterns which allow for broadening the role of special educators in a variety of settings to work in teams with other educators and children and youth with exceptionalities and for training the necessary supportive and ancillary personnel.

Para. 2 - Continuing Professional Development

As standards, practice, policy, and service delivery systems change, employing education agencies have a responsibility to assure that all professionals and others involved in the education of individuals with exceptionalities have the requisite knowledge and skills. Accordingly, CEC believes that both general and special education teachers and administrators, and other ancillary staff must have access to state-of-the-art knowledge and documented effective practices designed for students with exceptionalities. Therefore, access to the evolving knowledge base of effective practice is essential to maintaining programs that can respond to the needs of all students with exceptionalities. To this end, CEC calls upon the federal government and professional associations, states/provinces, local school districts, institutions of higher education, and other relevant entities to commit the necessary resources to professional development programs that are grounded in adult learning principles and reflect professional standards for continuing education.

Because effective special education is dependent on the continuous improvement of what special educators know and are able to do, CEC believes that all special education professionals must be committed to and engage in ongoing professional development that advances their practice. We further believe that professionals must have the opportunity to acquire knowledge and skills through a broad array of venues, including, but not limited to, institutions of higher education, professional associations, state/provincial education agencies, and local school districts. We further encourage collaboration among all of these entities in designing and implementing high quality professional development. Employing agencies must provide resources, including release time, to enable each special educator to engage in continuing professional development throughout her/his career. We further believe that employers and professional organizations should recognize and reward special education professionals for improving their knowledge and skills.

Para. 3 - Federal Role in Personnel Preparation

Through legislation, the federal government has played a dominant role in supporting initial efforts to prepare personnel for educating children and youth with exceptionalities. The Council believes that the federal government should continue and expand its efforts to train high-level leadership personnel, assist through leadership and financial support the development of agencies to prepare personnel, and conduct research in new systems of preparing and utilizing personnel and meeting personnel needs. Definitive data are needed concerning personnel utilization and retention and other factors of personnel usage.

Para. 4 - State, Provincial, and Local Role in Personnel Preparation

In recent years, state, provincial, and local governments, in order to improve professional competencies, have made greater efforts to support formal training programs in colleges and universities and facilitate inservice and workshop efforts. The Council believes that such activities should be increased and that greater state, provincial, and local financial support should be given to their development and operation. The Council advocates extension of state, provincial, and federal funding to new and emerging special education services.

Para. 5 - National Recruitment

Further efforts need to be undertaken to develop a national program to attract more qualified and motivated individuals into the field of special education. Such a program should include efforts to recruit more members from ethnic and multicultural groups into the field and to provide employment opportunities for those persons trained. The Council believes that such a program must be conducted through national leadership with full involvement and participation of all levels of government and professional organizations. It is only through such a well coordinated effort in recruitment that the field's needs for qualified and motivated personnel can ever be met.

Para. 6 - Responsibility of Higher Education

Colleges and universities have an obligation to develop and coordinate their resources in support of programs for exceptional children. The obligation comprises a number of factors:

a. To provide through scholarly inquiry an expanded knowledge base for special education programs.

b. To provide training for various professional and paraprofessional personnel needed to conduct programs for students with exceptionalities.

c. To cooperate in the development and field testing of innovative programs.

d. To provide for the coordinated development of programs across disciplines and professions so that training and service models are congruent with emerging models for comprehensive community services.

e. To provide all students, whether or not they are in programs relating specifically to children with exceptionalities, a basis for understanding and appreciating human differences.

f. To exemplify in their own programs of training, research, and community service—and even in their architecture—a concern for accommodating and upgrading the welfare of handicapped and gifted persons.

g. To cooperate with schools, agencies, and community groups in the creation and maintenance of needed special education programs.

Para. 7 - Government Role in Research

The Council recommends additional federal funding to bring about effective coordination of services and research efforts in order to provide a national information service encompassing curriculum methods and education technology. Funds from all levels of government should be made available for the development of more effective information and dissemination services. To facilitate more effective dissemination, an interchangeable coding and retrieval system compatible with educational enterprises and disciplines should be established across organization, agency, and government lines. Considering the exceptional child, through the teacher, as the ultimate recipient of services, The Council believes that information and dissemination systems should be coordinated so that a concerted and unified thrust is possible. Such systems should not be unique to geographic areas but national in scope.

Para. 8 - Dissemination of Research

The Council sees research and its dissemination as inextricably interrelated. No longer can these two functions be considered as separate entities if children and youth with exceptionalities are to benefit from such enterprises. The Council recommends that all government funded research projects include a means for dissemination that will contribute toward upgrading the instruction of children and youth with exceptionalities.

The Council strongly recommends that government-approved dissemination activities be provided for separately in the federal education budget and not subsumed under some other priority. Further, it is recommended that dissemination not only include information delivery, but also include the identification and implementation of better educational practices and a process to train school personnel in the implementation of the improved practices and procedures.

A coordinating process for such a system is mandatory in order to identify, redirect, and deliver information among the various parts of the system. The goal is to constantly survey the information needs of multiple audiences; inform appropriate agencies who can develop materials, methods, programs, and strategies to meet those needs; inform users of worthwhile and proven resources; and encourage their implementation.

Para. 9 - Focus of Research

The Council believes that greater emphasis needs to be given to improving educational methods and curriculum for children and youth with exceptionalities. It is suggested that government agencies give particular attention to applied educational research which would provide for the empirical evaluation of educational materials, analysis of teacher-pupil interaction, efficacy of media and technology as they relate to the instructional process, and development and evaluation of innovative instructional methods for children and youth with exceptionalities.

Equally important, as has been learned from the developing fields associated with the education of exceptional children, is the belief that research must be conducted regarding how the human service delivery system can be made available to formerly institutionalized persons with exceptionalities. The Council believes that such research should be highly programmatic in nature and should clearly focus on the development of new policies and approaches for the delivery and evaluation of needed and provided services. At a minimum, such research must focus upon the implementation and continuous evaluation of the utilization of the individualized educational program.

Para. 10 - Preparation of Personnel for Exceptional Children from Ethnic and Multicultural Groups

The Council supports the following personnel preparation policy recommendations to assist teachers and other professional personnel to improve their skills in meeting the needs of children from ethnic and multicultural groups:

a. Teachers and college faculty members and others who provide training should include information about the diversity of cultural and linguistic differences in their preservice and inservice training programs.

b. Professional personnel should be required to receive training in adapting instruction to accommodate children with different learning styles who are members of ethnic and multicultural groups.

c. College and university preservice training programs should include clinical, practicum, or other field experiences with specific focus on learning about exceptional children from ethnic and multicultural groups.

CHAPTER 02
PROFESSIONAL STANDARDS, RIGHTS, AND RESPONSIBILITIES

Para. 1 - Preamble

As public awareness increases and public policies expand, new sets of conditions are created under which professionals in special education must function. While such awareness and policies may be powerful forces for improvement in the field, they do not of themselves deliver appropriate education to persons with exceptionalities. Effective education for persons with exceptionalities is also dependent upon qualified professionals who work under appropriate standards and conditions and are able to ensure their own professional rights and responsibilities.

Professionals must be adequately prepared and have a supportive environment which enables them to meet new demands. As advocates for persons with exceptionalities they must have the right to be responsive to and responsible for the vulnerable persons whom they serve. Finally, professionals must continually advance the knowledge, skills, behaviors, and values that make up the collective basis for practice and decision making for those working in the field. The combined energies of the profession and The Council for Exceptional Children are needed to accomplish these goals.

Therefore, The Council believes that professionals practicing in the field should be able to do so according to recognized standards of practice and a professional code of ethics; and that only persons qualified to provide special educational services should be eligible for employment in instructional, administrative, and support roles in programs serving persons with exceptionalities.

For these reasons, The Council is committed to the development, promotion, and implementation of standards of preparation and practice, code of ethics, and appropriate certification and/or licensure in order to continue its leadership role in supporting professionals who serve persons with exceptionalities.

Para. 2 - Code of Ethics

We declare the following principles to be the Code of Ethics for educators of persons with exceptionalities. Members of the special education profession are responsible for upholding and advancing these principles. Members of The Council for Exceptional Children agree to judge and be judged by them in accordance with the spirit and provisions of this Code.

a. Special education professionals are committed to developing the highest educational and quality of life potential of individuals with exceptionalities.

b. Special education professionals promote and maintain a high level of competence and integrity in practicing their profession.

c. Special education professionals engage in professional activities which benefit exceptional individuals, their families, other colleagues, students, or research subjects.

d. Special education professionals exercise objective professional judgment in the practice of their profession.

e. Special education professionals strive to advance their knowledge and skills regarding the education of individuals with exceptionalities.

f. Special education professionals work within the standards and policies of their profession.

g. Special education professionals seek to uphold and improve where necessary the laws, regulations, and policies governing the delivery of special education and related services and the practice of their profession.

h. Special education professionals do not condone or participate in unethical or illegal acts, nor violate professional standards adopted by the Delegate Assembly of CEC.

Para. 3 - Standards for Professional Practice

3.1   PROFESSIONALS IN RELATION TO PERSONS WITH EXCEPTIONALITIES AND THEIR FAMILIES

a. Instructional Responsibilities

Special education personnel are committed to the application of professional expertise to ensure the provision of quality education for all individuals with exceptionalities. Professionals strive to:

(1) Identify and use instructional methods and curricula that are appropriate to their area of professional practice and effective in meeting persons' with exceptionalities needs.

(2) Participate in the selection and use of appropriate instructional materials, equipment, supplies, and other resources needed in the effective practice of their profession.

(3) Create safe and effective learning environments which contribute to fulfillment of needs, stimulation of learning, and self-concept.

(4) Maintain class size and case loads which are conducive to meeting the individual instructional needs of individuals with exceptionalities.

(5) Use assessment instruments and procedures that do not discriminate against persons with exceptionalities on the basis of race, color, creed, sex, national origin, age, political practices, family or social background, sexual orientation, or exceptionality.

(6) Base grading, promotion, graduation, and/or movement out of the program on the individual goals and objectives for individuals with exceptionalities.

(7) Provide accurate program data to administrators, colleagues and parents, based on efficient and objective record keeping practices, for the purpose of decision making.

(8) Maintain confidentiality of information except when information is released under specific conditions of written consent and statutory confidentiality requirements.

b. Management of Behavior

Special education professionals participate with other professionals and with parents in an interdisciplinary effort in the management of behavior. Professionals:

(1) Apply only those disciplinary methods and behavioral procedures which they have been instructed to use and which do not undermine the dignity of the individual or the basic human rights of persons with exceptionalities, such as corporal punishment.

(2) Clearly specify the goals and objectives for behavior management practices in the person's with exceptionalities Individualized Education Program.

(3) Conform to policies, statutes, and rules established by state/ provincial and local agencies relating to judicious application of disciplinary methods and behavioral procedures.

(4) Take adequate measures to discourage, prevent, and intervene when a colleague's behavior is perceived as being detrimental to exceptional students.

(5) Refrain from aversive techniques unless repeated trials of other methods have failed and only after consultation with parents and appropriate agency officials.

c. Support Procedures

(1) Adequate instruction and supervision shall be provided to professionals before they are required to perform support services for which they have not been prepared previously.

(2) Professionals may administer medication, where state/provincial policies do not preclude such action, if qualified to do so or if written instructions are on file which state the purpose of the medication, the conditions under which it may be administered, possible side effects, the physician's name and phone number, and the professional liability if a mistake is made. The professional will not be required to administer medication.

(3) Professionals note and report to those concerned whenever changes in behavior occur in conjunction with the administration of medication or at any other time.

d. Parent Relationships

Professionals seek to develop relationships with parents based on mutual respect for their roles in achieving benefits for the exceptional person. Special education professionals:

(1) Develop effective communication with parents, avoiding technical terminology, using the primary language of the home, and other modes of communication when appropriate.

(2) Seek and use parents' knowledge and expertise in planning, conducting, and evaluating special education and related services for persons with exceptionalities.

(3) Maintain communications between parents and professionals with appropriate respect for privacy and confidentiality.

(4) Extend opportunities for parent education utilizing accurate information and professional methods.

(5) Inform parents of the educational rights of their children and of any proposed or actual practices which violate those rights.

(6) Recognize and respect cultural diversities which exist in some families with persons with exceptionalities.

(7) Recognize that relationship of home and community environmental conditions affects the behavior and outlook of the exceptional person.

e. Advocacy

Special education professionals serve as advocates for exceptional students by speaking, writing, and acting in a variety of situations on their behalf. They:

(1) Continually seek to improve government provisions for the education of persons with exceptionalities while ensuring that public statements by professionals as individuals are not construed to represent official policy statements of the agency that employs them.

(2) Work cooperatively with and encourage other professionals to improve the provision of special education and related services to persons with exceptionalities.

(3) Document and objectively report to one's supervisors or administrators inadequacies in resources and promote appropriate corrective action.

(4) Monitor for inappropriate placements in special education and intervene at appropriate levels to correct the condition when such inappropriate placements exist.

(5) Follow local, state/provincial and federal laws and regulations which mandate a free appropriate public education to exceptional students and the protection of the rights of persons with exceptionalities to equal opportunities in our society.

3.2 PROFESSIONAL EMPLOYMENT

a. Certification and Qualification

Professionals ensure that only persons deemed qualified by having met state/provincial minimum standards are employed as teachers, administrators, and related service providers for individuals with exceptionalities.

b. Employment

(1) Professionals do not discriminate in hiring on the basis of race, color, creed, sex, national origin, age, political practices, family or social background, sexual orientation, or exceptionality.

(2) Professionals represent themselves in an ethical and legal manner in regard to their training and experience when seeking new employment.

(3) Professionals give notice consistent with local education agency policies when intending to leave employment.

(4) Professionals adhere to the conditions of a contract or terms of an appointment in the setting where they practice.

(5) Professionals released from employment are entitled to a written explanation of the reasons for termination and to fair and impartial due process procedures.

(6) Special education professionals share equitably the opportunities and benefits (salary, working conditions, facilities, and other resources) of other professionals in the school system.

(7) Professionals seek assistance, including the services of other professionals, in instances where personal problems threaten to interfere with their job performance.

(8) Professionals respond objectively when requested to evaluate applicants seeking employment.

(9) Professionals have the right and responsibility to resolve professional problems by utilizing established procedures, including grievance procedures, when appropriate.

c. Assignment and Role

(1) Professionals should receive clear written communication of all duties and responsibilities, including those which are prescribed as conditions of their employment.

(2) Professionals promote educational quality, and intra- and interprofessional cooperation through active participation in the planning, policy development, management and evaluation of the special education program and the education program at large so that programs remain responsive to the changing needs of persons with exceptionalities.

(3) Professionals practice only in areas of exceptionality, at age levels, and in program models for which they are prepared by their training and/or experience.

(4) Adequate supervision of and support for special education professionals is provided by other professionals qualified by their training and experience in the area of concern.

(5) The administration and supervision of special education professionals provides for clear lines of accountability.

(6) The unavailability of substitute teachers or support personnel, including aides, does not result in the denial of special education services to a greater degree than to that of other educational programs.

d. Professional Development

(1) Special education professionals systematically advance their knowledge and skills in order to maintain a high level of competence and response to the changing needs of persons with exceptionalities by pursuing a program of continuing education including but not limited to participation in such activities as inservice training, professional conferences/workshops, professional meetings, continuing education courses, and the reading of professional literature.

(2) Professionals participate in the objective and systematic evaluation of themselves, colleagues, services, and programs for the purpose of continuous improvement of professional performance.

(3) Professionals in administrative positions support and facilitate professional development.

3.3   PROFESSIONALS IN RELATION TO THE PROFESSION AND TO OTHER PROFESSIONALS

a.   To the Profession

(1) Special education professionals assume responsibility for participating in professional organizations and adherence to the standards and codes of ethics of those organizations.

(2) Special education professionals have a responsibility to provide varied and exemplary supervised field experiences for persons in undergraduate and graduate preparation programs.

(3) Special education professionals refrain from using professional relationships with students and parents for personal advantage.

(4) Special education professionals take an active position in the regulation of the profession through use of appropriate procedures for bringing about changes.

(5) Special education professionals initiate, support and/or participate in research related to the education of persons with exceptionalities with the aim of improving the quality of educational services, increasing the accountability of programs, and generally benefiting persons with exceptionalities. They:

(a) Adopt procedures that protect the rights and welfare of subjects participating in the research.

(b) Interpret and publish research results with accuracy and a high quality of scholarship.

(c) Support a cessation of the use of any research procedure which may result in undesirable consequences for the participant.

(d) Exercise all possible precautions to prevent misapplication or misutilization of a research effort, by self or others.

b.   To Other Professionals

Special education professionals function as members of interdisciplinary teams and the reputation of the profession resides with them. They:

(1) Recognize and acknowledge the competencies and expertise of members representing other disciplines as well as those of members in their own disciplines.

(2) Strive to develop positive attitudes among other professionals toward persons with exceptionalities, representing them with an objective regard for their possibilities and their limitations as persons in a democratic society.

(3) Cooperate with other agencies involved in serving persons with exceptionalities through such activities as the planning and coordination of information exchanges, service delivery, evaluation and training, so that no duplication or loss in quality of services may occur.

(4) Provide consultation and assistance, where appropriate, to both regular and special education as well as other school personnel serving persons with exceptionalities.

(5) Provide consultation and assistance, where appropriate, to professionals in nonschool settings serving persons with exceptionalities.

(6) Maintain effective interpersonal relations with colleagues and other professionals, helping them to develop and maintain positive and accurate perceptions about the special education profession.

Para. 4 - Standards for the Preparation of Special Education Personnel

4.1 GOVERNANCE OF BASIC PROGRAMS

a. Membership of the Governing Unit

Standard: The faculty and staff of the governing unit for basic programs possess scholarly preparation and professional experience appropriate to their assignments. They maintain an involvement in, and are well informed about, educational issues and are committed to the preparation of teachers to provide instruction in a multicultural society.

b. Functions of the Governing Unit

Standard: The governing unit is responsible for setting and achieving teacher education goals, establishing policies, fixing responsibility for program decision-making, identifying and utilizing resources, and facilitating continuous development and improvement of basic teacher education programs.

c. Relationship to Other Administrative Units

Standard: Policies are published that clearly delineate responsibility of the governing unit and the interdependent responsibilities of other policy-making groups and administrative offices within the institution for the overall administration and coordination of basic programs.

d. Official Representative

Standard: One person is officially designated to represent the teacher education unit. The authority and responsibility of this individual for the overall administration and coordination of basic teacher education programs are indicated in published policies.

e. Commitment to Exceptional Children

Standard: Members of the governing unit responsible for basic programs understand and are committed to the preparation of teachers capable of providing an appropriate educational program for exceptional students.

f. Representation by Special Education Administrative Units

Standard: Special education programs where established as administrative units shall be represented on the teacher education governing unit.

4.2 CURRICULA FOR BASIC PROGRAMS

a. Design of Curricula

Standard: Special education curricula are based on explicit objectives that reflect the institution's conception of the teacher's role. There is a direct and obvious relationship between these objectives and the components of the curriculum.

(1) Multicultural Education

Standard: The institution provides for multicultural education throughout the curriculum.

(2) Special Education

Standard: The institution provides its graduates with the knowledge and skills necessary to provide an appropriate education for learners with exceptionalities.

b. The General Studies Component

Standard: There is a planned general studies component requiring that at least one-third of each curriculum for prospective teachers consist of studies in the symbolics of information, natural and behavioral sciences, and humanities.

c. The Professional Studies Component

Standard: The professional studies component shall be sufficient to provide a preparation program requisite to the development of a competent professional and shall not constitute less than one-half of a student's total undergraduate program of study.

(1) Content for the Teaching Specialty

Standard: The professional studies component of each curriculum for prospective special education teachers includes: (1) the study of the content to be taught to pupils; and, (2) the supplementary knowledge, from the subject matter of the area of emphasis and from allied fields, that is needed by the teacher for perspective and flexibility in teaching.

(2) Humanistic and Behavioral Studies

Standard: The professional and specialty studies component of each curriculum for prospective special education teachers includes instruction in the humanistic studies and the behavioral studies.

Distribution of Humanistic and Behavioral Studies

Standard: The humanistic and behavioral studies shall be determined by the specialty area and may be achieved as part of, or separate from, the general component.

(3) Teaching and Learning Theory with Laboratory and Clinical Experience

Standard: The professional and specialty studies component of each curriculum includes the systematic study of teaching and learning theory with appropriate laboratory and clinical experiences.

(4) Practicum

Standard: The professional studies component for each specialty area curriculum offered shall provide prospective special education teachers with direct, qualitative, and intensive supervised teaching experience. Prospective special education teachers seeking multiple specialization shall be required to complete a practicum in each specialization area (as defined by individual teacher preparation programs and state education agencies).

(5) Supervision of Practicum

Standard: Each Area of Emphasis provides supervision to teacher candidates by university/college faculty qualified and experienced in teaching in the Area of Emphasis.

(6) Practicum Selection and Placement

Standard: Each Area of Emphasis has responsibility for assigning teacher candidates to approach placements. This responsibility includes the approval of cooperating teachers and supervisors. Criteria for the selection and retention of such persons are in writing and subject to ongoing evaluation.

d. Use of Guidelines Developed by National Learned Societies and Professional Associations

Standard: The institution's process for developing curriculum for the preparation of special education personnel includes procedures for the study of the recommendations of national professional organizations (e.g., CEC divisions, American Speech-Language-Hearing Association, American Nursing Association), as they may affect special education programs.

e. Student Participation in Program Evaluation and Development

Standard: The institution makes provisions for representative student participation in the decision-making phases related to the design, approval, evaluation, and modification of its teacher education programs.

4.3 FACULTY FOR BASIC PROGRAMS

a. Competence and Utilization of Faculty

Standard: An institution engaged in preparing teachers has full-time faculty members in teacher education whose preparation reflects rich and varied backgrounds appropriate to the programs offered. Each has post-master's degree preparation and/or demonstrated scholarly competence and appropriate specializations. Such specializations make possible competent instruction in the humanistic and behavioral studies, in teaching and learning theory, and in the methods of teaching in each of the specialties for which the institution prepares teachers. There are appropriate specializations to ensure competent supervision of laboratory, clinical, and practicum experiences. Institutional policy will reflect a commitment to multicultural education in the recruitment of full-time faculty members.

b. Faculty Involvement with Schools and Other Educational Agencies

Standard: The teacher education faculty members maintain a continuing interaction with educational programs and personnel working in both public and private schools, institutions, and state and local agencies in their specialty areas.

c. Conditions for Faculty Service

Standard: The institution enforces a policy which limits faculty teaching load and related responsibilities to make possible effective performance.

d. Conditions for Faculty Development

Standard: The institution provides conditions and services essential to continuous development and effective performance of the faculty.

e. Part-Time Faculty

Standard: Part-time faculty who meet all appointment requirements applicable to full-time faculty are employed when necessary to augment and/or enrich existing course or program offerings. No more than one-fourth or 25% of any specialty area should be delivered via the utilization of part-time faculty.

4.4 STUDENTS IN BASIC PROGRAMS

a. Admission to Basic Programs

Standard: The institution applies specific, published criteria for admission to teacher education programs.

b. Retention of Students in Basic Programs

Standard: The institution applies clearly stated evaluative criteria and establishes time frames for the retention of candidates in basic programs. These criteria are reviewed and revised periodically, in the light of data on the teaching performance of graduates, to increase the probability that candidates will become successful teachers.

c. Counseling and Advising for Students in Basic Programs

Standard: Counseling and advising provided to teacher education programs should be provided by persons qualified in and knowledgeable about the specialty area being pursued by the student. Advisement should provide for a total career understanding encompassing both preparation and practice.

4.5   RESOURCES AND FACILITIES FOR BASIC PROGRAMS

a. Library

Standard: The library quantitatively and qualitatively supports the instruction, research, and services pertinent to the needs of each teacher education program.

b. Materials and Instructional Media Center

Standard: An accessible instructional materials and media center shall be maintained to support all teacher education programs offered. The responsibility for the content, materials acquisition, and operation of the center shall be that of the teacher education program or shared with the library, depending upon its location.

c. Physical Facilities and Other Resources

Standard: The institution provides accessible physical facilities and instructional resources as well as other appropriate adaptations of them to assure maximal utilization by all students enrolled in teacher education programs.

4.6   EVALUATION, PROGRAM REVIEW, AND PLANNING

a. Evaluation of Graduates

Standard: The institution keeps abreast of emerging evaluation techniques and engages in systematic efforts to evaluate the quality of its graduates upon completion of their programs of study and after they enter the teaching profession. This evaluation includes evidence of their performance in relation to program objectives.

b. Evaluation of Results to Improve Basic Programs

Standard: The basic teacher education programs preparing persons to perform as teachers in public and private schools, institutions, and agencies offering educational programs shall be regularly and systematically evaluated in an effort to improve these programs and maximize their quality.

c. Long-Range Planning

Standard: The institution has plans for the long-range development of teacher education; these plans are part of a design for total institutional development.

4.7   GOVERNANCE OF ADVANCED PROGRAMS

a. Membership of the Governing Unit

Standard: The faculty and staff of the governing unit for basic programs possess scholarly preparation and professional experience appropriate to their assignments. They maintain an involvement in, and are well informed about, educational issues and are committed to the preparation of teachers to provide instruction in a multicultural society.

b. Functions of the Governing Unit

Standard: Primary responsibility for initiation, development, and implementation of advanced programs lies with the education faculty. The governing unit is responsible for setting and achieving advanced program goals, establishing policies, fixing responsibility for program decision-making, identifying and utilizing resources, and facilitating continuous development and improvement of advanced programs.

c. Relationship to Other Administrative Units

Standard: Where special education is identifiable as an organizational unit or program entity it shall be entitled to representation on the decision-making unit responsible for advanced program

4.8 CURRICULA FOR ADVANCED PROGRAMS

a. Design of Curricula

Standard: Curricula for advanced special education programs are based on explicit objectives that reflect the institution's conception of the professional roles for which the preparation is designed. There is a direct and obvious relationship between these objectives and the components of the respective curricula.

Multicultural Education

Standard: The institution provides for multicultural education in its advanced curricula—in the content for the specialty, the humanistic and behavioral studies, the theory relevant to the specialty, and with direct and simulated experiences in professional practices.

b. Content of Curricula

Standard: The curriculum for each advanced program includes (a) content for the specialty, (b) humanistic and behavioral studies, © theory relevant to the Area of Emphasis with direct and simulated experiences in professional practice, all appropriate to the professional roles for which candidates are being prepared and all differentiated by degree or certificate level.

c. Research in Advanced Curricula

Standard: Each advanced curriculum includes the study of research methods and findings; each doctoral curriculum includes study in the designing and conducting of research.

d. Use of Guidelines Developed by National Learned Societies and Professional Associations

Standard: The institution's process for developing curriculum for the preparation of special education personnel includes procedures for the study of the recommendations of national professional organizations (e.g., CEC divisions, American Speech-Language-Hearing Association, American Nursing Association), as they may affect special education programs.

e. Student Participation in Program Evaluation and Development

Standard: The institution makes provisions for representative student participation in the decision-making phases, related to the design, approval, evaluation, and modification of its advanced programs.

f. Individualization of Programs of Study

Standard: Each advanced curriculum provides for the individualization of teacher candidate's programs of study.

g. Quality Controls

Standard: Institutional policies preclude the granting of graduate credit for study which is remedial or which is designed to remove deficiencies in meeting the requirements for admission to advanced programs.

(1) Graduate Level Courses

Standard: Not more than one-third of the curricula requirements for the masters' degree and sixth-year certificate or degree may be met by the utilization of courses, experiences, and seminars open both to graduate and advanced undergraduate students. The institution has policies which stipulate that all courses granting credit toward the doctoral degree must be graduate level offerings.

(2) Residence Study

Standard: A full-time continuous residency on campus which consists of any two contiguous semesters or three contiguous quarters (or alternative pattern defined by the institution) shall be required for the doctoral degree.

4.9 FACULTY FOR ADVANCED PROGRAMS

a. Preparation of Faculty

Standard: Faculty members teaching at the master's level in advanced programs hold the doctorate with advanced study in each field of specialization in which they are teaching, or have demonstrated competence in such fields; those teaching at the sixth-year and doctoral levels hold the doctorate with study in each field of specialization in which they are teaching and conducting research. Faculty are teaching and conducting research. Faculty members who conduct the advanced programs at all degree levels are engaged in scholarly activity that supports their fields of specialization and have experience which relates directly to their respective fields.

b. Composition of Faculty for Doctoral Degree Programs

Standard: No less than one full-time qualified doctoral faculty member shall be provided for each specialty area (as defined by the institution) offered in special education. In addition, sufficient faculty shall be provided in those areas that directly relate to, or serve to augment, the specialty area programs.

c. Conditions for Faculty Service

Standard: The institution enforces a policy which limits faculty teaching load and related assignments to make possible effective performance and time for scholarly development and community service.

d. Conditions for Faculty Development

Standard: The institution provides conditions and services essential to the effective performance by the faculty in the advanced programs.

e. Part-Time Faculty

Standard: The number of part-time faculty utilized in the support of any one given doctoral specialty area shall not exceed one-fourth or 25% of the total curricula delivered.

f. Faculty Involvement with Educational Programs in Public and Private Schools, Institutions, and Local and State Agencies

Standard: Faculty who are assigned courses and/or who are required to supervise practicum shall have demonstrated past, present, and planned involvement with public and private schools, agencies, and other institutions providing educational programs and/or services in their specialization area.

4.10 STUDENTS IN ADVANCED PROGRAMS

a. Admission to Advanced Programs

Standard: The institution applies published specific criteria for admission to each advanced program at each level.

b. Retention of Students in Advanced Programs

Standard: The institution applies clearly stated evaluative criteria and establishes time frames for the retention of candidates in advanced programs. These criteria are reviewed and revised periodically in the light of data on the performance of graduates, to increase the probability that candidates will be successful in the professional roles for which they are being prepared.

c. Planning and Supervision of Students' Programs of Study

Standard: The program of study for each student in the advanced programs is jointly planned by the student and a member of the faculty; the program of study for each doctoral candidate is approved by a faculty committee; the sponsorship of each thesis, dissertation, or field study is the responsibility of a member of the faculty with specialization in the area of the thesis, dissertation, or field study.

d. Admission Policies

Standard: Students considered for admission to advanced programs shall not be discriminated against because of ethnicity, race, sex, creed, socioeconomic status, age, disability, sexual orientation, or exceptionality.

4.11 RESOURCES AND FACILITIES FOR ADVANCED PROGRAMS

a. Library

Standard: The library provides resources that quantitatively and qualitatively support instruction, independent study, and research required for each advanced program.

b. Materials and Instructional Media

Standard: Accessible materials and instructional media resources are provided to advanced programs by the teacher education program directly or on a shared basis by the library in both quantity and quality sufficient to support each specialty area.

c. Physical Facilities and Other Resources

Standard: The physical facilities, instructional resources, and other related services which are integral to the delivery of instructional and research activities related to advanced programs shall be fully accessible to all students. Appropriate adaptations necessary to maximize instructional opportunity for all students shall also be provided.

4.12 EVALUATION, PROGRAM REVIEW, AND PLANNING

a. Evaluation of Graduates

Standard: The institution keeps abreast of emerging evaluation techniques and engages in systematic efforts to evaluate the quality of its graduates upon completion of their programs of study and after they enter their professional roles. This evaluation includes evidence of their performance in relation to program objectives.

b. Evaluation Results to Improve Advanced Programs

Standard: The advanced preparation programs for practitioners in public and private schools, agencies, institutions, and higher education institutions shall be regularly and systematically evaluated in an effort to improve and/or modify these programs to assure maximum quality.

c. Long-Range Planning

Standard: The institution has plans for the long-range development of its advanced programs; these plans are part of a design for total institutional development.

Para. 5 - Standards for Entry Into Professional Practice

a. Requirements for professional practice should be sufficiently flexible to provide for the newly emerging and changing roles of special education professionals and to encourage experimentation and innovation in their preparation.

b. CEC and its divisions should be the lead organizations in establishing minimum standards for entry into the profession of special education. CEC should develop and promote a model that requires no less than a bachelor's degree which encompasses the knowledge and skills consistent with entry level into special education teaching.

c. Each new professional in special education should receive a minimum of a one-year mentorship, during the first year of his/her professional special education practice in a new role. The mentor should be an experienced professional in the same or a similar role, who can provide expertise and support on a continuing basis.

d. State and provincial education agencies should adopt common knowledge and skills as a basis for providing reciprocity for approval of professional practice across state and provincial lines.

e. Approval of individuals for professional practice in the field of special education should be for a limited period of time with periodic renewal.

f. There should be a continuum of professional development for special educators. The continuum for special education teachers should include at a minimum:

(1) Knowledge and skills required to practice as a teacher in a particular area of exceptionality/age grouping (infancy through secondary).

(2) Knowledge and skills required to excel in the instruction of a particular area of exceptionality/age group (infancy through secondary).

g. Each professional in the field of educating individuals with exceptionalities shall participate an average of 36 contact hours (or an average of 3.6 CEUs) each year of planned, organized, and recognized professional development activities related to the professional's field of practice. Such activities may include a combination of professional development units, continuing education units, college/university coursework, professional organization service (eg, CEC state and provincial units, chapters, divisions, subdivisions, and caucuses), professional workshops, special projects, or structured discussions of readings from the professional literature. Employing agencies should provide resources to enable each professional's continuing development.

Appendix 5

National Board for Professional Teaching Standards for Exceptional Needs
(for teachers of students ages birth–21+)

The National Board for Professional Teaching Standards has organized the standards for accomplished teachers of students with exceptional needs into the following 14 standards. The standards have been ordered to facilitate understanding, not to assign priorities. They each describe an important facet of accomplished teaching; they often occur concurrently because of the seamless quality of accomplished practice. These standards serve as the basis for National Board Certification in this field.

PREPARING FOR STUDENT LEARNING

I. Knowledge of Students: Accomplished teachers of students with exceptional needs consistently use their knowledge of human development and learning and their skills as careful observers of students to understand students' knowledge, aptitudes, skills, interests, aspirations, and values.

II. Knowledge of Special Education: Accomplished teachers of students with exceptional needs draw on their knowledge of the philosophical, historical, and legal foundations of special education and their knowledge of effective special education practice to organize and design instruction. In addition, they draw on their specialized knowledge of specific disabilities to set meaningful goals for their students.

III. Communications: Accomplished teachers of students with exceptional needs know the importance of communications in learning. They know how to use communication skills to help students access, comprehend, and apply information; to help them acquire knowledge; and to enable them to develop and maintain interpersonal relationships.

IV. Diversity: Accomplished teachers of students with exceptional needs create an environment in which equal treatment, fairness, and respect for diversity are modeled, taught, and practiced by all, and they take steps to ensure access to quality learning opportunities for all students.

V. Knowledge of Subject Matter: Accomplished teachers of students with exceptional needs command a core body of knowledge in the disciplines and draw on that knowledge to establish curricular goals, design instruction, facilitate student learning, and assess student progress.

ADVANCING STUDENT LEARNING

VI. Meaningful Learning: Accomplished teachers of students with exceptional needs work with students to explore in purposeful ways important and challenging concepts, topics, and issues to build competence and confidence.

VII. Multiple Paths to Knowledge: Accomplished teachers of students with exceptional needs use a variety of approaches to help students strengthen understanding and gain command of essential knowledge and skills.

VIII. Social Development: Accomplished teachers of students with exceptional needs cultivate a sense of efficacy and independence in their students as they develop students' character, sense of civic and social responsibility, respect for diverse individuals and groups, and ability to work constructively and collaboratively with others.

SUPPORTING STUDENT LEARNING

IX. Assessment: Accomplished teachers of students with exceptional needs design and select a variety of assessment strategies to obtain useful and timely information about student learning and development and to help students reflect on their own progress.

X. Learning Environment: Accomplished teachers of students with exceptional needs establish a caring, stimulating, and safe community for learning in which democratic values are fostered and students assume responsibility for learning, show willingness to take intellectual risks, develop self-confidence, and learn to work not only independently but also collaboratively.

XI. Instructional Resources: Accomplished teachers of students with exceptional needs select, adapt, create, and use rich and varied resources, both human and material.

XII. Family Partnerships: Accomplished teachers of students with exceptional needs work collaboratively with parents, guardians, and other caregivers to understand their children and to achieve common educational goals.

PROFESSIONAL DEVELOPMENT AND OUTREACH

XIII. Reflective Practice: Accomplished teachers of students with exceptional needs regularly analyze, evaluate, and strengthen the quality of their practice.

XIV. Contributing to the Profession and to Education: Accomplished teachers of students with exceptional needs work independently and collaboratively with colleagues and others to improve schools and to advance knowledge, policy, and practice in their field.

For more information check www.nbpts.org.

Appendix 6
CEC Professional Entry Level Standards: A Graphic

CEC Professional Entry Level Standards are built on research that informs the field on best practice in the education of children with exceptionalities. From this research, CEC developed Knowledge and Skill Standards that delineate the competencies that entry-level special education teachers need to master in order to effectively serve children with specific exceptionalities. Using the Knowledge and Skills as a base, CEC developed 10 Content Standards (aligned with the INTASC Core Principles) that describe, at a general level, what all special education teachers should know and be able to do. These different levels of standards are presented in graphic form on the next page.

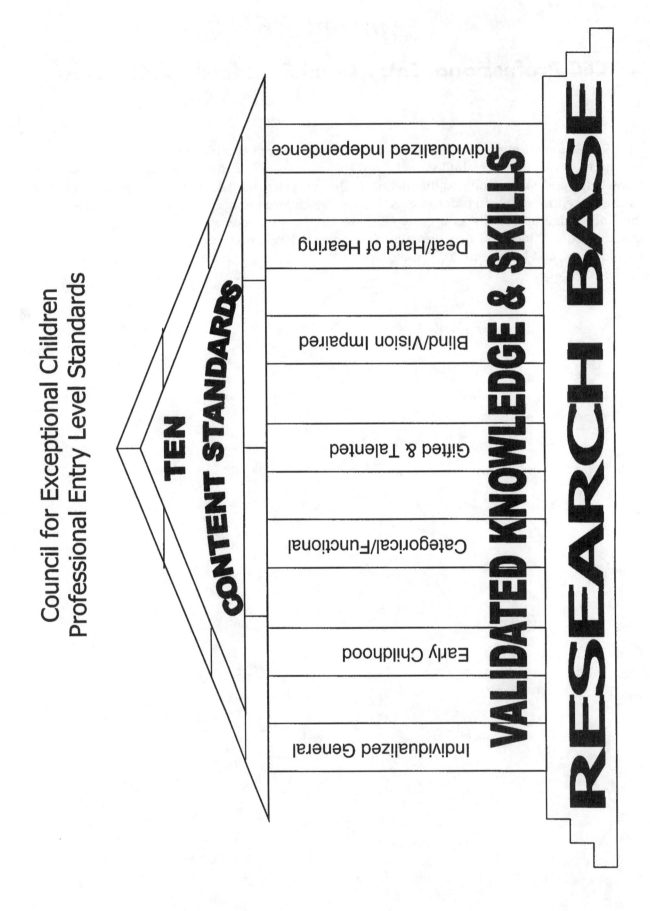

Council for Exceptional Children
Professional Entry Level Standards

TEN
CONTENT STANDARDS

Individualized Independence

Deaf/Hard of Hearing

Blind/Vision Impaired

Gifted & Talented

Categorical/Functional

Early Childhood

Individualized General

VALIDATED KNOWLEDGE & SKILLS

RESEARCH BASE

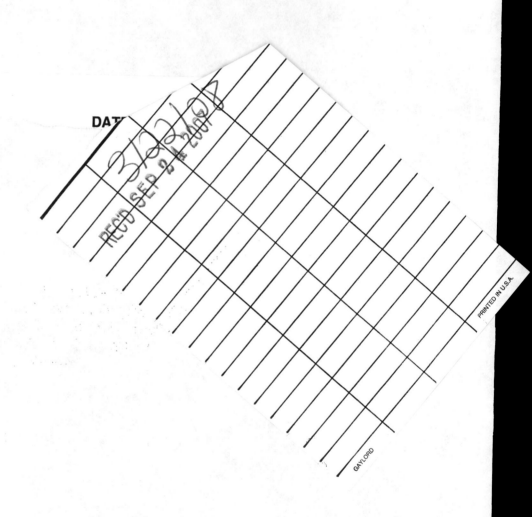